Studies in Economic Reform and Social Justice

Markets, Competition, and the Economy as a Social System

Edited by
Frederic S. Lee

WILEY

Studies in Economic Reform and Social Justice

Markets, Competition, and the Economy as a Social System

Edited by
Frederic S. Lee

WILEY

This edition first published 2013
© 2013 American Journal of Economics and Sociology, Inc.

Registered Office
John Wiley & Sons Ltd, The Atrium, Southern Gate, Chichester, West Sussex, PO19 8SQ, United Kingdom

Editorial Offices
350 Main Street, Malden, MA 02148-5020, USA
9600 Garsington Road, Oxford, OX4 2DQ, UK
The Atrium, Southern Gate, Chichester, West Sussex, PO19 8SQ, UK

For details of our global editorial offices, for customer services, and for information about how to apply for permission to reuse the copyright material in this book, please see our website at www.wiley.com/wiley-blackwell.

The rights of Frederic S. Lee to be identified as the author of the editorial material in this work has been asserted in accordance with the Copyright, Designs and Patents
Act 1988.

All rights reserved. No part of this publication may be reproduced, stored in a retrieval system, or transmitted, in any form or by any means, electronic, mechanical, photocopying, recording, or otherwise, except as permitted by the UK Copyright, Designs and Patents Act 1988, without the prior permission of the publisher.

Wiley also publishes its books in a variety of electronic formats. Some content that appears in print may not be available in electronic books.

Designations used by companies to distinguish their products are often claimed as trademarks. All brand names and product names used in this book are trade names, service marks, trademarks, or registered trademarks of their respective owners. The publisher is not associated with any product or vendor mentioned in this book. This publication is designed to provide accurate and authoritative information in regard to the subject matter covered. It is sold on the understanding that the publisher is not engaged in rendering professional services. If professional advice or other expert assistance is required, the services of a competent professional should be sought.

Library of Congress Cataloging-in-Publication Data

Markets, competition, and the economy as a social system / edited by Frederic S. Lee.
   pages cm
  Includes index.
  Originally published as: "The American journal of economics and sociology, November 2012 Issue."
   ISBN 978-1-118-69162-5 (casebound)—ISBN 978-1-118-69157-1 (pbk.) 1. Economics.
2. Economics–Sociological aspects. I. Lee, Frederic S., 1949- II. American journal of economics and sociology.
  HB71.M288 2013
  330—dc23
                                  2013007843

A catalogue record for this book is available from the Library of Congress.

Set in 10 on 13pt Garamond Light by Toppan Best-set Premedia Limited
Printed in Singapore by Markono Print Media Pte Ltd.

01—2013

Contents

Editor's Introduction 1

Economy as a Social System: Niklas Luhmann's Contribution
  and its Significance for Economics—*Ivan A. Boldyrev* 6

Social Network Analysis and the Sociology of Economics:
  Filling a Blind Spot with the Idea of Social Embeddedness—
  Dieter Bögenhold 34

Schmoller's Method as a Critique and Alternative to Marginalist
  Economics: a Comment to Louzek—*Carlo D'Ippoliti* 60

The Economic Deterioration of the Family: Historical
  Contingencies Preceding the Great Recession—
  Michael D. Gillespie 70

The Market Concept: A Characterization from
  Institutional and Post-Keynesian Economics—
  Eduardo Fernández-Huerga 102

The Organization, Operation, and Outcomes of Actually Existing
  Markets: A Suggested Approach for Empirical Analysis—
  Lynne Chester 127

Three Modes of Competition in the Marketplace—
  William Redmond 164

Saving Private Business Enterprises: A Heterodox Microeconomic
  Approach to Market Governance and Market Regulation—
  Tae-Hee Jo 188

Market Cycles: Bicycles, Riders, Industries, and Environments
  in France and the United States, 1865–1914—
  Thomas Burr 209

No End to the Consensus in Macroeconomic Theory?
  A Methodological Inquiry—*John McCombie and
  Maureen Pike* 238

Index 270

Editor's Introduction

In economics as well as sociology, there is an ongoing debate about conceptualizing and modeling the economy as a whole. One aspect of the debate concerns the degree or extent to which the economy is or is not socially embedded, while the other aspect concerns the "microfoundations" of macroeconomics. The former arose because Karl Polanyi thought that the emergence of capitalisms resulted in the actual economy being extracted from the social system in which it was previously embedded. However, he confused the words of the supporters of capitalism, such as Adam Smith, Jean-Baptiste Say, David Ricardo, and a whole host of neoclassical economists since the 1870s, with the actual facts of the situation. Once this is recognized and with it the admission that the economy has always been socially embedded, the interesting and most relevant theoretical question is: What is the best way to model the economy as a whole and as a social system? Such a question, it might be thought, would promote modeling investigations that would create a dense set of economic and social relationships constituting the social-economic system as a whole. Perhaps so for sociologists, but economists think quite differently, that is, in terms of microfoundations and macroeconomics. One response is to reduce the macro entirely to the micro, that is, reducing all social-economic relationships to a single asocial agent producing and consuming a single good produced by his/her hands. Another response is to separate the macro from the micro by visualizing the economy as a whole as being constituted by a few aggregate entities, such as income, effective demand, and employment, that are devoid of any agency and unconnected to the social-economic relationships at the level of markets, competition, business enterprises, households, the state, and trade unions. Both responses are equally preposterous.

The November 2011 issue of *The American Journal of Economics and Sociology* carried a number of articles dealing with modeling the economy as a historical-social, disaggregated system of economic activity with economic agents that cannot be aggregated. While the articles made important contributions to modeling the economy as a social system, there were many omissions, especially with regard to markets and competition. This issue of the *AJES* endeavors to correct this with several articles on markets, competition, and market governance. However, it starts with four articles that deal with issues impinging on modeling the economy as a social system. Ivan Boldyrev begins the issue with a critical discussion of Niklas Luhmann's work on the economy as a social system. What is significant is that (1) Luhmann conceives the economy as a social system that is unfamiliar to most economists but yet should command their attention; and (2) that his view of markets and competition are very much in terms of social engagement between competing enterprises. This is followed by Dieter Boegenhold discussion of the role of social network analysis in providing a way to concretely understand the irrevocable manner in which economic activities are socially embedded. In particular, he argues that social network analysis clearly illuminates the social relationships that govern market activities; or, in other words, it shows that markets are social institutions that encompass social-economic activities. Then, Carlo D'Ippoliti comments on Gustav von Schmoller's inductive-deductive, historically contingent methodology, suggesting that its fit quite well with modeling the economy as a social system. That is, as long as the capitalist economy has distinct historical stages, then the theoretical analysis of economic activity and the social provisioning process within each stage will differ to one degree or another from those of other stages. Hence, a Schmoller-like research strategy used to construct the theoretical analysis cannot promote universal, timeless "laws" or be completely and only based on deductive reasoning. Rather, as D'Ippoliti qua Schmoller suggests, a preferable research strategy must contain inductive and deductive reasoning, where the former provides the historically contingent facts and the latter provides the theoretical analysis based upon those facts. Finally, drawing upon the social structures of accumulation approach, Michael Gillespie argues that the New Deal provided the structures for understanding the post-1945 economic situation of the American family. He then shows that the structures changed and decayed in the post-war period, generating new "facts" about the household, which in turn requires new theoretical arguments. This supports Schmoller's position that theoretical explanations about the social-economic are always historically contingent.

All capitalist economies produce a differentiated array of goods and services and they are for the most part exchanged in markets. Because the economy is also a social system of production, markets and the exchange and competitive activities within them are also social activities. This conceptualization of markets as social institutions does not fit well with mainstream economics, which often sees markets as asocial, natural, timeless entities. On the other hand, it does fit well with various heterodox approaches to markets. Eduardo Fernandez-Huerga shows how the heterodox approaches of institutional and post-Keynesian economics deals with markets. He found that social acting individuals and enterprises combined with fundamental uncertainty generate an array of markets that are differentiated by their social structures and internal social relations between the participants. This in turn drove Fernandez-Huerga to argue that "market competition" comes in different varieties, many of which involve trust and values that control and govern competitive interactions. Drawing upon the contributions of the French Regulation School and others, Lynne Chester furthers this discussion with an eye towards conducting empirical research in actual markets. She illustrates her arguments with short stories on how the electricity, water, low-income housing, and employment services markets, being social institutions, can be transformed by government (neoliberal) public policies.

The conclusion emanating from Fernandez-Huerga and Chester is that markets are the site of socially structured competition, which means that variations in the social structures result in different kinds of competition within and across markets. William Redmond explores the former and comes up with three types of competition: competition between competing selling enterprises, competition between selling enterprises and buyers, and between buyers. He notes that competition between sellers is sufficiently regulated and governed so as to cause them no harm. In contrast, the vertical competition between sellers and buyers (consumers) through brand loyalty is one preferred strategy of enterprises because it enables them to get higher profits through setting higher prices without precipitating a price war with their "competitors." Finally, Redmond introduces a Veblenian conspicuous consumption-invidious comparison form of competition between consumers. That is, consumers compete for status and enterprises manipulate this behavior through creating products (with accompanying advertising) that they buy. So consumers use money to buy status while enterprises provide status in exchange for money. Redmond argues quite clearly that enterprises prefer the latter two forms of socially constructed competition because they do not threaten their existence as going concerns through reducing their income flows via price wars and generally destabilizing their markets. Tae-Hee Jo elaborates on these points in his article on saving private enterprise. Starting with the proposition that capitalism is inherently unstable, Jo argues that social mechanisms need to be established that both minimize the instability and specifically protect the business enterprise from its ravages. He outlines two forms of protection—market governance and market regulations. Both reduce the harmful effects of market competition by "structuring" and organizing the market so that competitive activities are directed at, as Redmond suggests, consumers and not at the "competing" enterprises.

One implication that can be drawn from Fernandez-Huerga, Chester, Redmond, and Jo is that markets must be carefully crafted and competition suitably regulated so that they can be a safe home for going enterprises. Thomas Burr provides a story of the pitfalls and successes of creating the consumer bicycle markets in the United States and France. The successful building of a permanent bicycle market involved the interaction of producers designing bicycles, consumers using bicycles and then communicating to the producers on how to improve them, and the use of advertising and bicycle clubs and road races to stimulate demand. As the markets grew in each country, enterprises created a national network of wholesalers and retailers, established trade journals, and created trade associations to help govern market activities. However, the combination of explosive demand followed by a sharp depression, relatively easy entry, and the decline of leisure cycling overwhelmed the governing mechanism in the U.S. market, resulting in market destabilizing, price wars, exit, and, eventually, market concentration as a way to reestablish market stability. In contrast, the French market enjoyed stability because the demand for bicycles continued to grow and its trade associations were able to successfully regulate price competition.

Modeling the economy as a whole is a theoretical exercise fraught with controversy. For example, the New Neoclassical Synthesis found in mainstream macroeconomics is, as John McCombie and Maureen Pike argue in their article, internally incoherent and unable to explain the recent economic crisis; but such shortcomings have not prompted mainstream economists to question the theory and replace it with, say, post-Keynesian macroeconomic theory (which is less incoherent and a little better at explaining the recession). Moreover, there are heterodox economists who model the current capitalist economy using a single non-basic good, homogenous labor power, and have no state; and they are also unwilling to change their modeling views even though they are contradicted by reality. It is not clear why macroeconomists are so rigid in their views. But it is safe to say that they would find faults with the modeling of the economy as a social system delineated in this *AJES* issue, as the strengths of the model lie in its disaggregation of the economy and in the heterogeneous nature of goods, enterprises, households, and labor power. In addition, with competition differentiated across markets and emergent market governance organizations, enterprises, and households, it is not possible to easily summarize the economy in a simple model. Consequently, macroeconomists would probably dismiss the model because it is too unwieldy, even though it is more coherent and better able to explain the recession than its competitors. Clumsy, coherent, and right versus simple, incoherent, and wrong are the model of the economy options facing economists. The articles in this issue of the *AJES* suggest that the former is the right choice.

FL

Economy as a Social System: Niklas Luhmann's Contribution and its Significance for Economics

By Ivan A. Boldyrev*

Abstract. Niklas Luhmann's (1927–1998) ambitious research project was aimed not only at describing society as a global social system, but it also analyzed various subsystems (including an economic one). The article assesses Luhmann's vision of the economy, summarized mainly in his *Wirtschaft der Gesellschaft*, wherein he addresses basic economic notions: the economic system, money, prices, rationality, and the market. I then interpret his ideas in the context of modern discussions in economics (intersubjective structures, complex systems, and evolutionary modeling). I also propose some heuristics implied by Luhmann's economic ontology, which are potentially interesting for methodological and theoretical strategies of modern economics.

Introduction

Niklas Luhmann (1927–1998) was a social thinker who tried to construct a universal social ontology of modern society. He developed a conceptual apparatus linking general systems theory, sociological insights on communication and the structure of society, conceptions from biology, and evolutionary ideas. Luhmann's general theory, which is still not very well known in the English-speaking world, is not discussed at length here. Instead, in this article, an attempt is made to assess Luhmann's vision of the economy, developed mainly in *Wirtschaft der Gesellschaft*, his first book devoted solely to one particular (sub)system[1] and to put his ideas on the agenda of modern economic theory and methodology.

The task of situating some of Luhmann's economic ideas within the history of modern economics is promising but has not yet received

*Department of Economics, National Research University Higher School of Economics, Moscow, Russian Federation; E-mail address: iboldyrev@hse.ru. The author is deeply grateful to Dirk Baecker, Alexander F. Filippov, and Nikita S. Kharlamov for their helpful comments on an earlier draft of this article.

American Journal of Economics and Sociology, Vol. 72, No. 2 (April 2013).
DOI: 10.1111/ajes.12013
© 2013 American Journal of Economics and Sociology, Inc.

much attention.[2] His theoretical style is rather unusual, his prose is often considered obscure and sometimes impenetrable. Luhmann does not easily fit into well-known domains of study, such as economic sociology. However, in view of the vast literature devoted to his ideas and a general reception of his work in social theory,[3] one might suppose that examining Luhmann's approach to economy might be useful for today's economics. In this article, a critical commentary is provided (without any claims for comprehensiveness, especially with respect to Luhmann's multiple sources and contexts), which may also contribute to understanding of economic thinking existing in various disciplines other than economics. Such analysis also allows for rethinking both the interaction between social theory and economics and the insights from a holistic way of describing economic reality.

Luhmann's social theory was introduced and critically discussed within evolutionary economics by Michael Hutter (1994), in economic methodology by Alex Viskovatoff (1998, 1999, 2000, 2004), and in economic sociology by Jens Beckert (2002: Ch. 4). However, it is still unclear whether Luhmann's conception of economy is an economic theory, a version of economic sociology, or simply an application of his general framework to economic themes.[4] His theoretical perspective lacks a more precise qualification. Are there themes and ideas in economics that would clarify or elaborate on Luhmann's insights? What lessons can be learned by economists from Luhmann's fundamental social theory applied to some basic economic ideas and categories? My article indicates parallel developments and discussions within economics and interprets Luhmann's insights in light of modern economic thought. It shows that some of those discussions, particularly the one of open and closed systems, autonomy of the economic, and rejection of methodological individualism, are surprisingly relevant both for the modern development of economic theory (institutional economics, game-theoretic modeling, and a complex systems approach) and economic methodology (for which the concept of an open system led to some interesting findings).

Several reservations are in order here. I do not claim that my account accurately represents the totality of Luhmann's writings on economic matters. Indeed, some important themes (such as the analysis of scarcity or risk as well as the texts on organizational theory) are deliberately omitted to focus on more general issues. I also did not intend to show that Luhmann can be used to solve *all* the problems faced by today's economists (both orthodox and heterodox) and economic methodologists/philosophers. Instead, I propose to look carefully at some aspects of his legacy and identify the ideas that may prove fruitful in the context of modern economics, which is, for the most part, isolated from contemporary social theory.

The article is organized as follows. The second section deals with the most general vision of the economic system in *Wirtschaft der Gesellschaft*. I briefly discuss the notions of system and environment and show how Luhmann unifies openness and closure of an economic system. In the third section, I provide a closer reading of the most basic economic categories employed by Luhmann (money and prices) and show some philosophical ambiguities in Luhmann's conception of the self-reproduction of the economy. The fourth section is a commentary on Luhmann's analysis of the market, illustrating his methods of working with concepts of environment and interpenetration. The penultimate section, which is followed by the conclusion, compares Luhmann's approach with some recent accounts provided by economic methodologists and discusses how Luhmann's rejection of methodological individualism and the "open/closed systems" divide may become a source of inspiration for modern economic theory and methodology, especially in light of the new developments in complexity economics.

Economic System

Luhmann uses his social systems theory to construct a coherent view of the economy as a *social system*. The concept of a "system" for Luhmann is determined first and foremost by the idea that there are objects that maintain the difference between themselves and their environment (Luhmann 1995: 2).[5] The most important feature of "the social" for Luhmann is that it deals with communication. Communications in the economy are payments regulated by money and prices. Any communication may be thought of and reproduced only by being linked to other communications.

Each social system is (functionally, not spatially) differentiated according to a symbolically generalized communication medium.

Here, "generalized" means establishing a relation between diverse phenomena *without making them identical* and, thus, preserving differences between them. In the case of an economic system, it is money (see below).

The economy represents a subsystem of a social system. Luhmann follows in various ways (mainly along Polanyian lines, but sometimes in an extremely abstract form) the paths of self-differentiation of an economic subsystem and its growing autonomy within society. The modern case is, for Luhmann, the one with a fully differentiated economy.[6] The emergence of this differentiated economy contributed to the emergence of "economy" as a proper subject matter of science in the 18th century.

Any differentiated subsystem has its own *code*, which constitutes its *differentia specifica*. Here, the concept of difference is fundamental because any (sub)system preserves and reproduces its difference from the environment and, at the same time, generates internal differences to manage itself. Various subsystems do not neglect each other—each of them "codes" all the incoming signals from outside with the help of its own code. The fact of law, for example, has an economic meaning within the economy after being appropriately "re-encoded" in terms of payments (see below). "Society," for Luhmann, is not a sum of various subsystems of a social system (as it was in Parsons), but rather a general term that represents "the social" existing in different forms. "Subsystem of a social system," thus, does not mean that the economy is a "part" of society, but it means that economic communication is a social activity. Any communication may be regarded from various standpoints, and the economic is just one dimension not to be confused with any other.

The ontological level of communication is beyond the levels of resources (in economics—goods, services, and natural resources) and mental states (in economics—preferences). The latter are both the objects and necessary conditions of communication. Thus, Luhmann *rejects methodological individualism,* insisting on the irreducibility of the social and the uselessness of looking for microfoundations. He does not acknowledge the logic of the reductionist argument, claiming that, together with general systems theory, any elementary social "atom" is conditioned by the system as a whole (Luhmann 1988:

48–49). "Elements are constituted by the systems that are composed of them" (Luhmann 1995: 215). At the same time, this rejection, which might seem questionable, is marked by an extraordinary flexibility in choosing concepts and redrawing traditional lines of opposition. The individual is considered an *environment of the social system*. The environment should not be understood as a spatial concept; it is a metaphor meaning everything from which the system differentiates itself.[7] Since social systems consist of communications we should differentiate between communications and individuals, the latter being therefore the environment for the former.

Luhmann does not defend equilibrium method.[8] On the contrary, as will be shown below, his interests lead economic thinking in another direction. However, his general intention, to *explain* the emergence of certain institutions, is (contrary to what Viskovatoff (2000: 137) suggests) characteristic even for modern mainstream economics.[9] The point of divergence here is the ontological views of the majority of economic theorists, who most likely would not subscribe to Luhmann's idea that systems exist and produce communications *independently* of individuals' desires and aspirations.

For Luhmann, an economic system is, at the same time, open (its self-reproduction is possible only in its environment and by differentiating itself from this environment) and closed (elements of the environment are not used as the basis for the system's reproduction process—only communications are forms of this process).[10] The closure means that the system's logic is not extended to its environment—the economy does not enter into a money exchange with it. The duality of closure and openness is, for Luhmann, an obsolete style of reasoning in social theory. As a subsystem that relates to other subsystems, the economy is adapting and trying to fulfil the tasks posed by its social environment, but in relation to the society as a whole, it is autonomous and evolves according to its own laws (Luhmann 1988: 63). The economy is also a complex—and even hypercomplex—system, which regards its own complexity as a problem and attempts to handle it within different contexts (for example, with production and consumption).[11] But, again, if some non-economic facts "enter" the economy they immediately get an economic meaning and are handled with the help of an economic code. An economic system cannot produce justice, truth, or beauty—only law, science, and art can do that, respectively.

Reproduction of the economy is not viewed in a teleological way. An economic system is *autopoietic*, meaning that it reproduces itself with the help of its own elements, which are in turn produced by the system.[12] It is no wonder then that an economic model Luhmann considers to be historically the first in an analysis of the economy as a differentiated subsystem is Quesnay's "Tableau" (Luhmann 1988: 79).[13]

Money and Prices

We now turn to the discussion of genuinely economic categories in *Wirtschaft der Gesellschaft*. The economy as a social system is differentiated when *money* appears (as a means of communication that, at the same time, enables communication or raises the probability of its occurrence). Money provides a distinct communicative mechanism—*payments*. Payments are time-restricted events that form the ontological basis of an economic system. They are "cells" enabling the "autopoietic" system to reproduce itself, and they, themselves, are being reproduced by that system.[14] At the same time, payments are transitory events, not substances. Payments condition other payments and form opportunities for these new payments and corresponding expectations, thereby securing the satisfaction of future needs and fulfilling the tasks of the economy. This process is ongoing, self-enforcing, and, therefore, potentially eternal or (at least) very robust to changes.

Payment is also a reflexive process—payments may be secured only by other payments. To pay means to enable payments by others but, at the same time, to lose the opportunity to pay afterwards (or to pay for an alternative good/service). This loss forces one to restore one's ability to pay; otherwise, one is excluded from the system (Luhmann 1988: 134–135). Luhmann calls it "double circular flow"—constituted not by money and goods but rather by interconnected code structures of payment and the inability to pay. The recovery is accomplished with the help of investment (if the agent pays to get money back), taxes (in terms of public spending), or labor (in the household).

Luhmann claims that the movement of goods and services emerges as a consequence of this movement of payments (Luhmann 1988: 137). This posited priority helps him to rationalize the paradox of closure and openness: the economic system should be closed; otherwise, it cannot be open to perform its functions for its various environments. The double circular flow should function according to its own logic of payments (economic rationality and efficiency); it is not governed by some external logic of political or familial life. However, government (with respect to the state) and labor (with respect to the household) are still important conditions of existence for this double circular flow of ability and inability to pay.

The flow of the ability to pay is visible in traditional economic theory—unlike the second flow, which streams in another direction, transmitting the inability to pay. One may accentuate the first flow, to emphasize solvency, or the second, to emphasize the satisfaction of needs. The banking system is the one that unifies these two aspects, creating the ability to pay and, at the same time, lucratively monetizing its debts, that is, the inability to pay. It secures the functioning of both flows by providing the opportunity to defer payments, on the one hand, and by providing deposit accounts to the customers, on the other—by having money, on the one hand, and not having money, on the other hand. To ensure the system's stability, both flows should be separated and conditioned differently (Luhmann 1988: 148).

To differentiate itself from other systems, the economy should contain an unfolding self-reference that reproduces it and gives it a stable economic meaning. Money refers and *should* refer (as the economy is an open system) to other objects (goods, needs, and consequences). It is a combination and mutual interdependence of self-reference and reference to other objects that, for Luhmann, marks the nature of an economic system as open and, at the same time, provides it with stability for the future. The economic system is closed, but it begs being opened, as each payment should find a reason, a grounding outside the pure logic of payments (to pay in order to provide other payments), and this reason is to be found precisely in the system's environment. Both sides are inextricably intertwined.[15]

The notion of payment is tightly connected to that of *price* as a mechanism that makes payments possible, transforms "encoding" into "programming" (Luhmann 1988: 227) and into concrete rules of action, and is the form in which those payments are expected to come (Luhmann 1988: 41). The economy's self-differentiation is both the cause and effect of the emergence of a price system. Reasoning in terms of prices becomes a hallmark of a disembedded, self-differentiated economy (Luhmann 1988: 111). A price system is a "sign," an ideal representation of real payment processes.[16] Prices solve the "paradox of payment," which means that once you have paid, you may not pay more (Luhmann 1988: 226–227). Prices give information; they both form and inform our expectations. These ideas, developed by economics, are also relevant for Luhmann, who makes no explicit reference to his precursors (Hayek, for example). He also distinguishes between values (as social indicators of economic activity showing the "real" significance of objects or processes for the society) and prices (as means of the system's autopoiesis) (Luhmann 1988: 55). However, the prices generalize as well and leave us with an economic system in which there is no place for irrelevant information on payments other than a simple code: to pay or not to pay. The system of prices must be flexible to reflect ever-changing money-communication procedures. The abstract character of prices is possible only when the very difference between an abstract price system and its multiple real factors is sustained and reproduced.

An enormous flexibility in the price system creates uncertainty that is associated with money (Luhmann here follows economic theorists such as Marx or Keynes). Inner uncertainty and price flexibility help to cope with an exogenous uncertainty. (The same logic is used in the case of organizations that face external instability and should be unstable as well.) The identity of price, the opportunity to fix the price and to use it as a reference point in acquiring information and making decisions is key to successful management of economic diversity and uncertainty (Luhmann 1988: 110–111). As Viskovatoff (2004: 10) points out, for Luhmann, it is important that prices are determinate at any given time. In fact, Luhmann rationalizes Adam Smith: "At the same time and place . . . money is the exact measure of the real exchangeable value of all commodities. It is so, however, at the same time and place only" (Smith 1778: 44). With the help of this determinate (but not necessarily stable) number, an agent can manage the complex situation (s)he faces at any point in time. However, after the payment is made, all contingencies concerning further use of the money received or utilization/consumption of acquired resources return.

Luhmann elaborates on two ways to cope with inner instability: either an observer moves one level higher and makes the credit scarce and the price of money (interest rate) unstable; or one uses a political system with its own instability. Note that each system should have its own logic, and Luhmann tries to show that any mixture of political and economic logic is an illusion. Both political and economic spheres produce instability, which is necessary to control the instability in their respective environments. Such a dependence has, in Luhmann's view, implications for economic policy; he urges not to confuse the economic with the political and not to place too much stress on either of the two spheres.

Prices thus constitute self-reference and self-representation, a self-description (Selbstbeschreibung) of a complex economic system, allowing it to acquire information about itself and its environment (Luhmann 1988: 113–114). In particular, prices as social facts (Luhmann 1988: 118) enable economic agents to observe economic activities and to observe these observations as well. Luhmann, however, is not ready to acknowledge that prices contain *all* of the relevant information about the system and its environment. One can imagine a situation in which being guided exclusively by prices means failure.

Prices are also a form in which money payments are expected to come. The systemic character of prices should be recognized in a structural way. When criticizing prices (for example, from the humanistic critical standpoint), one fails to criticize (structurally) the price mechanism itself. Such analysis needs a system-theoretic elaboration, based not on labor as a fundamental category (as in Marx) but on money as a code of economic communication.[17]

Luhmann draws on Parsons, considering *money* as a *symbolically generalized medium*. It is a social mechanism, a form of language that secures that the system of payments will work in the future. Participation in the global processes of exchange in society is mediated through money, which helps agents universalize their needs and interests but only under the condition that the natural scarcity of goods and resources be symbolically doubled in the scarcity of money, which itself should be scarce to reflect the real world adequately (although it is obvious that the two scarcities are quite different in nature). The economic system thus internalizes scarcity and reproduces it using the banking system (Hutter 1999). In the face of growing diversity and heterogeneity of motives, needs, and preferences, which can otherwise make economic communications (payments) more and more unlikely, money helps to manage this highly complex system, in which agents face too many alternatives and must select among them. One might use a metaphor of the Babylonian "Confusion of Tongues" to depict this chaotic movement that can emerge if our universal code is lost. The code itself works because of heterogeneity inherent in the interactions of goods/services and money, which are "asymmetrical." Money is a symbol, a physically present "identity in difference," which for Luhmann—who follows Parsons[18]—along with symbolization provides generalization as well (Ganßmann 1988). As a symbol, it is not only a sign that refers to something else (in economic theory one would deem it not to be a veil covering some fundamental relations of value or utility) but an autonomous entity that performs many functions, for example, helps us avoid conflicts over scarce resources, re-encoding violence into economic exchange (Luhmann 1988: 253). Money appears first as something existing outside the economic system but, in fact, it is produced within it (Hutter 1999).

The level of the economic system's development is marked for Luhmann by the generality of monetary code: in developed countries, not everything can be bought for money. This is the sign that the economic system is fully differentiated (Luhmann 1988: 239). Money, therefore—as any other symbolically generalized communication medium (though paradigmatic one)—helps to solve the problem of *double contingency* posed initially by Parsons: in social interaction, an individual's action is contingent not only on, for example, his (her) knowledge, cognitive capabilities, and states of nature but also on actions taken by others (see Parsons 1968: 436). This problem involves "radical uncertainty about the action intentions of the interaction partner" (Beckert 2002: 204) and, hence, makes communication increasingly difficult.

Accepting money, we accept different choices made by other individuals regardless of what they want to buy. This idea is clearly a deviation from Parsons's scheme of symbolically generalized communication media because Parsons appealed to some shared norms and values as means for stabilizing interaction processes. Luhmann, on the contrary, speaks about the growing subjectivation, and hence arbitrariness, of economic ends, which need to be managed. What is symbolic (unifying and integrating) in money can also be "diabolic" (disintegrating and dividing): the very notion of generalization implies a possibility of different points of view. Luhmann tries to incorporate into his theory a critique of money by emphasizing the "dark" sides of the monetary system as something that can cause alienation, hostility, and mistrust among people who see money as being owned by others, that is, as wealth that is not theirs. To unify these perspectives, Luhmann makes a speculative step: monetary generalization is symbolic in action, enabling exchange, but when we observe it as a regulatory instance for scarcity, it appears diabolic. One should integrate these two perspectives by incorporating observation into the system, that is, by making the system observe itself, which is precisely the case of money.

At the same time, notions of medium and code are insufficient for guiding action. Luhmann had to introduce programs for the agents to interpret codes in certain ways. Beckert (2002: 221–227) considers this idea as response to Luhmann's critics (for example, R. Münch), who claimed that economic action in Luhmann's treatment becomes a purely mechanical following of the certain (rather one-sided and primitive) rule, without taking into account other important "codes," mainly a moral one—a code of good/evil. Economic action is indifferent to this code. However, using programs (which are analogous to the utility maximization postulate in orthodox economics, in addition to the scarcity axiom), we may introduce extra-economic motives into the economic system, encoding them properly and thus contributing to the system's openness.

Luhmann's thinking faces a general philosophical problem. An event that constitutes the system is constantly reproduced in it and takes part in the system's reproductive process (autopoiesis). However, at the same time, each event (each payment) is unique in space and time. Each payment is both unique and refers to other payments, conditioning them and being conditioned by them. How can we reconcile a "reproductive" logic of payments and irreversible, historical character of economic development?[19] The logic of events occurring in time is clearly at odds with the autopoietic logic of systems theory. A more general question concerns dynamics—how does the economic system change over time? These are not questions for which we can find ready-made answers in Luhmann's work. However, they must be asked if we want to advance our understanding of the economic system.

We now turn to another economic concept—the concept of market, which is also fundamental to the economic system and is discussed in detail in *Wirtschaft der Gesellschaft*. The analysis of the market demonstrates Luhmann's peculiar style of thinking and drawing distinctions.

Market

The notion of the market is sometimes disturbing for economists. It may be regarded, for example, as a place of trade (trading area), as a purchasing power for a commodity, or as a specific mechanism of coordination and social structures supporting it. With reference to Harrison White (1981), Luhmann defines the market not as a place for trade or as a system of organizations necessary for the economic exchange to emerge, but as a mirror in which the firm sees both itself and its competitors, its context. This mirror shows to the producers (facing uncertainty about consumer motives[20]) the fact that consumers are scarce and should be fought for.[21]

Traditional economic theory, Luhmann claims, is not much concerned with the definitions of the market simply because "market" may stand for any empirical phenomenon, to which equilibrium theory refers (Luhmann 1988: 92). However, Luhmann proposes a more intricate definition. He uses the concept of a "participating system" (Luhmann 1988: 94). One may consider the economic system not only as a whole—and see a self-referential system—but also consider it as something internally heterogeneous that is differentiated within itself. To highlight internal differences inside the economy,

Luhmann uses the concept of *interpenetration* (borrowed from Parsons). The participating subsystem of an economic system (a household or a firm) regards the *market* as its own—often uncertain and somewhat "cloudy"—environment. The market is an economic system itself, considered not in its wholeness but in its "turning-itself-into-environment" for some of its "activities" (Luhmann 1988: 94). This internal "reflection" into itself (to use Hegel's language) helps the system *observe itself* by drawing internal lines between a ("small") system and an environment (indeed, to observe in Luhmann's language means to create a difference). That is why an adequate socio-theoretical analysis of the market is, for Luhmann, an observation of the second or even third order, i.e., an observation of an observation. These observations are a consequence of the aforementioned internal differentiations because only a relatively independent system differentiating itself from its environment can observe itself.

The system thus observes itself by turning itself into an environment for its own activities (Luhmann 1988: 125). Each payment as an action is conditioned by observations of the others' actions—those actions being, in turn, payments that inform us about themselves by means of prices. The unity of the system and its environment is sustained with the help of system/environment differentiation.

The market is seen therefore as a "polycontextual" system that forms an environment for any participating system—an environment that is different for each of the systems (as any system is a specific center of observation, and the contexts of observation differ among systems) *and yet* is still the same. Luhmann applies this "paradox of differentiation" (Luhmann 1988: 110) to prices, which have different meanings for different people and yet are still the same. The durability of a disembedded economy is based on the heterogeneity of needs and preferences, that is, on the complexity of the environment. This external complexity is regulated by the internal one, which consists of the uneven income (money) distribution within the economic system.[22] Note that, according to Luhmann, without systemic closure, no internal complexity can be built.

Within the framework of his theory of observation, Luhmann discusses *rational expectations* theory, defining it as a theory in which actors inside the system observe it as though they were outside it. The accent is placed not on the system that observes itself or the very possibility of such self-correcting self-observation, or "introspection," but rather on the process of observing a theoretical model (Luhmann probably means the process of rational decision making) that observes itself (Luhmann 1988: 125). Luhmann's emphasis on the system is partly justified by his appeal to studying not only the system itself but also its reactions to self-observation and self-description.[23] He accuses rational expectations theory (which is seemingly close to his own approach) of neglecting precisely this point: How is it possible that an economic system can observe itself and react to self-observation?

The market as an environment that is internal for the system is not a system itself, but unlike economy as a whole, it may be partially regulated by hierarchies and organizations (Luhmann offers the banking system as an example). Accordingly, Luhmann proposes to distinguish between market and non-market economies. However, he finds the oppositions "market/state" or "market/planned economy" as irrelevant to his notion of the market.[24] Furthermore, a complex, self-referential, learning system cannot be planned[25] due to its self-observing. This reasoning is very close to the famous Lucas critique (Lucas 1976) and concerns reflexivity of economic knowledge in general. Luhmann is well aware that economic science should intrude into the reality it depicts, and with the same act, it gradually loses its relevance (Luhmann 1988: 80).

The concept of competition receives a new interpretation as well. Luhmann thinks that competition is not a structure of a system because it cannot be imposed, communicated, and implemented but is rather a structure of the environment. He observes that competition is a structure that *minimizes conflict* and, indeed, any direct personal communication between agents, thus saving time and reducing other costs of interaction (in economic terms, transaction costs) but ensuring the homogenous reaction of all agents to some external event (he refers to the concept of social or mimetic contagion proposed by M. Aglietta and A. Orléan, who drew on ideas of R. Girard[26]). At the same time, he rejects the notion of maximal freedom associated with competition, noting that an agent faces the same imposition of prices (s)he cannot regulate, regardless of whether these prices are imposed by the market or by authority.[27] It is an important insight because it emphasizes, in the context of the economic system as a whole, the controversial nature of competition as something that avoids imposition and violence and, at the same time, should be (sometimes violently) imposed.

Luhmann's unusual conception of the market is still in line with modern economic sociology and especially game theory. One should only think of the notion of observation. It plays a fundamental role in Luhmann's approach and is indispensable for analysis of any communication, including an economic one. It is no wonder that analysis of observation is common in the modern game-theoretic accounts of economic interaction. However, Luhmann's perspective is more systemic. We do know that agents observe the other agents' actions, but what about self-reference of the economic system as a whole, which observes itself? Luhmann's perspective invites economists to move in that direction.

Luhmann and Economics: Implications and Heuristics

Luhmann's holistic perspective should not be considered a substitute for economics proper, as in some other approaches to economic sociology. Thus, Luhmann's theory is *not* an economic theory or a version of economic sociology among many others—it is pointless to question its epistemic status with respect to the data, for example. To take another example: the priority of communication over individual intentional action in social life is a strategic methodological choice on the part of Luhmann and theorists willing to follow him because to explain it conclusively is not a task Luhmann set for himself. His construction of the economy is thus a more general framework, a set of concepts that can perform *heuristic functions* in guiding research strategies both in orthodox and heterodox strands of modern economics. Luhmann thus proposes a social ontology of the economic world—an economic metaphysics (regardless of how ambiguous both these terms may seem in the context of Luhmann's work).

What are the heuristics relevant for economics that Luhmann's ontology implies? I distinguish three of them: a particular way of approaching (and hence abstracting) "the economic"; a methodological perspective radically different from that of methodological individualism common to modern economics; and a complex systems approach overcoming the open-closed systems dichotomy. We will address these three issues in order.

First, Luhmann suggests a specific understanding of *the economic* generally. His views differ from standard ideas expressed by "economic imperialists," who consider "economic" to be an adjective referring to intentional rational actions in different contexts (which can be, for example, political or familial). Luhmann does not emphasize individual rational behavior. Instead, he seeks a more "genuine" foundation of economic phenomena (payments, prices, and money), which would be closer to the actual economy. Indeed, it is an invitation for economists *to change the type of abstraction* they commonly use: not to move from individual rationality to various social phenomena (including institutions), but rather to approach the economy as an autonomous complex system and to abstract it from the other systems in society. The strategy is not to impose the logic of the economic on the other domains of the social but to carefully detach this logic (understood literally to be communications following a certain code) from all the other logics in the social life. This is not to mean, however, that Luhmann just wants to detach economic logic from all the others and leave economists alone with their models and theories. As we have seen, Luhmann's view of the social permits one to see the economy as a subsystem that differentiates itself but continues to be linked to the social system as a whole. Moreover, the economic logic for him does not boil down to formal (game-theoretic) rationality that is indifferent with respect to the subject matter at hand—be it law, politics, economics, or the Bible—and that long ago became a refuge for economic imperialists. Unlike them, Luhmann looks at the economic system from the holistic point of view.

Hence, second, Luhmann's approach is far from methodological individualism (understood as the position that economic phenomena must be explained in terms of intentional actions of individual economic agents[28]). Interestingly, this heuristic seems to be in line with many developments and various theoretical strategies in modern economics.[29] On the one hand, we can observe the reduction of individual characteristics to mental states (behavioral economics) and, on the other hand, the analysis emphasizing group behavior, direct interactions (see Kirman and Zimmerman 2001; Dawid and Fagiolo 2008), and various diffused cognitive structures, which are not to be associated exclusively with an individual who makes decisions according to his/her beliefs and preferences (Ross 2005; Kirman 2008). It also means that the economists of the 1970–1980s and Luhmann, who thought of an individual as an outdated concept fluctuating between a physical organism, cognitive system, and socially constructed person (Viskovatoff 2004: 2), followed similar intellectual paths.

An instructive example of these affinities concerns the concept of rationality. Luhmann claims that one needs an economic theory that would recognize the causal effects of economic activity on the economy's environment (Luhmann 1988: 38)—a claim that comes very close to modern discussions in ecological economics.[30] Inequality, conflict between the economic system and its environment, is resolved with the help of the price instability. However, precisely due to such simplicity, prices are unable to provide full information about the system's environment—to understand which resources are truly scarce one cannot rely on prices only. Therefore, Luhmann refuses to ascribe the title of rationality to the price system itself (as a means to differentiate the economic system), whereby rationality is defined in the language of a social system theory, as the situation in which "unity of difference between system and [its] environment is reproduced within the system" (Luhmann 1988: 42). Rationality, for Luhmann, is not to be gained by efficiency or optimization, but is rather the feature of a robust system that corrects internal and external errors in the face of growing uncertainty (Luhmann 1988: 122). It is *not individuals* who are rational *but the whole system* that is stable and acts in an appropriate way. "No one would think of trying to describe the activity of an ants' nest by examining the behavior of the 'representative ant', yet many would describe the allocation of effort and resources as 'efficient' " (Kirman 2008).[31] Some economists think similarly and look not for "microfoundations" for macroeconomics (as they used to do in the 1950s) but for macrofoundations of micro (Colander 1996), thus following Luhmann's dictum that communications are conditioned by the system as a whole.

Luhmann rejects methodological individualism (and the notion of action his teacher Parsons suggested[32]) on the grounds that the concept of *communication* is better suited to grasp the nature of social interactions. A statement that the "agent communicates" makes, for Luhmann, little sense, unlike the following: "Socially determined agents communicate with each other reproducing communication and reacting on each other's action"; therefore, the "social system produces communication." Modern economics, with its interest in mechanism design, incentives (as intersubjective constraints), contracts, networks, strategies, and institutions, appears to manifest precisely the same shift in attention from merely individual behavior to interactions (still conceptualized mainly as games) and to relatively stable structures of interactions (conceptualized as equilibria, institutions, and conventions) as something existing alongside minds and mental states of individual agents. Moreover, for modern complex systems theorists, "[h]ow individual agents decide what to do may not matter very much. What happens as a result of their actions may depend much more on the interaction structure through which they act—who interacts with whom, according to which rules" (Arthur, Durlauf, and Lane 1997: 9).

Luhmann's ontological stance and his attention to communication instead of intentional actions are reproduced (perhaps unconsciously) in some modern discussions, for example, in the "portrait of markets as software machines evolving in an environment of people towards no ultimate or final *telos*" (Mirowski 2004: 506). (Interestingly, Mirowski uses Luhmannian terminology without referring explicitly to Luhmann.) Games, conventions, and other intersubjective structures in economics can be analyzed taking into account their systemic and self-referential nature.[33] A system reproducing itself through *communications* (a concept virtually nonexistent in economics[34]) and observing itself is a nice metaphor that captures all of these developments in economics and in philosophy of economics.

Third, as I showed above, Luhmann does not recognize the sharp distinction between open and closed systems and approaches the economy as a system that is closed and open at the same time. I will turn to some remarkable recent discussions of closed and open systems in economic methodology (Chick and Dow 2005) and contrast them with Luhmann's perspective. The idea is to find theoretical and methodological commitments that would make sense of Luhmann's ideas in the context of modern economics. By no means do I suggest that Chick and Dow provide the only way to approach this complicated issue, but they nevertheless communicate some important insights from both economic theory and economic methodology.

In addressing systems, Chick and Dow distinguish between the level of reality and the level of theory. Real-world open systems are not atomistic—agents in them may learn, structures and interactions may evolve, outcomes of actions cannot be reduced to the results of individual actions (hence methodological individualism fails), the set of connections in any system is incomplete, and internal and external boundaries of the system may shift. For theory, it means that the number of relevant variables and their characters (endogenous/exogenous) may not be fixed, the relationships between them may be unstable, and our knowledge about the system's boundaries and environment is imperfect. In fact, many of the ideas summarized by Chick and Dow are inspired by Tony Lawson's (1997, 2003) account of open and closed systems.[35]

Chick and Dow realize that real-world systems are open but allow for usage of closed-system theorizing when open-system effects remain "at the back of one's head" and constant restructuring, re-design of a theory is practiced. Another idea is that there are no perfectly open or perfectly closed systems, but rather degrees of openness.

Both Luhmann and open-system methodology propose *to start from complexity*, not from simple premises. The constructive nature of Luhmann's theorizing (the observer defines differences and therefore creates his/her object of inquiry) is close to the flexibility of shifting boundaries and to the open system's incompleteness with respect to the theorist's needs in Chick and Dow's approach. Both Luhmann and Chick and Dow refuse to accept a strict duality between open and closed systems, although on different grounds: for Luhmann, any system is "fully" closed and "fully" open at the same time, whereas for Chick and Dow, there is a spectrum from perfect closure to perfect openness as ideal cases.

Luhmann proposes a vision of an economy that reconciles its openness and autonomy and can stop fruitless discussions of whether it is better to theorize open systems or closed ones. It also makes sense of what Chick and Dow (2001) mean by "keeping at the back of one's head" complex interactions stemming from the system's openness. For Luhmann, the system does not "see" its environment; rather, the environment triggers change within a system, and the system reacts to this change within itself, following its code. Luhmann's model of the system, which only sees itself, thus permits economists (following the first heuristic) to conduct economic analysis *per se*—an analysis that concentrates specifically on *economic* interactions—while being aware of the environment that clearly affects economic processes.

Of course, these themes are not the only ones that deserve being mentioned when we try to establish important links between Luhmann and modern economics. His clear emphasis on uncertainty (Beckert 2002), on the role of autopoiesis (related to the idea of enforcement familiar in economic theory), and on the importance of observation[36] are further themes that are of significance for the advancement of modern economic analysis.

Luhmann's economic metaphysics stresses deficiencies of standard two-valued logic for economic analysis (Luhmann 1988: 120)—due partly to the complexity of the economic system in which self-fulfilling prophecies emerge. He also emphasizes the pragmatic nature of economic agency—the urgency of making a decision despite any uncertainty one faces.[37] All of these ideas clearly diverge from standard economic thinking and are simply other arguments in favor of abandoning old stereotypes. They are also fully in line with modern ideas of applying formal logical reconstruction to economics and of questioning standard logical foundations of economic analysis (see, for example, Stigum 1990; Dow and Ghosh 2009).

What lessons can we draw from Luhmann's approach to economy? I would propose three of them. First, economic communications are not paradigmatic for any other communications; economists should concentrate on their own subject matter, being aware of the fact that they deal with an autonomous social system with its own particular logic. Second, this system observes, describes, and regulates itself, and its responses to its complex environment as well as its adaptation are to be discussed within a complex systems approach. Hence, evolutionary economics (or, more explicitly: agent-based modeling) is a promising way of conceptualizing the economy as an autonomous complex system (in Luhmann's sense). Third, economic theory in the "Luhmannian" spirit would involve a detailed analysis of ways to manage complexity in this autonomous economic system. The most appropriate theoretical language would be a holistic (institutional) one, analyzing evolving structures of communication that are designed to cope with uncertainty.

Conclusion

In this article, I have shown the richness and diversity of Luhmann's ideas. The analysis of some categories discussed in *Wirtschaft der Gesellschaft* shows that Luhmann's economic thinking is only one application of a much more general research program. Luhmann's ideas were *not* conceived as an economic theory. He distinguishes his work from what he terms "state-descriptions" (Zustandsbeschreibungen) of economic systems (Luhmann 1988: 127–130). Instead, he develops a set of concepts, attempting to capture fundamental (but generally unobservable) properties of the economic world and principles of economic life and to translate them into the language of his social theory. This approach is not something modern economists are inclined to take.

However, it does not mean that this enterprise does not make sense. Indeed, the very notion of the system, which follows its specific code, is an interesting way to show how a genuinely holistic perspective in economics may be adopted. I claimed that the discussion of a modern "economy as a complex system" has been moving along the same theoretical path. It means that Luhmann's social theory may inform contemporary economists and their research strategies, help in resolving long and seemingly fruitless methodological controversies in economics, and give them a general perspective on how the society as a whole may be conceptualized and what implications it has for their own research. Presumably, that should be the role of any deep social theory, and in this regard, various social theories are not mutually exclusive.

Does it all mean that economists have to wholly adopt a Luhmannian perspective? I doubt that such an outcome would be pleasant even for Luhmann himself. However, it does mean that Luhmann should occupy a firm place in our historical and methodological narratives, especially if we wish not only to have a picture of one science but also to view modes of economic thinking evolving over time and across disciplines.

Notes

1. The book (Luhmann 1988), which is clearly an allusion to Max Weber's "Wirtschaft und Gesellschaft," was followed by similar treatises covering science, risk, law, mass media, and art. Some other fundamental themes, such as love and education, were considered before the economy. Unlike these treatises, it was conceived not as a book but as a collection of articles written for the most part during the beginning of the 1980s. On the ambiguous status of subsystems in Luhmann, see below.

2. For general introductions to Luhmann, see, for example, Kneer and Nassehi (1993), Baraldi, Corsi, and Esposito (1997), and Krause (2005).

3. Luhmann is mentioned and discussed in many popular social theory textbooks—see, for example, Ritzer and Goodman (2003) and Baert and Carreira da Silva (2010).

4. When using the labels "economic theory," "social theory," and "economic sociology" I stick to the crudest of possible definitions, that is, I propose to name the discipline following the way it has been institutionally stabilized. Perhaps it is not the best way, but at least it helps avoid confusion and elaboration of disciplinary boundaries, which is an important theme in itself, although beyond the scope of this article. Economic theory is something taught at universities as "economics" or "political economy" (both orthodox and heterodox, including the study of classics like Marx or Schumpeter); social theory can be also derived from classics from Weber to Durkheim to Parsons but also has some modern classics (Luhmann is among them); and economic sociology is today for the most part associated with the "new" economic sociology (James Coleman, Marc Granovetter, Richard Swedberg, Harrison White, and some others being the founding fathers). But Luhmann's economic writing has not been adopted either by "economic theory" or by "economic sociology." Further distinctions (like game theory or institutional economics) are taken as various aspects of modern economic thinking that necessarily overlap but may nevertheless be distinguished.

5. "The point of departure for all system-theoretical analysis must be the *difference between system and its environment*" (Luhmann 1995: 16).

6. The remarkable ideological feature of a fully autonomous economy is that salvation, political appointments, and love cannot be bought and sold and are not subject to economic calculation (Baecker 2012).

7. Luhmann distinguishes between two types of environment—ecological and social (communicative). "For a functionally differentiated social system (economy, politics, etc.), all other subsystems are the environment, like the natural environment and psychological systems (processes of consciousness)" (Beckert 2002: 315). The ecological environments do not consist of communication. Subsystems of a social system also form (social) environments for each other since they differentiate themselves from one another. They are open both within the natural and the social environment.

8. Luhmann criticized equilibrium theorizing, with reference to Kornai (1971).

9. This tendency is evident, for example, in the works of Shleifer and Glaeser (2002, 2003), Acemoglu and Robinson (2006), and, of course, North (2005).

10. "The . . . distinction between 'closed' and 'open' systems is replaced by the question of how self-referential closure can create openness" (Luhmann 1995: 9).

11. This is the reason Luhmann calls it a "polycontextual" system (Luhmann 1988: 96, 126), a concept borrowed from the logic of Gotthard Günther.

12. Luhmann borrows the concept of an autopoietic system from the works of biologists Maturana and Varela (1980).

13. The circle of Quesnay's circular flow has to be "broken" by introducing land as the only means for creating the surplus, but at the same time, the economy reproduces itself according to its own autonomous logic, following economic laws.

14. Luhmann's emphasis on reproduction seems to place him virtually in the Sraffian camp because it is not an equilibrium but rather a self-reproduction, which is a starting point and, at the same time, a framework for his analysis. This version is also indirectly suggested by his idea that only the production sphere can form subsystems within an economic system because consumption forms a part of the whole of society (Luhmann 1988: 72–73).

15. It does not mean, however, that the system itself has a perfect a priori knowledge about what exactly its environment is. Luhmann stresses that the market success decides what the system's environment will be after trial-and-error activities in face of uncertainty (Luhmann 1988: 113).

16. Parallel to "payment" and "price" (and purportedly more general) may well be the concepts of "transaction" and "contract," respectively (Hutter 1994).

17. An owner of commodities "must . . . lend them his tongue, or hang a ticket on them, before their prices can be communicated to the outside world" (Marx 2000: 74).

18. Note that for Parsons, symbolically generalized media provided a means of communication *between* subsystems of a social system, whereas for Luhmann, money is a purely *internal* medium because economy for him represents *the whole* of society (encoded in a certain way).

19. Walter Benjamin's ([1928] 1991: 343) image of a "Totenkopf" (dead head) taken from Baroque drama is one version of such a mediation, showing both the transient character of a unique human existence and the recurring, inexorable course of natural processes, which constantly replicate themselves. However, it is only a metaphor that resolves the problem on a poetic and not a theoretical level.

20. The lack of information forces producers to mainly observe competitors and not consumers. See White (1981) and Luhmann (1988: 109).

21. Another, somewhat obscure, definition refers to the market as the difference between internal (and therefore certain, manageable) and external (uncertain) complexity (Luhmann 1988: 73). The uncertainty of the latter is attributed to the fact that it is the result of complex interactions of a given firm with its competitors in an ongoing process of mutual interdependence (and therefore of dependence upon one's own actions). It is this tension between internal and external complexity—along with the need to regulate it—that constitutes the market.

22. See Hildenbrand (1983) and Grandmont (1987) for the formalization of a similar intuition in mainstream economics.

23. As Viskovatoff (2000: 152) argues, Luhmann himself adopts a sort of constructivist perspective of the theoretician who observes observing systems and therefore constructs his object of inquiry. In fact, Beckert (2002: 209) describes orthodox economics in the Luhmannian sense, claiming that the maximization postulate is merely a heuristic, a cognitive structure invented by an observer (that is, a scientist) and imposed onto reality to cope with uncertainty.

24. A "market" in Luhmann's sense—as a systemic environment within an economy where competition, cooperation, and exchange emerge—exists and "works" in a socialist economy as well. Such economies are also able to reproduce themselves and thus, as Viskovatoff (2004: 10) remarks, to observe themselves. Luhmann suggests instead the subsistence economy as a counter-example to the market economy.

25. Arthur, Durlauf, and Lane (1997) make the case for the complex systems approach with their "no global controller" condition.

26. He also criticizes Aglietta and Orléan's (1982) theory of violence for the lack of a clear idea about whether to abandon the capitalist system for some alternative or to leave it as it is.

27. It is tempting to situate Luhmann among different economic ideologies and to name him, for example, a liberal or interventionist, but it is a misguiding intention: his theory is clearly beyond ideological oppositions. Even if he did

adopt a particular political attitude (for instance, an anti-interventionist one, on the grounds that the economy should function as an autonomous subsystem without any external restrictions, or an interventionist one, on the grounds that to cope with uncertainty, we have to consciously construct regulating institutions), it is largely irrelevant for our tasks.

28. There is a vast literature on the ambiguous and controversial nature of this concept in economics and in other social sciences. See, for instance, Udéhn (2001), Kincaid (2004), and Hodgson (2007).

29. For parallel discussions in economics, see, for example, Janssen (1993) and Hartley (1997).

30. Luhmann would claim, however, that ecological and economic systems should be distinguished since the natural environment of economic processes does not consist of communications unless they become part of the economy (as, for example, in the case of emissions trading).

31. Compare also Davis (2003) for a notion of rationality ascribed not to the individual, but rather to the rules of the game.

32. By no means do I suggest here that Parsons was a methodological individualist. His position was complex and evolved over time. The relationships between Parsons's theory of action and Luhmann's notion of communication are complicated and go beyond our concerns in this context.

33. Intersubjectivity and reflexivity of economic action have only recently become a part of the methodological discussion in modern economics (Fullbrook 2002; Davis and Klaes 2003).

34. Deirdre McCloskey's (1985, 1990) emphasis on communication could be an exception, but Luhmann's view is far wider than it appears to be in McCloskey, who has in mind verbal (rhetorical) communication as a primary model of communication as such.

35. Lawson defines a close system as a kind of experimental world with stable event regularities in place and proposes to use instead the methodology of demi-regularities that may or may not get realized.

36. It is only recently that historians of economics have begun to address the issue of observation in economics (this is the topic of the 2011 History of Political Economy (HOPE) conference).

37. In his analysis of agency, Luhmann tries to make sense of Gotthard Günther's "rejection value" as the third value in a multivalued logic, a value implying the refusal to assume the very choice between true and false. Compare in economics Samuelson's solution of a St-Petersburg paradox (Samuelson 1960).

References

Acemoglu, D., and J. Robinson. (2006). *Economic Origins of Dictatorship and Democracy.* Cambridge: Cambridge University Press.

Aglietta, M., and A. Orléan. (1982). *La violence de la monnaie*. Paris: PUF.
Arthur, W. B., S. N. Durlauf, and D. Lane. (1997). "Introduction." In *The Economy as an Evolving Complex System II*. Eds. W. B. Arthur, S. N. Durlauf, and D. Lane, pp. 1–14. Reading, MA: Addison-Wesley.
Baecker, D. (2012). "Die Wirtschaft der Gesellschaft." In *Luhmann-Handbuch: Leben—Werk—Wirkung*. Eds. A. Nassehi, O. Jahraus, I. Saake, M. Grizelj, Ch. Kirchmeier, and J. Müller, pp. 219–223. Stuttgart: Metzler.
Baert, P., and F. Carreira da Silva. (2010). *Social Theory in the Twentieth Century and Beyond*. London: Polity.
Baraldi, C., G. Corsi, and E. Esposito. (1997). *GLU. Glossar zu Niklas Luhmanns Theorie sozialer Systeme*. Frankfurt am Main: Suhrkamp.
Beckert, J. (2002). *Beyond the Market. The Social Foundations of Economic Efficiency*. Princeton: Princeton University Press.
Benjamin, W. (1991). "Ursprung des deutschen Trauerspiels." In *Gesammelte Schriften*. Bd. I, 1. Frankfurt am Main: Suhrkamp.
Chick, V., and S. Dow. (2001). "Formalism, Logic and Reality: a Keynesian Analysis." *Cambridge Journal of Economics* 25(6): 705–721.
———. (2005). "The Meaning of Open Systems." *Journal of Economic Methodology* 12(3): 363–381.
Colander, D. (1996). "The Macrofoundations of Micro." In *Beyond Microfoundations: Post Walrasian Macroeconomics*. Ed. D. Colander, pp. 57–68. Cambridge: Cambridge University Press.
Davis, J. B. (2003). *The Theory of the Individual in Economics*. London: Routledge.
Davis, J., and M. Klaes. (2003). "Reflexivity: Curse or Cure?" *Journal of Economic Methodology* 10(3): 329–352.
Dawid, H., and G. Fagiolo. (eds.) (2008). Special Issue on "Agent-Based Models for Economic Policy Design." *Journal of Economic Behavior and Organization* 67(2): 351–544.
Dow, S., and D. Ghosh. (2009). "Fuzzy Logic and Keynes's Speculative Demand for Money." *Journal of Economic Methodology* 16(1): 57–69.
Fullbrook, E. (ed.) (2002). *Intersubjectivity in Economics: Agents and Structures*. London: Routledge.
Ganßmann, H. (1988). "Money—A Symbolically Generalized Medium of Communication? On the Concept of Money in Recent Sociology." *Economy and Society* 17(3): 285–316.
Grandmont, J. M. (1987). "Distributions of Preferences and the Law of Demand." *Econometrica* 55(1): 155–162.
Hartley, J. (1997). *The Representative Agent in Macroeconomics*. London, New York: Routledge.
Hildenbrand, W. (1983). "On the Law of Demand." *Econometrica* 51(4): 997–1019.

Hodgson, G. (2007). "Meanings of Methodological Individualism." *Journal of Economic Methodology* 14(2): 211–226.

Hutter, M. (1994). "Communication in Economic Evolution: The Case of Money." In *Evolutionary Concepts in Contemporary Economics*. Ed. R. W. England, pp. 111–136. Ann Arbor: University of Michigan Press.

———. (1999). "Wie der Überfluß flüssig wurde. Zur Geschichte und zur Zukunft der knappen Ressourcen." *Soziale Systeme* 5(1): 41–54.

Janssen, M. C. W. (1993). *Microfoundations; A Critical Inquiry*. London, New York: Routledge.

Kincaid, H. (2004). "Methodological Individualism and Economics." In *Elgar Companion to Economics and Philosophy*. Eds. J. B. Davis, A. Marciano, and J. Runde, pp. 299–314. Cheltenham: Edward Elgar.

Kirman, A. P. (2008). "Economy as a Complex System." In *The New Palgrave Dictionary of Economics*. 2nd edition. Eds. S. N. Durlauf and L. E. Blume. London etc.: Palgrave Macmillan.

Kirman, A., and J.-B. Zimmerman. (eds.) (2001). *Economics with Heterogeneous Interacting Agents*. Heidelberg: Springer.

Kneer, G., and A. Nassehi. (1993). *Luhmanns Theorie sozialer Systeme. Eine Einführung*. München: Fink.

Kornai, J. (1971). *Anti-Equilibrium*. Amsterdam: North Holland.

Krause, D. (2005). *Luhmann-Lexikon*. 4. Aufl. Stuttgart: UTB.

Lawson, T. (1997). *Economics and Reality*. London, New York: Routledge.

———. (2003). *Reorienting Economics*. London, New York: Routledge.

Lucas, R. (1976). "Econometric Policy Evaluation: A Critique." In *The Phillips Curve and Labor Markets, Carnegie-Rochester Conference Series on Public Policy* 1: 19–46.

Luhmann, N. (1988). *Wirtschaft der Gesellschaft*. Frankfurt am Main: Suhrkamp.

———. (1995). *Social Systems*. Trans. by J. Bednarz Jr. with D. Baecker. Stanford: Stanford University Press.

Marx, K. (2000). *Das Kapital*. Vol. I. Washington: Gateway Editions.

Maturana, H. R., and F. J. Varela. (1980). *Autopoiesis and Cognition: The Realization of the Living*. Dordrecht: Reidel.

McCloskey, D. (1985). *The Rhetoric of Economics*. Madison: University of Wisconsin Press.

———. (1990). *If You're So Smart: The Narrative of Economic Expertise*. Chicago: University of Chicago Press

Mirowski, Ph. (2004). "Philosophizing with a Hammer." *Journal of Economic Methodology* 11(4): 499–513.

North, D. C. (2005). *Understanding the Process of Economic Change*. Princeton: Princeton University Press.

Parsons, T. (1968). "Interaction: Social Interaction." In *International Encyclopedia of the Social Sciences*, pp. 429–441, Vol. 7. New York: Macmillan.

Ritzer, G., and D. J. Goodman. (2003). *Sociological Theory.* 6th ed. New York: McGraw-Hill.

Ross, D. (2005). *Economic Theory and Cognitive Science: Microexplanation.* Cambridge, MA: MIT Press.

Samuelson, P. (1960). "The St. Petersburg Paradox as a Divergent Double Limit." *International Economic Review* 1(1): 31–37.

Shleifer, A., and E. Glaeser. (2002). "Legal Origins." *Quarterly Journal of Economics* 117(4): 1193–1229.

———. (2003). "The Rise of the Regulatory State." *Journal of Economic Literature* 41(2): 401–425.

Smith, A. (1778). *An Inquiry into the Nature and Causes of the Wealth of Nations.* 2nd ed. London: Pr. for W. Strahan & T. Cadell.

Stigum, B. (1990). *Toward a Formal Science of Economics.* Cambridge, MA: MIT Press.

Udéhn, L. (2001). *Methodological Individualism: Background, History and Meaning.* London and New York: Routledge.

Viskovatoff, A. (1998). "Two Conceptions of Theory." *Research in the History of Economic Thought and Methodology* 16: 91–122.

———. (1999). "Foundations of Niklas Luhmann's Theory of Social Systems." *Philosophy of the Social Sciences* 29(4): 481–516.

———. (2000). "Will Complexity Turn Economics into Sociology?" In *Complexity and the History of Economic Thought.* Ed. D. Colander, pp. 129–154. London: Routledge.

———. (2004). "The Market as an Environment." *Journal des Economistes et des Etudes Humaines* 14(2): Article 4.

White, H. (1981). "Where Do Markets Come From?" *American Journal of Sociology* 87(3): 517–547.

Social Network Analysis and the Sociology of Economics: Filling a Blind Spot with the Idea of Social Embeddedness

By Dieter Bögenhold*

Abstract. Today, social networks analysis has become a cross-disciplinary subject with applications in diverse fields of social and economic life. Different network designs provide different opportunities to communicate, to receive information, and to create different structures of cultural capital. Network analysis explores modes and contents of exchanges between different agents when symbols, emotions, or goods and services are exchanged. The message of the article is that social network analysis provides a tool to foster the understanding of social dynamics, which enhances recent debate on a micro-macro gap and on limitations of the cognitive and explanatory potential of economics.

Introduction[1]

Many social sciences, but especially economics and sociology, are arranged in faculties, courses, and textbooks on the basis of macro and micro analysis. Research on the connection between micro and macro perspectives has been scarce and the subject is virtually neglected (see Hoover 2009, 2010; Colander 1993). In economics, no consensus exists as to whether macro follows micro or vice versa. While a macro perspective dominated for a long time since Wicksell "more or less founded macroeconomics" (Blaug 1986: 274), recently Rodgers (2011: ch. 2), who puts some of the discussed theoretical trends in a wider social perspective of thought, argues that micro views have gained some advantages nowadays.

In many respects, network analysis may be a tool to bridge both perspectives. Social embeddedness seems to have become "economic

*Alpen-Adria University Klagenfurt, Department of Sociology, Faculty of Management and Economics, Universitätsstrasse 65-67, 9020 Klagenfurt, Austria; E-mail address: Dieter.Boegenhold@aau.at

sociology's most celebrated metaphor" (Guillén et al. 2002: 4). Social network analysis may be able to translate and to exemplify those popular formulations. Different network designs provide different opportunities to communicate and to receive information and, as a result, they create different structures of social contacts and an unequal distribution of knowledge, which serve as a kind of social capital for individual agents. Network analysis enquires of the modes and content of exchanges between people, where symbols (concepts, values, and norms), emotions (love, respect or hostility), or goods or services (especially financial subsidies and gifts) are exchanged. Network research has become an evolving cross-disciplinary subject with applications in many diverse fields of social and economic life. Even physicists show an increasing interest in network research (Scott 2011).

The aim of the article is to present a compelling argument for social network analysis as a valid way to illuminate the idea of social embeddedness, since it provides dynamic aspects that are inherent in structures often commonly treated as blueprints. Social network analysis sits comfortably alongside recent discussions within the field of philosophy of economics, examining the limitations of mainstream economics. It has been argued that economics should be open to the integration of behavioral and cognitive elements (Akerlof 2007; Akerlof and Kranton 2000; Akerlof and Shiller 2009; Kahneman 2003) in order to assist the movement of economics from the world of abstract modeling to real-world phenomena. Viewing economics as a box of tools (Schumpeter 1954: Preface) permits one to identify social network analysis as an economic technique with the potential to map with economic behavior, institutions, and economic and social change. That is because social network analysis will foster a shift from abstract economics towards an economics dealing with real people.

If sociology can claim that traditional network research belongs on sociological terrain, then the improving reception of the literature on social networks and the growing acceptance of interdisciplinary network research necessarily requires sociological competency in the subject. In other words, institutional academic sociology can use the subject of network sociology as a positive example to demonstrate the comparative strengths of academic sociology.

By referring to the network issue in a broader sense and at different levels, one can show that specific regions, related companies, and economies differ in terms of their network structures, implying that they have specific family structures and structures of interaction, communication, and exchange. Consequently, different structures reflect the issue that has been expressed by the formulation of "Culture Matters" (Harrison and Huntington 2000). In contrast to sterile neoclassical economics, which aims at universal principles in a capitalist economy, the topic of network structures, which by definition includes corresponding variability, must be regarded as a counterweight to abstract theorizing in economics (Jones 2006).

The current article addresses the challenges brought out in two major areas of discussion. First of all, the article tries to provide a survey of positions in the history of intellectual debate on network research. Moreover, the composition of arguments and related references is more concerned with a sociology of science. In contrast to, and in critique of, formal and abstract attempts of theorizing in economics and in sociology, the article wants to show that social network research highlights what cultural sciences want to express, which is that *culture matters*. Networks integrate the level of action and communication with issues of structural selection and social change, which is the reason that social networks can be viewed as both a theoretical and methodological concern simultaneously. Different network structures in different cultures frame individual decision making and choice (Becker 1974) by providing specific sets of preferences (Ellison 1995). Cultures within related times and spaces provide a differing calculus of individual rationality.

Network Research and Academic Innovation: Against the *Homo Oeconomicus*

When discussing sociological network theory, we follow an innovative script that invites academic and economic and policy issues of *real* societies and economies (as opposed to abstract societies and economies) as subjects for research. Network research, especially when applied, is increasingly interdisciplinary and provides an adequate response to the limitations of mono-disciplinary approaches (Marcovich and Shinn 2011), which are always in danger of being quasi-autistic. It is just the intensive study of the economic development that illustrates our genuine understanding of Schumpeter, namely, that innovation is the enforcement of "new combinations" (Schumpeter [1911] 1963: 100–102) of ways to produce.

Referring to differences in economic structures between countries and within countries, many of the differences to be found may reflect different culture-related organizational principles of economic life that are reflected by divergent social network structures, which mirror divergent training, education, and employment arrangements and, ultimately, different family structures, different systems of industrial relations, and economic mentalities. As a result, a variety of social actors can be found that cannot be reduced to the simple idealized figure of *homo oeconomicus* as the ideal model of a "clean" economics would have it. The idea of *homo oeconomicus* itself is a stereotype that does not acknowledge properly the semantic changes over time (Pearson 2000). Nevertheless, historian David Landes (2000: 2) put it concisely: "Culture makes almost all the difference."

Thinking along those lines, the intersection between a perspective on social network analysis and research on institutional economics and socioeconomic systems becomes visible; both aim to understand the object of analysis in its social and historical context. Instead of referring to stereotypical classifications that emphasize generalized statements on nature, the role and function of *the* society or *the* economy, independent of specific cultural and historical contexts, economic life never takes place without an interplay with its real social and economic environment. Peter Berger put it this way: "Economic institutions do not exist in a vacuum but rather in a context of social and political structures, cultural patterns, and indeed, structures of consciousness (values, ideas, belief systems). An economic culture then contains a number of elements linked together in an empirical totality" (Berger 1986: 24).

This position is constitutive for new economic sociology, which takes up a tradition going back to *old institutionalism* that intersected the *new historical* school in the German-speaking world (Schmölders

1984) and also works simultaneously in North America (see Dorfman 1946–1959). There is an inherent common logic between modern works in sociology and those in economics that criticize the status of mainstream economics. The term "heterodox economics" (Lee 2009) stands for this form of critique. In the center of the related critique is the model of the *homo oeconomicus* as it is used in neoclassical theory. The basic assumptions are: "1. The assumption of rational, maximizing behavior by agents with given and stable preference functions, 2. A focus on attained, or movements toward, equilibrium states, 3. The absence of chronic information problems (there is, at most, a focus on probabilistic risk: excluding severe ignorance, radical uncertainty, or divergent perceptions of a given reality)" (Hodgson 1994: 60).

In our discussion, it is the first and third items of Hodgson's notion that are of interest: human beings have motives, which may be viewed as rational *or* irrational by observers (Lauterbach 1962; Rabin 1998), and people have emotions by which they are governed positively or negatively (Elster 1998, Scherer 2011). Love, hate, or envy are expressions of human activity that are real. Human beings love human beings, yet they kill people on occasion, they take part in lotteries, or they present gifts and cheat elsewhere (see, for emotions, Turner and Stets 2009; Stets and Turner 2007). Human beings do not share the same network structures but have divergent communication structures and related modes of interaction. Communication processes are asynchronous—everybody cannot speak with everybody else, but only a few people in specific groups communicate regularly with selected others, and consequently information in society is not shared equally. The topic of social networks tries to highlight the blind spots of neoclassical theory (Smelser and Swedberg 1994). Society is conceptualized as a configuration of different patterns of interactions that party overlap and partly coexist. The question of the institutional framing and of the relevance of culture is not only the legitimacy of doing appropriate analysis on economies and societies (Jones 2006), but it is a *conditio sine qua non* if one wants to avoid a sterile economic discussion that neglects diverse social networks and structures of motivations in order to arrive at generalized statements.

Society *in Abstracto* Versus *in Concreto*: An Epistemological View

Differentiation of academic subjects and disciplines, especially in the second part of the 20th century, brought increasing autonomy to the disparate sections of social sciences, and consequently academic communication between individual branches of the subject decreased. An archipelago of new academic islands emerged, most with an intensive island life, but the communication traffic between each was scarce and almost silent. Economics suffered from a loss of access to sociological and behavioral contexts, and came to favor *a priori* assumptions regarding human action. The trend ran parallel with a shift in economic theorizing towards formalized modeling and theory building instead of real-world analysis (Mikl-Horke 1999: ch. 13) but modeling itself became differentiated and contradictory (Morgan 2011).

As scientific theorems became more formal and abstract, dimensions such as space and time lost their significance, theorizing became increasingly non-historical and non-cultural since sterility was precisely the aim. In economics, a substantial number of positions neglected culture for that very reason, and often with quite offensive arguments. In that respect, there is a parallel between the approach of Karl Marx and formulations in neoclassic theory and its related idea of *homo oeconomicus*. Marx thinks human actors are treated simply as agents of roles, as personifications of economic categories, which function like actors interpreting a specific script (Marx 1977: 16). In terms of their methodological procedures, economists engaged in marginal utility theory proved to be quite similar. Karl Menger and associates assumed that human needs that are relevant for economic life occur at different stages, which lead—from stage to stage—to decreasing ratios of satisfaction and finally to the marginal utility of the last available unit. This idea was not based upon empirical psychological research because it was not regarded as necessary. Deductive reasoning came up with *a priori* statements instead.

Arguing against Menger, there was Gustav Schmoller, who opposed Menger in what came to be called the first battle of methods in social sciences. Schmoller's intention was to criticize the abstract nature of those models solely based on non-empirical assumptions. Schmoller argued institutionally in favor of the cultural and historical embeddedness of observations.[2] The 20th century represented the triumph of Menger's thought and his marginal utility theory became a foundation of a neoclassical economics clearly distinct from sociology and historicism (Hodgson 2001).

Today, the works of Max Weber and Werner Sombart are better known both in terms of their theoretical impact and empirical content. Religious dispositions and economic mentalities were discussed in relation to the establishment of socioeconomic systems and Weber elaborated a typology of four ideal types of social action, which are the rationality of traditional action, of affective action, of value orientation, and of purposive-rational utilitarian action (Weber 1972: pt. 1, ch. 1) of which only the last point of classification matches with the supposed rationality of *homo oeconomicus*.[3] Being distant to a procedure as provided in theoretical economics, Max Weber concluded that economics "argues with a non-realist human being, analogous a mathematical ideal figure" (Weber 1990: 30). The questioning of the institutional framework of economic phenomena and the relative autonomy of networks corresponds with the recognition of the impact of culture within the process of economic development. According to Sombart (1982), all economies and their inherent economic lives are related to specific times and spaces, which are always embedded in a historical flux. The perspective comes very close to that of a modern interdisciplinary program, both claiming a dialogue between economics and neighboring academic fields.

The Idea of "Social Embeddedness"

As ideas about an economy and society *in concreto* are increasingly accepted, so the relative autonomy of culture and its specification in different historical variations is also increasingly accepted. A plea for the academic existence of sociology must be the ultimate consequence. In particular, historical and comparative sociology, socioeconomics and economic sociology, and, of course, social network research prove to be innovative when highlighting national and international variations and specifics. In general, one can also argue that history, economics, business administration, and sociology should try to reintegrate because their topics are among the items in a complex web of reciprocal thematic interaction. The concept of the "social embeddedness" of institutional actors and human behavior is a common label for approaches that attempt to deal with the interplay of individual and corporate actors in a dynamic and joint process. "Social embeddedness," as a term and conceptual idea, goes back to Karl Polanyi, who became especially well-known through his book, *The Great Transformation* (2001), which elaborates on the genesis of a self-regulatory market in Europe, and particularly in England. Polanyi's concept shows clear links to Durkheimian thought (Carroll and Stanfield 2003).

Polanyi contends that all societies are regulated and limited by economic factors. Parallel to the course of the establishment of free and self-regulatory markets, Polanyi observes a process of social differentiation. Status and community dominate where an economy is integrated in non-economic institutions, but contract and society are characteristic of a separation of economy and society.

According to Polanyi, an economy is a process embedded in economic and non-economic institutions. The integration of economic life runs in three different ways, namely, through the mode of reciprocity, which is dedicated to social networks and kinship relations, through the mode of redistribution, which depends on a central organization in society, and through processes of exchange integrating the economy into a system of market prices. The semantic use of "social embeddedness" originated from anthropology (and is still to be found in substantive anthropology) but it has now been adopted by a range of other disciplines.

The impact of such a perspective is that modern economics could be linked with a constructive view that provides a new division of work between economics and the other social sciences (Granovetter 1993). Granovetter's formulation of a "social embeddedness of economic behavior and institutions" (Granovetter 1985) has subsequently become widely known. Granovetter focuses explicitly on the work of Polanyi and his argumentation is based upon three premises, namely, that economic action is a special case of social action, secondly, that economic action is socially situated and embedded, and thirdly, that economic institutions are social constructions. A synthesis is sought between conceptions of over-socialized and under-socialized human beings in order to articulate a theorem that takes into account both the determination of society and the relative openness of human activities as a process (Granovetter 1993, 2002). Granovetter argues against the concept of a *homo oeconomicus* as used in neoclassical thought and against a model of a *homo sociologicus* in which an individual agent is controlled by social norms and roles.

Social network research has, partly implicitly and partly explicitly, adopted Granovetter's preambles as a research program. Economy and society are permanently "in the making" and they are best interpreted as the socially structured and motivated interaction of actors. Social actions are constituted along existing ties of contacts, which are based upon social experiences within different social circles of communication.

The Genesis of Network Research: Some Retrospective Observations

Geometry of Social Relations and Structures of Reciprocity

The earliest network research is attributed to Georg Simmel. Although Simmel was not strictly a network researcher, he was a researcher who thought in categories quite similar to network approaches found today. Simmel portrayed society in dualistic terms, exemplified by the word pairs of universality and particularity, continuity and change, or conformism and distinction. In addition, people are dualistic and Simmel thinks of dualism as a driving force of development, which creates change.

The earliest sociologists thought of society in terms of the *geometry of social relations*. In the same way that geometry deals with forms capable of becoming bodies, the analysis of abstract forms was a major task for Simmel's work. Social formations are characterized and constituted through continuous repetition. Simmel's view of the cross-pressures of social circles ("Kreuzung sozialer Kreise"; Simmel 1908) appears very similar to the modern analysis of cliques in contemporary network analysis. The dispositions of individual actors differ according to their positions in a network, and personality, in the sense of individuality, is a result of the cross-pressures of circles. Networks function as modes of social differentiation *and* societal trends of standardization. Finally, social structures are conceptualized as *relational*—and principally changing—links between human actors and organizations.

A different origin of contemporary network discussion can be seen in anthropology, where structural attributes of societies will be discussed in the context of processes of gift giving, marriages, or authority and violence. Mauss (2002, 2006) demonstrates how the giving and exchanging of gifts is organized along social norms and processes. Often, no specific economic advantage is connected to the exchange of gifts and sometimes the same things are even exchanged between two parties, suggesting that beyond the economic rationalities a specific social logic must be working.

Individual agents, families, and tribes combine with each other through the exchanges of gifts and of "throats to be cut which are 'lent' and 'repaid' " (Collins 1988: 419). As a consequence, social relations emerge and are intensified so that circles of reciprocal connections between families and tribes are constructed. Although the terminology of networks is not used, the topic is obviously close. Reciprocal *ties* based upon different manners of exchange between actors constitute the structure of societies.

Structure as a term also has substantial meaning in the works of Lévi-Strauss.[4] In the societies he analyzed, families form alliances through marriages of dependent family members that lead to reciprocal commitments. Such alliances provide for the distribution of goods and services. Since the patterns of kinship exchange vary between societies, Lévi-Strauss addresses the dynamics of the structures by asking for specific rules for marriage practices (Lévi-Strauss 1987) and by distinguishing between "short cycles," which unify a small number of families and that are stable over a few generations, and "long cycles," which unify many more families indirectly and families that may also be geographically separated (Collins 1994: 231).

The works of Mauss and Lévi-Strauss are antecedents of modern network research but their perspective is already clear and convincing. Families establish *ties* and create simple and complex networks. This structural approach describes the structure of societies and related dynamics and changes to these societies. The argumentation is in no way restricted to agrarian or tribal societies, but can be applied to modern societies as well.

Later, other anthropologists produced more elaborate theoretical and empirical work on networks, trying to deal with particular units and relations. British structural functionalists like Radcliffe-Brown and the "Manchester anthropologists"—John Barnes, Clyde Mitchell, Elizabeth Bott—focused on cultural systems of normative rights and duties, which govern behavior within specific ensembles like tribes, villages, or working groups (Wellman 1988: 21).

Radcliffe-Brown is often credited as the originator of the term *social network*: he wrote that "direct observation does reveal to us that these human beings are connected by a complex network of social relations. I use the term 'social structure' to denote this network of actually existing relations" (Radcliffe-Brown 1940: 2). Radcliffe-Brown's terminology inspired other anthropologists to discuss contemporary metaphors such as "fabric," "web," "interweaving," and "interlocking" and to extend them to formal concepts like "density" and "texture" (Scott 2010).

The work of anthropologists in the 1950s focused on cultural systems, which had limitations when relations occurred that were transitory to close groups or categories. "*Concrete ties*" and "*cross-cutting ties*" were discussed, and network analysis started in earnest by developing systematic network concepts. In his study of a Norwegian island on which he discovered hidden networks of friendship and kinship, which sometimes crossed the hierarchical, administrative, and industrial structures, Barnes (1954) produced pioneering work. His network of relations was built upon intentional choices made by individual actors that partially reflected the class system of the island. Barnes initiated a change from a metaphoric network to a network term corresponding to modern network analysis, which is close to graph theory (Scott 2010: 27).

The research program of these anthropologists was focused on particular social relations to determine structures with inherent patterns of action. A crucial advance was added by structuralists like Harrison White and associates (White, Boorman, and Breiger 1976), who introduced the block-model analysis, which is still on the agenda in evolved form and is used by mathematicians and physicists and members of other disciplines (see Scott 2010: 33). The basic premise was to use network concepts in order to arrive at a theory of social structures:

The presently existing, largely categorical description of social structure has no solid theoretical grounding; furthermore, network concepts may provide the only way to construct a theory of social structure (White, Boorman, and Breiger 1976: 732). Many subsequent network-related studies and research topics tried to foster "a broadly comprehensive structural analytic approach" (Wellman 1988: 29).

Social Network Research as Research of Social and Economic Dynamics

Social network analysis has become a cross-disciplinary subject with applications in many diverse fields of social and economic life, and it continues to evolve. One of the most challenging fields to investigate is market dynamics, a subject very often regarded as a black box by mainstream economists (Swedberg 2003). Markets function upon the basis of communication and social rules, which may be addressed by social-network-oriented research perspectives. At least two of the crucial research conclusions Fligstein (2001) drew in his *Architecture of Markets* are relevant for network research; these are: "What social rules must exist for markets to function, and what types of social structures are necessary to produce stable markets?" and "What is a 'social' view of what actors seek to do in markets, as opposed to an 'economic' one ?" (Fligstein, 2001: 11, 14). Markets are always in transition, they come up, they go down, and they change. The markets are populated by actors utilizing sets of people they know and in whom they trust, while regarding other people as potentially hostile competitors. However real markets are portrayed, they always have very social traits, and economics researchers would be neglecting their duties if they were not to ask about their effects. Competition processes must also be analyzed and understood as ongoing social processes that are involved in the continual reorganization (see Shackle 1972) of choices and decisions in relation to uncertainty.

The analysis of markets and processes of innovation has involved a variety of approaches, of which just three are mentioned here. Besides the works of White, it is worth mentioning network studies interpreting markets as networks (White 1981, 1988; Granovetter 1985; Baker 1984, 1990). A specific issue of research is how structures of a network *influence* markets and the different chances individual actors have according to their specific position in a network (Burt 1995). The starting point of the structural approach is the assumption that "markets may be viewed as social rather than exclusively economic structures" (Baker 1984: 776).[5] Burt summarizes the research idea programmatically when talking about the "social structure of completion" (Burt 1995, later broadly reformulated as Burt 2007).

Granovetter (1973, 1974) started to do labor market research in the 1970s, inquiring of the social processes involved in finding new jobs. His theorem of *"the strength of weak ties"* has since become a classic formulation. Granovetter referred to informal channels of getting information, which were introduced through micro structural perspectives. Later, Granovetter (1985, 2002) extended his argumentation to a discussion of macro-level structures when examining the social embeddedness of institutions and behavior and when discussing different modes of structures.

Baker (1984) performed network research on the social structure of stock markets. His study distinguishes between different markets and types of markets, which are carried out by different forms of social relations. This perspective holds that network structures serve as both cause *and* result of social processes. Finally, when referring to the ideas of Burt (1995), Baker (1984), or Granovetter (1974), it is important to note that they all center on the question "Where do markets come from ?" (White 1981) and favor a type of answer with a strong link to social foundations. New information, ideas, and opportunities come up through different forms of strong or weak ties between people in different clusters (see Bögenhold and Marschall 2008).

Social Network Analysis: Innovation, Theory, and Methods

The modern social-science-based understanding of how economy and society are linked seems to confer legitimacy upon social network research, owing to its offering a package of different perspectives and insights. The argumentation in the current article travels a long line within the history of thought in social network analysis. The evolution of research in the field has become remarkable and a series of journals and research committees have been founded worldwide. In the meantime, the *International Network for Social Network Analysis* (www.insna.org) has more than 1,700 members with very diverse academic backgrounds in 78 countries. Reading contributions in the field sometimes demands very specialized expertise in specific academic areas. Over time, the complexities increase and the applications multiply (Dehmer 2010). While network analysis started in anthropology and sociology, employing qualitative methods and local community studies, in the last few decades, quantitative methods have made strong advances in network research. In some disciplines, like physics, large-scale analysis has become the predominant method. However, even today, qualitative studies remain a useful and valuable field for social network research, ranging from anthropology to conversation and discourse analysis and other applications. In addition, historians increasingly refer to network concepts (see, for example, Rota 2007; Laird 2006).

Network research studies usually strengthen and highlight the inner dynamics of societies (for an overview, see Scott 2010; Carrington, Scott, and Wasserman 2009; Wasserman and Faust 2009; Carrington and Scott 2010; Stegbauer 2008; Häußling and Stegbauer 2010; Newman 2010; Easley and Kleinberg 2010; Burt 2010). Orthodox and heterodox economics could both take advantage of these conceptual ideas in order to instigate innovative research programs; other disciplines, like sociology, already do so.

Social network analysis now makes a constructive contribution in many academic fields. To neglect network structures bears the risk that the social figuration processes of interaction and the basic principles that underpin them are ignored. If one does not know the modes of interaction and communication, one does not know the ways in which signs, symbols, and contents are transported. To be able to study processes of diffusion requires information about ties and links of exchange. All processes of innovation and the diffusion of innovation are highly dependent upon communicative acts of people belonging to different networks, sharing and providing information through different media (Rogers 2003). Whether related to the innovation of production systems in diverse commercial fields, or to customers and their consumer behavior and social lifestyles, all hierarchies of preferences are crystallized in and through networks and constructed by opinion leaders. Networks are always the media holding (diverse) knowledge and the media through which that knowledge is modified.

One of the most intriguing questions is whether the way networks function has changed over time. Due to the increased prevalence of modern electronic communication systems, we not only have electronic markets but also new forms of private exchange through the Internet or by cell phone (Wellman and Haythornthwaite 2002). Does this development create new patterns of communication and network structures? How are network structures linked to increased social and occupational mobility? Has the relevance of family-based ties decreased in the era of individualization and globalization or is the opposite in fact evident? Do demographic changes have an impact on network structures? Will the increasing number of elderly people in society lead to changing network structures? Catalogues of questions could be formed to provide grounds for justifiable further research.

Since social network research has evolved so rapidly in recent decades, two specific questions have assumed great importance and must be answered explicitly: (i) Does network research still fit into one single academic subject? The answer must promptly follow that network research has become too diverse to be identified as part of *one* discipline. Network research has become a kind of cross-disciplinary way of thinking and, as such, it might become a new academic area in its own right. (ii) What is the status of social network research? Is it a theory or is it a research method?

To answer, one should first clarify what is meant by theory. Half a century ago Schumpeter (1954) wrote that a scientific economist can be distinguished from a simple economist by a command of techniques classified in different fields, that is, economic history, statistics, economic sociology, and theory and applied fields. In this context the word theory is always written with quotation marks—as "theory"—to underline that it is problematic to talk about theory as if a common understanding of the term existed. In fact, there is no unanimously agreed definition of theory at all, different types of theory coexist (see, for recent contributions, Bunge 1996; Haller 2003: ch. 1; Schülein 2009: 42–65) and the question of when an academic statement acquires the status of theory remains a moot point (Turner 1988: 4).

Reviewing several existing pieces of literature dealing with the question of whether social network analysis is primarily theory or instead a method shows that we have not yet found any coherent answers. The basic denominator is that social network analysis seems to be something of a hybrid (Bögenhold and Marschall 2010). Universally, network research is qualified as an important instrument, but the difficulty remains of how to describe the status of network analysis. More than 20 years ago Wellman (1988: 20) said: "Some have hardened it into a method, whereas others have softened it into a metaphor" and Collins referred to network analysis as a "technique in search of a theory" (Collins 1988: 412).

Ten years later Turner (1998: 528) says that the potential for network analysis as a theoretical approach is great because it captures an important property of social structure—patterns of relations among social units, whether people, collectivities, or positions. However, Turner's judgment is that network analysis is still overly methodological in nature and that it is concerned with generating quantitative techniques for arraying data in matrices and then converting the matrices into descriptions of particular networks (whether as graphs or as equations). As long as that is the case, network sociology will remain primarily a tool for empirical description. Second, there has been little effort to develop principles of network dynamics, *per se*. Few seem to ask theoretical questions within the network tradition itself. For example, how does the degree of density, centrality, equivalence, bridging, and brokerage influence the nature of the network and the flow of relations among positions in the network? There are many empirical descriptions of events that touch on this question but few actual theoretical laws or principles (Turner 1998: 529).

Strategically, networks provide a link between micro and macro perspectives. They integrate the level of action and communication with issues of structural selection and social change. Networks serve as "sets" of preferences and social contacts between individual agents and groups of people. The bloodstream of society runs through networks. Whereas many writers treat the functioning of markets as something close to a black box, in which offer and demand equalize somehow, network analysis sheds far more light on the processes and informs us of how economic dynamics are often based upon social dynamics in which personal experiences and trust play important roles. Markets as well as many other institutions provide resources to human actors through different levels of inclusion, which function through principles of social networks (Burt and Talmud 1993). That the status of social network analysis remains unresolved and weak (the theory versus method debate) implies that there is room for further input here.

From Social Network Analysis to Social Capital

Discussion of social network analysis often elicits mention of the term social capital, as if both terms are interchangeable. It seems appropriate to conclude the current article by adding some brief reflection on the relationship between social networks and social capital. The answer is very simple, since social networks *can* serve as social capital for individuals or groups of people. Sets of specific networks, which one actor has compared to those of another actor, may be understood and used as a kind of economic resource.

Even the debate on social capital is marked by a long history of ideas going back to early neighborhood and community studies, starting in the middle of the 20th century. However, the works of Bourdieu (1983) and Coleman (1988, 1990) addressed social capital more specifically and conceptually. Addressing "capital as power" (Nitzan and Bichler 2009), Bourdieu (1983) is primarily interested in inquiring of the analytical position of social resources and strategies in the context of economy and society. How can individuals, groups, or classes enhance their life-chances, careers, and quality of life? What many previous social network researchers have thought about, but rarely articulated, is explicitly elaborated as a conceptual perspective embedded in a broader scenario. Bourdieu (1983) distinguishes between economic capital, which he interprets in a classic sense as material and financial capital and assets, cultural capital, which includes an interpretation of human capital, and can be further split into subsections, and, finally, social capital. Individuals or collectives own different amounts of capital consisting of different compositions of the three sources of capital. Finally, capital of one sort can partly be instrumentalized to realize capital profits of another sort. Bourdieu's perspective left behind a narrow social network perspective and started focusing on the more principal issues of order and restructuring of complex societies and their social inequalities. Social capital is interpreted as the volume of social resources of a person's networks.

Coleman (1990) searches for the "social foundations of social theory" and has devoted a substantial chapter (chapter 12) of his *Foundations of Social Theory* to a discussion of social networks. He says that social capital and human capital are often complementary (Coleman 1988).

> Social capital, in turn, is created when the relations between people change in ways that facilitate action. Physical capital is wholly tangible, being embodied in observable material form; human capital is less tangible, being embodied in the skills and knowledge acquired by an individual; social capital is even less tangible, for it is embodied in the *relations* between people. Physical capital and human capital facilitate productive activity, and social capital does so as well. (Coleman 1990: 304)

Coleman (1990) does not restrict social capital to resources based upon social networks, but includes in his definition institutional interpretations as well. Those include family structures, societal forms of trustworthiness, systems of production and regulation, religion, education, and language. All these dimensions differ between and within societies and generate different levels of social capital.

The potential for further applications, and also for problems, becomes obvious as basic social network research starts to become diversified, opening itself to societal mentalities and their religions, social and psychological dispositions, and different institutions of societal order. Social capital became open to being multiplied and instrumentalized (Ostrom and Ahn 2001; Burt 1997). Policy studies, management and organization theory, and the practical policies of national and global policymakers started to employ social capital as a strategic concept for the use of an increasing number of associations. Putnam's (Putnam, Leonardi, and Nanetti 1993) networks of civic engagement, Fukujama's (1995) comparisons between different social structures in different societies as sources of different economic competitive structures of economies, and many other studies followed that analyzed links between social networks, social capital, and economic development (Sabatini 2008; Barr 2009; Chamlee-Wright 2008; Chalupnicek 2010), as did monographs, handbooks, and encyclopedias (Easley and Kleinberg 2010; Field 2008; Svendsen and Haase Svendsen 2009).

Debate on social capital has emerged and the term has become a policy instrument, and sometimes social capital sounds like a hackneyed phrase. It refers to political economy and some further distinct thematic areas but all of the applications are grounded on the premise that the procedures of a complex economic and social life have serious social roots that together constitute a powerful plea for an integrated *socio*economics in research and in teaching, which can only be understood as part of an institutional interpretation linking different academic areas. Recent ideas stem from their own history of ideas and economic and social thought. As always, it is fruitful to start from a broader perspective to see the conceptual lines of continuity and change. We started with the idea that cultures matter and that sterile conceptions close to central ideas of neoclassic economics fail. Accepting that premise and moving forward logically, we can see that network analysis and research on social capital provide useful arguments as to why these "social dimensions" fit with institutional thought.

Different capital structures correspond with different network designs and vice versa. Divergent network arrangements provide different opportunities to communicate, to receive information, and to create different structures of cultural capital. Network analysis explores modes and contents of exchanges between different agents when symbols, emotions, or goods and services get exchanged. The article tried to argue that social network analysis has become a cross-disciplinary subject with applications in diverse fields of social and economic life. The message of the article was to highlight that social network analysis provides a tool to foster the understanding of social dynamics by looking between micro and macro areas and by filling the gap. Social network analysis enhances recent debate on social and economic changes and may get rid of some limitations of the cognitive and explanatory potential of economics.

Notes

1. The article was written during a research stay at Turku School of Economics, Turku University, Finland, where the author found a stimulating research environment. Valuable comments were provided on the occasion of my talk at the Turku Center for Welfare Research (TCWR), April 28, 2011, and at the "Management and Social Networks Conference," Geneva, February 15–17, 2012. Further thanks are due to anonymous referees at the *AJES*, who encouraged a rethink and reformulation of some thematical issues.
2. Pearson (1999) argues that the concept of a German Historical School of Economics is itself infelicitous. For a substantial discussion of Schmoller's position, see Schumpeter (1926).
3. Weber (1988) noted the coincidence between the Protestant ethic and the rise of capitalism. It is interesting to see that Weber quoted Th. Veblen (1899) who—vice versa—already had a frequent exchange with contemporary European authors (see Loader and Rick 1995).
4. See Wiseman (2009) for an overview.
5. The cultural approach employs ethnographic (Abolafia 1998) or historical (Zelizer 1985, 1988) methods and the political approach underlines the role of institutions and the role of governmental influences for the functioning of markets (Fligstein 2001).

References

Abolafia, M. Y. (1998). "Markets as Cultures. An Ethnografic Approach." In *The Laws of the Markets*. Ed. M. Callon, pp. 69–85. Oxford: Blackwell Publishers.

Akerlof, G. A. (2007). "The Missing Motivation in Macroeconomics." Presidential Address, Paper Prepared for the Conference of the American Economic Association, Chicago.

Akerlof, G. A., and R. E. Kranton. (2000). "Economics and Identity." *Quarterly Journal of Economics* 115: 715–753.

Akerlof, G. A., and R. J. Shiller. (2009). *Animal Spirits: How Human Psychology Drives the Economy, and Why it Matters for Global Capitalism*. Princeton: Princeton University Press.

Baker, W. E. (1984). "The Social Structure of a National Securities Market." *American Journal of Sociology* 89: 775–811.

———. (1990). "Market Networks and Corporate Behavior." *American Journal of Sociology* 96: 589–625.

Barnes, J. A. (1954). "Class and Committees in a Norwegian Island Parish." *Human Relations* 7: 39–58.

Barr, T. (2009). "With Friends Like These. Endogenous Labor Market Segregation with Homogenous, Nonprejudiced Agents." *American Journal of Economics and Sociology* 68(3): 703–746.

Becker, G. S. (1974). "Theory of Social Interaction." *Journal of Political Economy* 82(6): 1063–1093.
Berger, P. L. (1986). *The Capitalist Revolution*. New York: Basic Books.
Blaug, M. (1986). *Great Economists Before Keynes. An Introduction to the Lives and Works of One Hundred Great Economists of the Past*. New York: Cambridge University Press.
Bögenhold, D., and J. Marschall. (2008). "Metapher, Methode, Theorie. Netzwerkforschung in der Wirtschaftssoziologie." In *Netzwerkanalyse und Netzwerktheorie. Ein neues Paradigma in den Sozialwissenschaften*. Ed. C. Stegbauer, pp. 387–400. Wiesbaden: VS-Publishers.
——. (2010). "Weder Methode noch Metapher. Zum Theorieanspruch der Netzwerkanalyse bis in die 1980er Jahre." In *Handbuch Netzwerkforschung*. Eds. R. Häußling and C. Stegbauer, pp. 283–291. Wiesbaden: VS-Publishers.
Bourdieu, P. (1983). "Forms of Capital." In *Handbook of Theory and Research for the Sociology of Education*. Ed. J. G. Richardson, pp. 214–258. New York: Greenwood Press.
Bunge, M. (1996). *Finding Philosophy in Social Science*. New Haven & London: Yale University Press.
Burt, R. S. (1995). *Structural Holes: The Social Structure of Competition*. Cambridge: Harvard University Press.
——. (1997). "The Contingent Value of Social Capital." *Administrative Science Quarterly* 42: 339–365.
——. (2007). *Brokerage and Closure: An Introduction to Social Capital*. Oxford: Oxford University Press.
——. (2010). *Neighbor Networks. Competitive Advantage Local and Personal*. Oxford: Oxford University Press.
Burt, R. S., and I. Talmud. (1993). "Market Niche." *Social Networks* 15: 133–149.
Carrington, P., and J. Scott. (Eds.) (2010). *Handbook of Social Network Analysis*. London: Sage.
Carrington, P. J., Scott, J., and S. Wasserman. (2009). *Models and Methods in Social Network Analysis*. Cambridge: Cambridge University Press.
Carroll, M. C., and J. R. Stanfield. (2003). "Social Capital, Karl Polanyi, and American Social and Institutional Economics." *Journal of Economic Issues* 37(2): 397–404.
Chalupnicek, P. (2010). "The CAPITAL in Social Capital: An Austrian Perspective." *American Journal of Economics and Sociology* 69(4): 1230–1250.
Chamlee-Wright, E. (2008). "The Structure of Social Capital: An Austrian Perspective on its Nature and Development." *Review of Political Economy* 20(1): 41–58.
Colander, D. C. (1993). "The Macrofoundations of Micro." *Eastern Economic Journal* 19(4): 447–457.

Coleman, J. (1988). "Social Capital in the Creation of Human Capital." *American Journal of Sociology* 94: 95–120.
———. (1990). *Foundations of Social Theory.* Cambridge: Harvard University Press.
Collins, R. (1988). *Theoretical Sociology.* San Diego: Hartcourt Brace Jovanovich.
———. (1994). *Four Sociological Traditions.* New York: Oxford University Press.
Dehmer, M. (Ed.) (2010). *Structural Analysis of Complex Networks.* Boston: Birkhäuser.
Dorfman, J. (1946–1959). *The Economic Mind in American Civilization.* 5 Vols. New York: Viking Press.
Easley, D., and J. Kleinberg. (2010). *Networks, Crowds, and Markets: Reasoning About a Highly Connected World.* Cambridge: Cambridge University Press.
Ellison, C. G. (1995). "Rational Choice Explanations of Individual Religious Behavior: Notes on the Problem of Social Embeddedness." *Journal for the Scientific Study of Religion* 34(1): 89–97.
Elster, J. (1998). "Emotions and Economic Theory." *Journal of Economic Literature* 36: 47–74.
Field, John. (2008). *Social Capital.* New York: Routledge 2008.
Fligstein, N. (2001). *The Architecture of Markets.* Princeton: Princeton University Press.
Fukuyama, F. (1995). *Trust: The Social Virtues and the Creation of Prosperity.* New York: Free Press.
Granovetter, M. S. (1973). "The Strength of Weak Ties." *American Journal of Sociology* 78: 1360–1380.
———. (1974). *Getting a Job: A Study of Contact and Careers.* Cambridge: Harvard University Press.
———. (1985). "Economic Action and Social Structure: The Problem of Embeddedness." *American Journal of Sociology* 91: 481–510.
———. (1993). "The Nature of Economic Relationships." In *Explorations in Economic Sociology.* Ed. R. Swedberg, pp. 3–41. New York: Russell Sage Foundation.
———. (2002). "A Theoretical Agenda for Economic Sociology." In *The New Economic Sociology. Developments in an Emerging Field.* Eds. M. F. Guillén, R. Collins, P. England et al., pp. 35–60. New York: Russell Sage Foundation.
Guillén, M. F., Collins, R., England, P. and M. Meyer. (2002). "The Revival of Economic Sociology." In *The New Economic Sociology: Developments in an Emerging Field.* Eds. M. F. Guillén, R. Collins, P. England et al., pp. 1–32. New York: Russell Sage Foundation.
Haller, M. (2003). *Soziologische Theorie im systematisch-kritischen Vergleich.* Stuttgart: UTB.

Harrison, L. E., and S. P. Huntington. (Eds.) (2000). *Culture Matters. How Values Shape Human Progress.* New York: Basic Books.

Häußling, R., and C. Stegbauer. (Eds.) (2010). *Handbuch Netzwerkforschung.* Wiesbaden: VS-Publishers.

Hodgson, G. M. (1994). "The Return of Institutional Economics." In *The Handbook of Economic Sociology.* Eds. N. J. Smelser and R. Swedberg, pp. 58–75. Princeton and New York: Princeton University Press and Russell Sage.

——. (2001). *How Economics Forgot History.* London: Routledge.

Hoover, K. D. (2009). "Microfoundational Programs." Paper Prepared for the First International Symposium on the History of Economic Thought: "The Integration of Micro and Macroeconomics from a Historical Perspective," University of São Paulo, 2009.

——. (2010). "Idealizing Reduction: The Microfoundations of Macroeconomics." *Erkenntnis* 73: 329–347.

Jones, E. L. (2006). *Cultures Merging. A Historical and Economic Critique of Culture.* Princeton: Princeton University Press.

Kahneman, D. (2003). "A Perspective on Judgment and Choice: Mapping Bounded Rationality." *American Psychologist* 58: 697–720.

Laird, P. W. (2006). *Pull: Networking and Success Since Benjamin Franklin.* Cambridge: Harvard University Press.

Landes, D. (2000). "Culture Makes Almost All the Difference." In *Culture Matters. How Values Shape Human Progress.* Eds. L. E. Harrison and S. P. Huntington, pp. 2–13. New York: Basic Books.

Lauterbach, A. (1962). *Psychologie des Wirtschaftslebens.* Reinbeck: Rororo.

Lee, F. S. (2009). *A History of Heterodox Economics. Challenging the Mainstream in the Twentieth Century.* London: Routledge.

Lévi-Strauss, C. (1987). *Anthropology and Myth.* Oxford: Blackwell.

Loader, C., and T. Rick. (1995). "Thorstein Veblen's Analysis of German Intellectualism: Institutionalism as a Forecasting Method." *American Journal of Economics and Sociology* 54(3): 339–355.

Marcovich. A, and T. Shinn. (2011). "Where is Disciplinarity Going? Meeting on the Borderland." *Social Science Information* 50: 582–606.

Marx, K. (1977). *Das Kapital. Kritik der politischen Ökonomie [1864].* (MEW Vol. 23.) Berlin: Dietz Publishers.

Mauss, M. (2002). *The Gift: The Form and Reason for Exchange in Archaic Societies.* London: Routledge.

——. (2006). *A General Theory of Magic.* London: Routledge.

Mikl-Horke, G. (1999). *Historische Soziologie der Wirtschaft.* Munich: Oldenbourg.

Morgan, M. (2011). *The World in the Model.* Cambridge: Cambridge University Press.

Newman, M. (2010). *Networks: An Introduction.* New York: Oxford University Press.
Nitzan, J., and S. Bichler (2009). *Capital as Power. A Study of Order and Reorder.* London: Routledge.
Ostrom, E., and T. K. Ahn (2001). "A Social Science Perspective on Social Capital: Social Capital and Collective Action." Research Paper, Indiana University.
Pearson, H. (1999). "Was There Really a German Historical School of Economics?" *History of Political Economics* 31: 547–562.
———. (2000). "Homo Economicus Goes Native, 1859–1945: The Rise and Fall of Primitive Economics." *History of Political Economy* 32: 933–998.
Polanyi, K. (2001). *The Great Transformation: The Political and Economic Origins of Our Time.* Boston: Beacon Press.
Putnam, R. D., Leonardi, R., and R. Y. Nanetti. (1993). *Making Democracy Work: Civic Traditions in Modern Italy.* Princeton: Princeton University Press.
Rabin, M. (1998). "Psychology and Economics." *Journal of Economic Literature* 36: 11–46.
Radcliffe-Brown, A. R. (1940). "On Social Structure." *Journal of the Royal Anthropological Institute of Great Britain and Ireland* 70: 1–12.
Rodgers, D. T. (2011). *Age of Fracture.* Cambridge: Harvard University Press.
Rogers, E. M. (2003). *Diffusion of Innovations.* New York: Basic Books.
Rota, M. F. (2007). *Is Social Capital Persistent? Comparative Measurement in the Nineteenth and Twentieth Centuries.* London: London School of Economics, Working Paper 103.
Sabatini, F. (2008). "Social Capital and the Quality of Economic Development." *Kyklos* 61(3): 466–499.
Scherer, K. R. (2011). "On the Rationality of Emotions: Or, When are Emotions Rational?" *Social Science Information* 50: 330–350.
Schmölders, G. (1984). "Historische Schule." In *Geschichte der Nationalökonomie.* Ed. O. Issing, pp. 107–120. Munich: Franz Vahlen.
Schülein, J. A.. (2009). "Soziologische Theorie und ihr Gegenstand." In *Soziologie für das Wirtschaftsstudium.* Eds. J. A. Schülein, G. Mikl-Horke, and R. Simsa, pp. 14–115. Vienna: UTB.
Schumpeter, J. A. (1926). "Gustav von Schmoller und die Probleme von heute." In *Jahrbuch für Gesetzgebung, Verwaltung und Volkswirtschaft im deutschen Reich,* pp. 337–388. Leipzig: Duncker & Humblot.
———. (1954). *History of Economic Analysis.* Oxford: Oxford University Press.
———. (1963). *The Theory of Economic Development.* New York and Oxford: Oxford University Press.
Scott, J. (2010). *Social Network Analysis.* London: Sage.
———. (2011). "Social Network Analysis: Developments, Advances, and Prospects." *Social Network Analysis and Mining* 1(1): 21–26.

Shackle, G. L. S. (1972). *Epistemics and Economics*. Cambridge: Cambridge University Press.
Simmel, G. (1908). "Die Kreuzung sozialer Kreise." In *Soziologie. Untersuchungen über die Formen der Vergesellschaftung*. Ed. G. Simmel, pp. 305–344. Berlin: Duncker & Humblot.
Smelser, N. J., and R. Swedberg. (1994). "The Sociological Perspective on the Economy." In *Handbook of Economic Sociology*. Eds. N. J. Smelser and R. Swedberg, pp. 3–26. New York & Princeton: Russel Sage Foundation and Princeton University Press.
Sombart, W. (1982). "Wirtschaft." In *Handwörterbuch der Soziologie [1931]*. Ed. A. Vierkandt, pp. 209–216. Stuttgart: Enke.
Stegbauer, C. (Ed.) (2008). *Netzwerkanalyse und Netzwerktheorie. Ein neues Paradigma in den Sozialwissenschaften*. Wiesbaden: VS-Publishers.
Stets, J. E., and J. Turner. (Eds.) (2007). *Handbook of the Sociology of Emotions*. New York: Springer.
Svendsen, Gert Tinggaard, and G. L. Haase Svendsen. (Eds.) (2009). *Handbook of Social Capital*. Cheltenham: Edward Elgar.
Swedberg, R. (2003). "Economic and Sociological Approaches to Markets." In *Principles of Economic Sociology*. Ed. R. Swedberg, pp. 104–131. Princeton: Princeton University Press.
Turner, J., and J. E. Stets. (Eds.) (2009). *The Sociology of Emotions*. Cambridge: Cambridge University Press.
Veblen, T. B. (1899). *The Theory of the Leisure Class. An Economic Study in the Evolution of Institutions*. New York: Macmillen.
Wasserman, S., and K. Faust. (2009). *Social Network Analysis*. Cambridge: Cambridge University Press.
Weber, M. (1972). *Wirtschaft und Gesellschaft*. Tübringen: Mohr.
———. (1988). "Die protestantische Ethik und der Geist des Kapitalismus [1904]." In *Gesammelte Aufsätze zur Religionssoziologie*. Ed. M. Weber. Vol. 1, pp. 17–206. Tübingen: Mohr.
———. (1990). *Grundriß zu den Vorlesungen über Allgemeine (theoretische) Nationalökonomie*. Tübingen: Mohr.
Wellman, B. (1988). "Structural Analysis: From Method and Metaphor to Theory and Substance." In *Social Structures. A Network Approach*. Eds. B. Wellman and S. D. Berkowitz, pp. 19–61. Cambridge: Cambridge University Press.
Wellman, B., and C. Haythornthwaite. (Eds.) (2002). *The Internet in Everyday Life*. London: Blackwell.
White, H. C. (1981). "Where Do Markets Come From?" *American Journal of Sociology* 87: 517–547.
———. (1988). "Varieties of Markets." In *Social Structures: A Network Approach*. Eds. B. Wellman and S. D. Berkowitz, pp. 226–260. Cambridge: Cambridge University Press.

White, H. C., S. A. Boorman, and R. L. Breiger. (1976). "Social Structures from Multiple Networks I: Blockmodels of Roles and Positions." *American Journal of Sociology* 81: 730–780.
Wiseman, B. (Ed.) (2009). *The Cambridge Companion to Lévi-Strauss*. Cambridge: Cambridge University Press.
Zelizer, V. A. (1985). *Pricing the Priceless Child. The Changing Social Value of Children*. New York: Basic Books.
———. (1988). "The Proliferation of Social Currencies." In *The Laws of the Markets*. Ed. M. Callon, pp. 58–68. Oxford: Blackwell Publishers.

Schmoller's Method as a Critique and Alternative to Marginalist Economics: a Comment to Louzek

By Carlo D'Ippoliti*

ABSTRACT. This article comments upon Louzek (2011) in this journal, claiming that the analysis of Schmoller's method, as evidenced by his practice, allows us to highlight a few themes that are relevant not only in reconstructing his critique of Menger's methodological proposal but also for an extension of such critique to the current mainstream economics.

In an interesting article in this journal, Professor Louzek reconsiders the century-old Methodenstreit (the "battle of methods" between the Younger German Historical School and the nascent marginalist Austrian School), highlighting those issues that should still concern present-day economists (Louzek 2011). Louzek singles out three themes as particularly relevant for contemporary economics: the legitimacy and usefulness of a deductive versus an inductive method of enquiry; the existence of "exact laws" in economics; and the correctness and expediency of methodological individualism vis-á-vis methodological collectivism.

Louzek rightly emphasizes that, as the relatively recent literature shows (see, for example, the debate between Pearson 1999 and 2001 and Caldwell 2001), for a long time both the debate and its participants' positions in the Methodenstreit have been oversimplified by many historians of economics, and he devotes special attention to a careful reconstruction of Menger's point of view—that which, concerning the three above-mentioned issues, we may consider as close to contemporary mainstream economics. Louzek explains:

> Menger spoke out against Schmoller at the moment when he felt that Schmoller was putting the methodology itself—the inductive procedures, the historical empiricism and methodological collectivism—in absolute terms and was making them the only justified approach in social sciences

*E-mail address: Carlo.dippoliti@uniroma1.it

in general. This criticism was justified in relation to the "factual" Schmoller, not to the "ideological" one . . . . The ideological Schmoller, when attacked, of course, insisted on the principle of methodological pluralism. (Louzek 2011: 453)

Such an interpretation of Schmoller's method deserves a more precise historical reconstruction, due to its heavy bearing upon the method and content of contemporary economics. I shall summarize my main points of disagreement with the claim that Menger's criticisms are "justified" by referring to Schmoller's major economic work, the *Grundriß der allgemeinen Volkswirtschaftslehre* (*Principles of Political Economy*, two volumes, 1900 and 1904, untranslated in English), in order to focus on Schmoller's practice as supposedly distinct from his methodological reflections.[1]

Concerning the issue of induction versus deduction, in the long introduction to the *Grundriß* Schmoller defines three moments, or tasks, of scientific enquiry (Schmoller 1904: 150): (1) observing well; (2) defining well and classifying; and (3) finding typical forms and explaining their causes. Throughout the work, Schmoller's typical approach to a new topic is first to precisely (even pedantically) define a concept, including its treatment by the previous literature, then to provide a comparative overview of the historical development of the phenomenon, in Europe and elsewhere, developing an original interpretation of the underlying cause-effect relations (this was usually accomplished by developing a theory of stages of the phenomenon). This may at first look like a purely inductive process, but it is not so, in so far as Schmoller's conceptualization phase is prior to the (analytical) historical analysis and indeed it is necessary in order to define its content and boundaries, the parallel phenomena that may be involved as causes or consequences, and other characteristics of it. That is, Schmoller was aware that a theory (a basic and rough one, at least) is necessary to any observation, already in the stage of selecting the variables to be observed and those to be related to the observed one (Schumpeter's pre-analytical vision).

Indeed, Schmoller's criticisms of the deductive method should be qualified in light of his historical method. By Schmoller's time, history had firmly established itself as a method of the social sciences rather than (or in addiction to) being considered a field of enquiry to be pursued for its own sake. To contextualize this statement, it is convenient to refer to John Stuart Mill, whose contribution in the field of methodology will be recalled later on from other respects. "Even" Mill, often incorrectly pointed out as the proposer of a purely deductive method in economics (D'Ippoliti 2011), sanctioned that

> from this time any political thinker who fancies himself able to dispense with a connected view of the great facts of history . . . must be regarded as below the level of the age. (Mill 1872: 308)

Schmoller clarifies that in his view (and in his practice) "historicism" encompasses two main features of social analysis:

(i) theoretical relativism: the conscience that a certain theory can emerge from detecting regularities that are specific to a certain time and space; therefore, a resulting theoretical law may fit a certain society at a certain time but no theory can fit all societies at all times;

(ii) evolutionism: the recognition that any social phenomenon must be in some sense a consequence of what came before, that is, the causes of change must be sought in the previous social situation and not (only) in some exogenous process.

Thus, Schmoller's criticism of a purely deductive method as proposed by Menger, even if complemented and not in opposition to an inductive one, as Louzek (2011) highlights, is twofold. On the one hand, Schmoller criticizes the assumption of ex ante given hypotheses (and this criticism applies *a fortiori* to present-day "convenience hypotheses," only aimed at making the subsequent mathematical reasoning possible) because they abstract from the specific reality of a certain society in a certain time and space, and they supposedly apply to a "general case." Thus they violate point (i) above. In *Grundriß* this criticism is, for example, very clear with respect to classical political economists (Schmoller 1904: 84–99) in so far as they assumed the "acquisitive instinct" to be a prime driver of human behavior. According to Schmoller, while such a hypothesis may in first approximation hold true with respect to certain spheres of the English society of the time, it was certainly inapplicable to most Continental European societies, despite what classical British economists seemed to assume. On the other hand, the assumption of certain fixed hypotheses (for example, our use still today of the assumption that the acquisitive instinct via utility maximization is the prime motive of behavior (see D'Ippoliti 2010), violates point (ii) above, in so far as it disregards the non-static and evolutionary nature of the social world. Indeed, from a methodological point of view, a "stage" of any historical phenomenon is defined precisely as the time/space window within which a certain social or economic law holds true (D'Ippoliti 2011).

In the end, the economists of the German Historical School criticized "Smith's disciples" (but the same holds for their Austrian counterparts) because they were interested in developing a theory that would be applicable to their own society, and to do so they firstly needed to understand the "empirical laws" of such a different society. Thus, it is not the case that Schmoller objected to the use of deductive reasoning in economic analysis, but rather he deemed necessary to identify first the right context-specific hypotheses of any such deductive process. This identification follows a process of learned observation (that, as mentioned, is not void of theory itself) that is qualitatively different from a shallow juxtaposition of facts or, in Louzek's words, empiricism.

Schmoller repeatedly stressed that this process of accumulation of factual knowledge is a slow and painful one (besides a certain polemic aim on the side of Schmoller, it must be recognized that the limited statistical tools of the time certainly posed great challenges to such a methodological approach). For example, criticizing the Older Historical School:

> The difference between the new historical school and Roscher is that the former is more cautious in generalizing, and feels a much stronger need to shift from the polyhistoric collection of data to the specific investigation of single epochs, single populations, single economic conditions. (Schmoller 1900: 119)[2]

Such a large share of time and effort being devoted to the phase of observation led many commentators to accuse the Younger German Historical School of vain empiricism. However, it should be noted that—both by our standards and in Schmoller's view—*Grundriß* is from all respects a theoretical work. Indeed, within the historical method the difference between description and interpretation of a certain phenomenon lies, as mentioned, in the identification of cause-effect relations, which requires the application of one or more theoretical laws (that is, it is a deductive analytical process). Thus, what emerges from an analysis of Schmoller's method in *Grundriß* is a spiral of induction and deduction, mutually reinforcing: the deductive part of the analytical process allows the scientist to pass from a simple chronicle of disconnected facts to a proper historical theory, with the identification of cause-effect relations; and the inductive part provides both the content of the analysis and directs the choice of hypotheses, which under no occasion can be arbitrary or ex ante.[3]

In conclusion, when considering the scientific endeavor as a dynamic process of approaching a useful knowledge, rather than a one-shot production of theories, there is no opposition between inductive and deductive methods and, to use Louzek's terminology, only exact laws that at least are liable of being translated into empirical laws are acceptable theoretical instruments (and only provided that these laws do not aim at general validity, for the reasons under (i) and (ii) above).

By analyzing Schmoller's practice and substantive economic theory, a further argument against exclusively deductive methods may be discerned, unrelated from the historical method and linked to Louzek's third theme (the issue of methodological individualism vs. holism). According to Schmoller, ex ante hypotheses of the axiomatic kind necessarily isolate a fragment of reality, through the ceteris paribus clause implicit in any model (including general economic equilibrium models). Such isolation is, however, a risky process in the face of a unique complex social reality, since it may lead the researcher to take inappropriate or inapplicable deductive steps. Also from this point of view Schmoller recommends, in his methodological considerations, and employs in his practice, a mixture or rather a sequence of induction and deduction.

Indeed, at least since the Middle Ages debate on "Universals" (recalled in this respect by Schumpeter 1954; Roncaglia 2005) scholars are confronted with the issue of reconciling the real world, in which each individual is singular and unique, with the human mind's inability to account for every phenomena simultaneously. Some sort of analytical aggregation is always implied by the very use of theoretical concepts—returning to J. S. Mill: "as soon as we employ a name to connote attributes, the things... which happen to possess those attributes, are constituted *ipso facto* a class" (Mill 1872: 118, italics in original).

Thus, for example, economic models employing the representative agent hypothesis, that is, a single individual or a household unit that is assumed to work, consume, and save with no interpersonal interactions (or a continuum of similarly characterized heterogeneous agents), are an example of models collecting all different individuals into a single analytical class (for example, abstracting from their gender, race, and other factors). As such, apart from certain heterodox streams of literature (such as agent-based computational modeling, for example) all macroeconomic models—even the microfounded ones—employ collective categories and therefore methodological holism of some sort, despite Louzek's claim that such an approach is now the proper domain of sociology (which indeed comprises several authors supporting methodological individualism), in the face of a supposedly purely methodologically individualistic economics.[4]

However, while economists and sociologists (but also mainstream and heterodox economists) share some methods, they mostly differ in the ontological status they accord to such aggregates. From this point of view, Schmoller is surely to be classified among those that recognize in social aggregates (such as social classes properly defined, but not only) both a positive analytical and ontological status.

As may be inferred from Schmoller's analysis in *Grundriß*, there are at least two senses in which social aggregates exist in reality and not only in the researcher's mind. On the one hand, there are examples of purely collective behavior, such as collective production or consumption:

> The idea that economic life has ever been a process mainly dependent on individual action—an idea based on the impression that it is concerned merely with methods of satisfying individual needs—is mistaken with regard to all stages of human civilization, and in some respects it is more mistaken the further we go back. (Schmoller 1897: 3)

On the other hand, social aggregates exist in individuals' (and collective) consciousness and self-consciousness. This does not imply that science should start out from these aggregates without ever considering their derivation from individuals' consciousness, but only that social considerations such as class belonging affect individuals' actions and therefore, in some sense, classes actually exist in society and are not just a researcher's invention:

> There is not, as however the Historical School had maintained, an objective popular spirit, independent of the individuals, overarching them and mystically reigning upon them; as there is not a superior general will, as Rousseau dreamt about; there is in every people a series of spheres of conscience, co-ordinated, each determining the other, tending to a certain unity.... Such an Objective Spirit ... does not live out of the individuals, but within the individuals, as each individual with a smaller or greater part of his or her self is part of some or many circles of the Objective Spirit. (Schmoller 1897: 16)[5]

While not everyone would agree with this specific ontological claim, most social scientists would agree that collective action and self-consciousness are two arguments for the rejection of a purely individualistic method. Indeed, it is in this very respect that J. S. Mill's methodological works should be recalled because, while as mentioned he was not an advocate of a purely deductive method in the social sciences, he did advocate for a disciplinary specialization whereby economists would not consider the whole social realm. As a consequence, in his view, in its application to the real world economic theory should always be complemented by the results of other social sciences (D'Ippoliti 2011). Mill's influence upon the subsequent evolution of the social sciences led to the current situation in which it is not—as Louzek seems to maintain—a difference of methods to distinguish economics from sociology, but the distinction is rather based on conventional and traditional boundaries of content (boundaries that while arguable and blurred since the beginning, are increasingly violated by both economists and sociologists: see, for example, Fine and Milonakis 2009). Mainstream economists, apart from possibly the most radical ones, do not deny the particular nature of their analysis but rather delegate its integration to other social scientists.

However, for his opposition to Mill's "isolating method" and by consequence to the current economic mainstream Schmoller should not properly be considered as a precursor of sociology, as Louzek does, but rather of several heterodox economic approaches (*in primis* the institutionalist tradition) that deny such strong disciplinary boundaries between the social sciences and most specifically that do not rely (or do not exclusively rely) on methodological individualism. On the one hand, as mentioned, mainstream macroeconomists are bound to consider aggregates despite their appeal to microfoundations. On the other hand, several non-mainstream economic traditions do resort to aggregate categories (such as race, gender, class) in their properly economic production.

In conclusion, the analysis of Schmoller's method, as evidenced by his practice rather than by his programmatic statements, allows us to highlight a few themes that are relevant not only in reconstructing his critique of Menger's methodological proposal, but also for an extension of such critique to the current mainstream. First, there is no sharp opposition between deduction and induction, provided that knowledge production is understood as a process of successive approximations to useful information. It is thus the marginalists' emphasis on deduction only, that is, on deduction unchecked by induction in the determination of its hypotheses and in some cases (for example, general equilibrium theory) not even in the falsification of its results, that should be regarded as radical single-mindedness. Second, methodological monism and specifically the acceptance of methodological individualism only (though as we saw this is in practice almost impossible in the field of macroeconomics) is a characteristic of mainstream economics, possibly dictated by its reliance on the marginal method, but it does not extend to all schools of economics and, in the face of social complexity, is probably a mischievous self-imposed limitation.

Notes

1. For a thorough analysis of Schmoller's method by the present writer, see D'Ippoliti (2011), especially Chapters 2–5.
2. "Der Unterschied der jüngeren historischen Schule von ihm ist der, daß sie weniger rasch generalisieren will, daß sie ein viel stärkeres Bedürfnis empfindet, von der polhistorischen Datensammlung zur Specialuntersuchung der einzelnen Epochen, Völker und Wirtschaftszustände überzugehen" (Schmoller, 1900: 119, our translation).
3. It is crucial to distinguish this inductive and deductive process of theory refinement and hypothesis development from the process of theory falsification by empirical tests, which, as Louzek (2011) points out, pertains to the inductive method only.

4. It should be noted that Louzek provides a very peculiar and restrictive definition of methodological individualism, basically referring to only a part (though the largest part) of mainstream economics: "Methodological individualism requires that social science should base the explanations of social phenomena on individual preferences" (Louzek 2011: 444).

5. "Nicht einen objektiven, unabhängig von den einzelnen und über ihnen waltenden, sie mastisch beherrschenden Volksgeist giebt es, wie die historische Rechtsschule lehrte; ebenso wenig einen allgemeinen Willen, der in allem übereinstimmte, wie Rousseau träumte. Aber es gibt in jedem Volke eine Reihe zusammengehöriger, einander bedingender und nach einer gewissen Einheit drängender Bewußtseinkreise, die man als Volksgeist bezeichnen kann. . . . dieser objektive Geist] nicht außerhalb der Individuen, sondern in ihnen lebt, daß jedes Individuum mit einem größeren oder kleineren Teil seines Selbst Bestandteil mehrerer oder vieler solcher Kreise, solcher Teile des objektiven Geistes ist" (Schmoller 1897: 16, our translation).

References

Caldwell, B. (2001). "There Really Was a German Historical School of Economics: A Comment on Pearson." *History of Political Economy* 33(3): 649–654.

D'Ippoliti, C. (2010). "Saggio recensione di Apps & Rees (2009) e Todorova (2009)." *Moneta e Credito* 63(250): 165–178.

——. (2011). *Economics and Diversity*. New York: Routledge.

Fine, B., and D. Milonakis (2009). *From Economics Imperialism to Freakonomics: The Shifting Boundaries Between Economics and Other Social Sciences*. New York: Routledge.

Louzek, M. (2011). "The Battle of Methods in Economics. The Classical Methodenstreit—Menger vs. Schmoller." *American Journal of Economics and Sociology* 70(2): 439–463.

Mill, J. S. (1872). *A System of Logic, Ratiocinative and Inductive*. London: Longmans (first edition 1843). Republished in Robson, J. M. (1969). *The Collective Works of John Stuart Mill*. Toronto: The University of Toronto Press, vols. 8–9.

Pearson, H. (1999). "Was There Really a German Historical School of Economics?" *History of Political Economy* 31(3): 655–661.

——. (2001). "Response to Bruce Caldwell." *History of Political Economy* 33(3): 649–654.

Roncaglia, A. (2005). *The Wealth of Ideas. A History of Economic Thought*. Cambridge: Cambridge University Press.

Schmoller, G. (1897). *The Mercantile System and Its Historical Significance*. New York: Macmillan. Available online at: http://socserv2.socsci.mcmaster.ca/~econ/ugcm/3ll3/schmoller/mercant

———. (1900). *Grundriß der allgemeinen Volkswirtschaftslehre*, Book 1. Leipzig: Duncker & Humblot (second edition 1908). Reprinted 2010. Milton Keynes, UK: Nabu Press.

———. (1904). *Grundriß der allgemeinen Volkswirtschaftslehre*, Book 2. Leipzig: Duncker & Humblot. Reprinted 2010. Milton Keynes, UK: Nabu Press.

Schumpeter, J. A. (1954). *History of Economic Analysis*. Oxford: Oxford University Press.

The Economic Deterioration of the Family: Historical Contingencies Preceding the Great Recession

By Michael D. Gillespie, Ph.D.*†

ABSTRACT. The "Great Recession" in the United States exposed contradictions between the economic well-being of families and capital that developed in the decades prior to this latest downturn. Using social structure of accumulation theory, a qualitative institutional analysis, and quantitative time-series models, this article investigates historically contingent relations between the nature of public assistance, family economic deterioration, and capital accumulation. To sustain the circuit of capital, I argue that the family propped up economic growth first through public cash assistance and then through private expenditures, the latter of which lead to the economic deterioration of families dependent on unprecedented levels of debt.

Introduction

The "Great Recession" of the United States that began in December 2007 was preceded by mounting social and economic problems of middle- and working-class families. While those who perpetually live in or near poverty are further marginalized during deep recessions, the most recent economic downturn swelled these ranks with middle-income households. These "typical" American families, who contributed to the resurging U.S. economy following the Great Depression and World War II, now exemplify the economic deterioration leading to the most recent recession.

When compared historically, contradictions emerge between the economic conditions for the reproduction of families and for the

*Eastern Illinois University; E-mail address: mgillespie@eiu.edu
†I extend my gratitude to Susan M. Carlson for her ongoing support, feedback, comments, and camaraderie. I would also like to thank Steve Pressman and Robert Scott for their comments, Terrence McDonough for his encouragement, and the important and critical comments received from the peer reviewers.

reproduction of profitability within an expanding capitalist society. Family income from employment has experienced a decades-long decline as both capital accumulation and consumer debt have dramatically increased. For example, between 1948 and 2007, the proportional share of total income held by poor and working-class families, the lowest 40 percent, decreased by 18.8 percent as the top 5 percent, the economic elite, experienced a 17.5 percent increase (U.S. Census Bureau 2009). Moreover, the ratio of total household debt to asset values increased from 18 cents to 55 cents per dollar as after-tax corporate profits rose over 600 percent (Bureau of Economic Analysis 2009; Federal Reserve Board of Governors 2010a). As the latest validation of these trends, the "Great Recession" exposed the ongoing deteriorating conditions of existence for low-, working-, and middle-income families as a social class.

Therefore, this research investigates these contradictions and their historical conditions by asking: *Why has the economic condition of the family in the United States deteriorated after World War II?*

A growing body of work on the political and economic shifts prior to the "Great Recession" concentrates on financial programs devised by investors, often in relation with governmental bureaucrats or elected officials (McLean and Nocera 2010; Sorkin 2009). Inclusive of historical and comparative accounts of economic crises (Reinhart and Rogoff 2009) and the ongoing housing crisis (Kotz 2009), a broad, historical concept of the family is missing from most of this work. Some social-economic research reflects the importance of banking and credit for low-wage households (Blank and Barr 2009), and the associated growth of debt poverty (Goodman 2009; Pressman and Scott 2009b), yet literature on the macro-economic links between financial institutions and the family institutions within the circuit of capital is inadequate (Barba and Pivetti 2009).

To address this gap and the research question, I first present an historical-institutional conception of the family and, using social structure of accumulation theory, conduct a qualitative institutional analysis of the political economy of the family in the United States after World War II. Next, four quantitative time-series models investigate historically contingent relations between family economic deterioration, shifts in income assistance, and financial deregulation.

I argue that the family, when needed, was once able to access public support and cash assistance to reproduce labor in the circuit of capital. However, conditioned by financial deregulations, waning public welfare, and stagnating wages from employment in the late 1970s to the "Great Recession" institutionalized consumer lending practices maintained the family as a durable market, even as its economic well-being was mired under unprecedented levels of debt.

Theoretical Frame: The Historical Institutional Family and SSA Theory

Typical attention by the social sciences on the economic conditions of families is on the lived experiences of poor, near poor, or low-income families (Collins and Mayer 2010; Wilson 1996), especially single-mother families in the welfare system (Hays 2003; Sidel 2006; Turner, Danziger, and Seefeldt 2006) and the downward mobility of middle-class families within changing labor markets (Newman 2006; Pattillo-McCoy 1999; Warren and Tyagi 2003). Where the literature includes certain family groups within specific social institutions, minimal attention has been given to the economic conditions of the family combining the poor, near-poor, and working and middle classes.

These limitations could stem from traditional family research that concentrates on individuals within families, broader kinship groups, and their immediate social milieu (White and Klein 2008). Other social-institutional analyses range from rational choice and econometric models of probable individual behavior (Almond 2006; Becker 1991) to grand, functionalist conceptions within an interdependent cohesive system (Parsons and Bales 1955; Swenson 2004). When applied, these approaches often link the economic deterioration of families to inferior investments in human capital or the requirements of social differentiation (Collins 1975).

The family as a political and economic social institution is more complex, and to analyze the contradictions between capital accumulation and family economic deterioration, an historical institutionalist approach is preferred. This approach links qualitative circumstances with quantitative associations to analyze the structural, historical, and material conditions of existence for families (Marx 1998; Mills 1959).

As U.S. capitalist society developed over time, the economy became its major organizing factor and extended periods of prosperity and growth link the *needs* of capitalist profit and accumulation to the supportive contributions of families. The political economy impacts the nature of institutions as the capitalist mode of production shapes the development of the family as a social institution within the circuit of capital (Creed 2000). Foremost, no other enterprise or industry exists within capitalist society specializing in the production and reproduction of human labor as an input to the production of commodities and services or for their subsequent consumption. The political and economic realities of the U.S. capitalist system following WWII promoted a middle-class family as an ideal through marriage and childbearing norms, patterns of socialization, and expanding consumer credit to foster consumption. Backed by educational, housing, financial, and other social programs, the family was reestablished in somewhat changed form as the primary institution for social reproduction (Coontz 1992).

At historical moments, the competitive and innovative nature of capitalist development promoted, supported, and benefitted unevenly from these essential reproduction, socialization, or consumption roles of the family institution (Dickinson and Russell 1986; Engels [1884] 2001; Zaretsky 1976). Therefore, this framework analyzes such historically contingent political and economic shifts in the family-capital relationship, and the dialectical character of circumstances that both shape and are shaped by families attempting to fulfill their institutional roles while within their conditions of existence.

Social structure of accumulation theory posits that at particular historical moments a distinctive set of economic, social, and political institutions, a social structure of accumulation (SSA), come together in a phase of *consolidation* providing conditions necessary for strong and persistent capital accumulation by regulating class conflict and competition. Over time, SSAs become ever more complex due to inherent contradictions and labor/citizen unrest, and ultimately break down, leading to economic decline during the *decay phase*, which overlaps with a following lengthy period of institutional restructuring during the *exploration phase*. Eventually a new SSA consolidates, fostering renewed economic growth (Gordon, Edwards, and Reich 1982). SSA theory, anchored in Marxist economics, combined capital-labor relations within the mode of production with historically contingent social institutions that mitigate contradictory social conditions.

SSA theorists (Bowles, Gordon, and Weisskopf 1990) have provided a detailed analysis of the period of sustained economic growth immediately after World War II—the post-WWII SSA in the United States.[1] This SSA has four institutional pillars—a limited capital-labor accord, the capitalist-citizen accord, Pax Americana, and muted inter-capitalist rivalry. Supported by a financial regulatory structure, these core institutions impinge most directly on capital accumulation (Gordon, Edwards, and Reich 1982; Wolfson 1994). The critical position of the state to support accumulation has been discussed within core SSA institutions, but has been undertheorized. O'Connor's (1973) theory of the capitalist state is argued here to be consistent with the SSA approach, where stable conditions amenable for accumulation are a product of the state's contradictory fiscal legitimization and accumulation roles (Carlson, Gillespie, and Michalowski 2010). However, these roles are not solely fiscal, but part of broader strategic policy interventions attempting to balance relations between class factions (Gough 1979; Jessop 2007). The capitalist state is therefore a *welfare state* within a modified capitalist-state-citizen accord to balance the well-being of capital and citizens and generate conditions necessary for a vigorous circuit of capital.

Theoretically, the family intersects the capital-labor and capitalist-citizen accords, and the financial regulatory structure. However, SSA theory, rooted in Marxist economics, has focused on class conflicts between labor and capital, with minimal consideration of household labor and internal family dynamics below an institutional level (Kotz 1994; O'Hara 1995). To supplement SSA theory, the historical institutional family reproduced current and future labor power for the capital-labor accord, socialized members within the capitalist system, and provided a durable market for consumption. Bolstered by access to credit and banking, middle-class families supported system stability and legitimacy within their conditions of existence.

Institutional Analysis: Family Economic Deterioration Over the Post-WWII SSA

Preceding Exploration: 1933–1948

A consolidated SSA is the product of its preceding exploration phase. For the post-WWII SSA, the 1933–1948 period of exploration, including core years of the Great Depression and World War II, generated high levels of structural unemployment and labor unrest, conditions addressed by the National Labor Relations Act, Fair Labor Standards Act, and Taft-Hartley Act. This capital-labor accord targeted enterprises most fundamental to economic growth, allowed labor to organize and bargain collectively, provided job safety and security, and, for families, real wages and cost-of-living increases were indexed to productivity, balancing production with new norms of consumption. The capitalist-state-citizen accord, through the Social Security Act, mediated labor-market risks for families with social insurance for the unemployed and in old age and means-tested public assistance through Aid to Dependent Children (ADC) and General Assistance when breadwinners were displaced from the labor force. To generate confidence and stabilize demand the Glass-Steagall Banking Act compartmentalized the banking industry and restrained interest rates, the Securities and Exchange Act established federal oversight of banks and markets, and the Federal Deposit Insurance Corporation promoted thrift. Finally, the National Housing Acts of 1934 and 1938 institutionalized the Federal Housing Administration (FHA) and Federal National Mortgage Association (FNMA) to promote home ownership.

In sum, the New Deal created a *capitalist welfare state* and the means for laboring and middle-class families to support the reproduction of labor power with the consumption of capitalist goods, simultaneously fortifying the circuit of capital and aggregate demand. However, the post-WWII SSA only included those families covered by the capital-labor and capitalist-state-citizen accords. Access to real living wages, job security, health, education, and a family home left agricultural workers, domestic servants, the self-employed, and small business owners and their employees at the margins. For the latter, work was reinforced by restricting aid and relief necessitating their labor power in low-wage sectors. Through both sets of relations, capital was provided an adequate supply of labor for stratified positions, and durable, but unequal, markets for consumption (Katz 1996).

Consolidation: 1948–1966

The consolidation phase of the post-WWII SSA was a period of rising productivity, corporate profits and investments, low inflation and unemployment, and increasing real wages (Bowles, Gordon, and Weisskopf 1990). Accordingly, labor rights, employment for displaced workers, and pay equity expanded the capital-labor accord through the Landrum-Griffin Act, Manpower Development and Training Act, and the Equal Pay Act. Social Security Act amendments replaced ADC with Aid to Families with Dependent Children (AFDC) and, with the Federal Food Stamp Program, and Medicare and Medicaid health insurance programs for the aged and the poor, broadened the capitalist-state-citizen accord to previously excluded families. For the first time, poor mothers were given access to public assistance despite linking most benefits to community service or work obligations (Neubeck 2006). Provisions to support reproduction and socialization were built into the financial regime, which separated commercial banking and insurance and extended interest rate caps on savings accounts. Finally, civil rights reforms created rent supplements and banned housing discrimination.

Despite these placative measures, the capitalist welfare state continually rebalanced private profitability with class compromises to maintain a surplus of low-wage labor. Families at the margins of the economic trajectory endured inequalities between capital and the lower classes, between men and women, and between whites and non-whites. By 1966, the post-WWII accords provided a selective safety net for working- and middle-class families but challenged poor families to sufficiently perform their reproduction, socialization, and consumption roles within these contradictions of capital accumulation.

Decay: 1966–1979

SSA theorists argue that the decay of the post-WWII SSA occurred in two distinct sub-phases, the first from 1966 overlapping in 1973 with the second, which ended in 1979 (McDonough 2008). In the first sub-phase of decay, a race- and gender-based wage gap developed between the core manufacturing and industrial firms and secondary sector of marginalized labor propelling civil and welfare rights, black power, and feminist groups to demand economic justice by directly challenging the capital-labor and capitalist-state-citizens accords. A series of court rulings ended restrictive practices denying poor single mothers and families of color access to public assistance, stressing welfare rolls with a stark increase in recipients. In turn, capital could no longer depend on this marginal pool of low-wage labor and, in 1967 the Work Incentives Program (WIN) offered recipients work opportunities in exchange for certain welfare benefits. Four years hence, amendments to the WIN program required recipients to work for welfare; directly benefitting capital, work was no longer voluntary for families.

The second sub-phase of decay was in part the result of strategic challenges to power relations between capital, the state, citizens, and families. Growing inflation and rising citizen unrest contributed to a severe recession in the early 1970s. Social spending was constrained at the same time capital cut wages, formally challenged union power, and relocated manufacturing to areas in the West, Southwest, and abroad where labor was weak (Piven and Cloward 1997). As a result, the fates of working- and middle-class families generated a dilemma for the federal government—sustain legitimacy by upholding the post-WWII SSA, or address the economic imperative for capital accumulation. The response signaled a shift in the conditions of existence for families.

Demands for consumption now outweighed demands for labor power. Capital, seeing corporate profits threatened by increased production costs and underconsumption, sought to stabilize its own reproduction and productivity by cutting wages and entire positions. Under these conditions, relief for families promoted consumption and managed demand with programs such as the supplemental food program for poor mothers. However, the most important program mirrored the profit motives of capital; by augmenting the annual earnings of low-income families, the Earned Income Tax Credit (EITC) incentivized low-wage work with much-needed means of consumption (Goldberg and Collins 2001).

In addition, with the rising number of dual-income households, access to and use of credit supported family consumption. The Equal Credit Opportunity Act banned discrimination in consumer loan and credit applications, providing for the first time new means of consumption for non-whites and women, the Community Reinvestment Act obligated federally insured depository institutions to invest in and serve their local populations, and a series of other consumer protections for credit reports, bankruptcy, and data disclosures legitimized credit and debt. Finally, the U.S. Supreme Court's 1978 *Marquette v. First of Omaha* ruling dismantled state interest rate caps, opening the credit industry to use higher rates. With jobs and living wages becoming more elusive, the reproductive role of families waned and the capitalist welfare state sanctioned consumption with consumer credit and weakened financial regulations.

Prolonged Decay and Initial Exploration: 1979–1992

The 1980s marked the emergence of a new era of exploration, even as the old SSA continued to decay. Stagflation surfaced as minimal wage growth and productivity regenerated low levels of investment and corporate profits. The exploration for institutional alternatives targeted the widespread underconsumption of families by attempting to reinvigorate capital accumulation with access to low-wage work and banking and credit services. In this phase of "business ascendency," as the post-WWII SSA continued to decay, a liberal structure of institutional alternatives (Wolfson and Kotz 2010) explored means to promote accumulation and consumption through work, not welfare.

For example, the 1981 Omnibus Budget Reconciliation Act cut public assistance rolls while expanding mandatory WIN requirements, and subsequent amendments increased the age for full Social Security benefits while delaying cost-of-living increases. The 1988 Family Support Act replaced WIN with the JOBS Program, requiring women on welfare, even with children younger than three, to find work or enroll in training programs in exchange for basic benefits. Characteristic of the shift toward work for welfare—workfare—under this conservative liberalization, the EITC was simultaneously expanded and indexed to inflation.

Beginning with the 1980 repeal of regulations on state usury laws by the Depository Institutions Deregulation and Monetary Control Act, an environment of deregulation to promote capital mobility began to emerge. Subsequently, the Garn-St. Germain Act and Alternative Mortgage Transaction Parity Act eased mortgage interest rates and created a market that promoted household debt as a mechanism for economic growth. Later legislation followed this trend; the Secondary Mortgage Market Enhancement Act lessened restrictions on mortgage-backed securities, the Tax Reform Act allowed for investments in these securities at different levels of risk, the Financial Institutions Reform, Recovery and Enforcement Act opened the housing sector to private mortgage firms, and in 1992 the Federal Housing Enterprises Financial Safety and Security Act charged Fannie Mae and Freddie Mac to increase credit market access for underserved populations (Bostic and Lee 2009).

With a growing number of families necessarily seeking multiple incomes to supplement low wages and tax credits, easing mortgage market restrictions managed demand by arming financial capital with variable interest rates for consumer credit and mortgage loans, financing the most important family asset, the home.

Neoliberalism 1992–2007

The liberal institutional structure of the 1980s and early 1990s bridged the former period of long-term stable human relations with this phase of short-term contracts and private economic gain (Harvey 2005). Workfare became the hallmark of the capitalist welfare state as Social Security and welfare benefits were increasingly restricted. Most profound, 1996 "welfare reform" replaced AFDC with the Temporary Assistance for Needy Families program (TANF). TANF exemplifies neoliberalism's mandate on short-term, market-based contractual relations by obligating recipients to work despite increasing competition for even the most marginal jobs (Morgen et al. 2006). As norms of reproduction, socialization, and consumption were increasingly harder to meet, the capitalist welfare state fixated on accumulation, leaving middle-class, working-class, and poor families impaired to act on their own behalf.

Neoliberal financial deregulation progressed by lifting barriers restricting bank acquisition and merger activities. In 1999, the Graham-Leach-Bliley Act repealed Glass-Steagall, driving the growth of investment, commercial, and insurance banking conglomerates. Later, the Commodity Futures Modernization Act expanded the activities of financial firms that, coupled with HOME Investment Partnerships for low-income housing, the American Homeownership and Economic Opportunity Act, and American Dream Downpayment Initiative, and the promotion of homeownership and consumer debt, continually invigorated the expansion of credit markets. Together, banks packaged these liabilities into derivatives—credit- and mortgage-backed securities—then sold, and resold, these debt obligations to willing investors (Kotz 2009).

Ultimately, the neoliberalization of the banking industry made it possible for financial capital to offer mortgage loans and consumer credit to risk-adverse, but willing families, historically discriminated against in housing and credit programs. These subprime markets allowed families to contribute to the circuit of capital by refinancing old loans or originating new obligations under expanding consumption norms catalyzed by an industry ready to benefit from these marginalized groups (Howell 2006). Finance capital balanced these risky loans with variable interest rates and potential profits by transferring the risk into securities markets.

Summarized in Table 1, this institutional analysis argues that changes to capitalist welfare state assistance, from cash welfare for the economically marginalized to consumer credit and low-wage labor tax credits, led in part to the deterioration of families after World War II. Underlying this shift is the changing primary relationship of the family as a capitalist institution from reproducing labor power to the consumption of goods and services. As languishing incomes exacerbated inequalities and the downward mobility of middle, working, and poor families, consumer credit supplied financial assistance for the means of consumption, and ultimately the deterioration of families through unprecedented levels of consumer debt.

Table 1
Institutional Conditions Across Phases of the Post-WWII SSA

SSA Phase	Institutional Conditions				Family Conditions of Existence
	Capitalist-State-Citizen Accord	Capital-Labor Accord		Financial Regime	
Consolidation 1948–1966	*Cash Assistance and Capitalist Welfare State Provisions* • Social Security Expansion • AFDC Expansion • Civil Rights Reforms • Community Action Agencies	*Industrial Democracy and Full Employment* • Landrum-Griffin • MDTA • Affirmative Action and Equal Pay		*Fiscal Stabilization and Urban Support* • Low-Income Housing Programs • Urban Redevelopment Initiatives • Regulation Q	*Structural:* • Normative family promotes stability *Institutional:* • Social reproduction *Economic:* • Rising median family incomes • Decreasing poverty rates • Unemployment less than 4% • Low, but growing debt obligations
Decay 1 1966–1973	*Increase in Assistance; First Work Mandates* • Work Mandated for Public Assistance (WIN) • Jobs Training Programs (CEP/JOBS) • SSI Established	*Employability and Jobs Training* • CETA • Equal Employment and Civil Rights Amendments		*Mortgage Promotion and Credit Protection* • Fannie Mae and Secondary Mortgage Markets • Consumer Protection • Fair Credit Regulations	*Structural:* • Civil rights and market diversity; • Rise of single-parent mothers *Institutional:* • Social reproduction *Economic:* • Slowly rising median incomes • Poverty rates under 10% • Unemployment near 5% • Stable consumer spending

Table 1 Continued

SSA Phase	Capitalist-State-Citizen Accord	Capital-Labor Accord	Financial Regime	Family Conditions of Existence
Decay 2 *1973–1979*	*Enforcement of Welfare and Work Provisions* • Supplemental Food Program (WIC) • EITC		*Credit and Debt for the Middle Class* • Lending as Community Reinvestment • Fair Credit and Debt Regulations, cont. • Bankruptcy Protections • Supreme Court's *Marquette* Decision	*Structural:* • Women entering workforce; • Dual-income households *Institutional:* • Reproduction waning; consumption promoted *Economic:* • Stagnating median incomes • Poverty rates over 9% • 6% Unemployment • Consumer credit increases
Prolonged Decay and Initial Exploration *1979–1992*	*Growth of Workfare and Welfare Retrenchment* • Welfare Roll Reductions; Spending Cuts • Workfare Through FSA and JOBS	*Business Ascendancy* • Liberalization of Labor Relations • Declining Unionization	*Financial Deregulation* • Easing Credit Controls • Tax Reforms to Promote Mortgage Debt • Federal Housing Assistance and GSE Expansion	*Structural:* • Rebalancing labor and household norms *Institutional:* • Consumption *Economic:* • Flat median incomes • Poverty rising to 12% • 7% unemployment • Growing household debt
Neoliberal Exploration *1992–2007*	*End of Cash Assistance and Institutionalization of Workfare* • Welfare Reform and TANF • American Dream Downpayment Initiative		*Fiscal Mechanisms* • Financial Product Innovation • Relaxing Barriers Between Financial Institutions • Bankruptcy Reform • Growth in Subprime Markets	*Structural:* • Financial capacity promoted despite labor market status *Institutional:* • Deregulated consumption *Economic:* • Slow median income growth • Poverty rate near 10% • Unemployment between 4–7% • Rapid growth in debt obligations

Models and Variables

Models and Expectations

The following expectations compare changes to public cash assistance and the rate of consolidation by financial capital as exogenous variables with four endogenous measures of family economic deterioration in the post-WWII period. Model 1 assesses total consumer credit outstanding; Model 2 estimates the ratio of household debt to disposable income; Model 3 measures the ratio of income inequality between the top 5 percent and bottom 40 percent of families; and Model 4 estimates the ratio of household liabilities to their asset values.

Expectation #1: As the family's primary institutional role shifts from reproduction to consumption, public cash assistance expenditures will have a negative relationship with outstanding consumer credit, as well as debt compared to disposable income, but a positive relationship with debt compared to assets.

Expectation #2: Through the phases of the post-WWII SSA, changes in public cash assistance expenditures from welfare to workfare are expected to exacerbate a negative relationship with income inequalities between families.

Expectation #3: Increased access to consumer credit through the deregulated financial sector contributes to family economic deterioration.

Variables

National U.S. annual time-series data on public assistance, family deterioration, financial deregulation, and unemployment begin with the 1948 consolidation of the post-WWII SSA in the United States through the start of the recession in December 2007.[2]

Independent Variables
Total public cash assistance expenditures on relief is the sum of capitalist welfare state expenditures through ADC/AFDC, TANF, EITC,

and historical Aid to the Aged, Blind, Permanently and Totally Disabled, General Assistance, and Supplemental Security Income (SSI) programs.

The *number of total unassisted mergers of commercial banks* provides a gauge of the deregulated finance industry's impact on the circuit of capital. As a measure of the pace of financialization, unassisted merger and acquisition activities promote profits by building a geographically broad clientele, constraining competition, and diversifying financial products (Spiegel and Gart 1996).

The not seasonally adjusted *unemployment rate* is included to control for labor market fluctuations and business cycles.

Dependent Variables

For Model 1, the *total consumer credit outstanding* is the level of new and ongoing private credit obligations for consumption and subsistence, and incidence of debt poverty (Pressman and Scott 2009b).

In Model 2, the *household debt ratio* compares the sum of new and outstanding home mortgage and consumer credit loans assumed by families with their ability to pay down these obligations through their disposable personal income. Household credit liabilities allow families to supplement or replace income and guarantee some level of purchasing power and effective demand (Blundell, Pistaferri, and Preston 2008). Disposable personal income is the money available to households after taxes and transfers are deducted from their annual income.

The *liabilities-to-assets* ratio in Model 4 compares outstanding household liabilities, as above, to the total current value of their assets by replacing disposable personal income with the total value of the family home and consumer durable goods. This ratio measures the relative change in family debt-to-assets, an indicator of the economic imbalance of families described as being "underwater" (Goodman 2009; Pressman and Scott 2009a).

For Model 3, *family income inequality* compares changes in the aggregate share of total income going to the top 5 percent of families to that going to the bottom 40 percent. Often, changes in family income are measured for the "middle class," however little agreement exists on a definition for this fluid demographic (Danziger and Haveman 2001). Juxtaposing the economic elite with the working poor and impoverished reflects relative changes in the gap between the most affluent and most vulnerable families.

Results

Table 2 presents the results of the four multivariate time-series regression analyses, which demonstrate, to varying degrees, the relationship between family economic deterioration and changes in the capitalist welfare state through the progression of the post-WWII SSA. For each model, estimates of the unstandardized slope and standard coefficients (in parentheses), the processes responsible for autocorrelation in the residuals (error), the adjusted-R^2 values and y-intercepts (constant), and the Chow breakpoint tests (Chow LR Test) are provided.[3] These observed relationships are not causal but correlational, and show the pattern of historically contingent effects, most evident by considering the Chow breakpoint tests where the null hypothesis of stability across SSA phases is rejected for each model.

The first empirical expectation anticipated that as the family's primary institutional role shifts from reproduction to consumption, public cash assistance expenditures will have a negative relationship with consumer credit and the household debt ratio, but have a positive relationship with debt to assets. The pattern of effects for total consumer credit outstanding (Model 1), the household debt ratio (Model 2), and the liabilities-to-assets ratio (Model 4) provide support for this expectation. The standardized coefficients in Model 1 indicate that this relationship is very strong during both decay sub-phases ($\beta = -0.867$ and $\beta = -0.837$, respectively), and in the decay 2 sub-phase in Model 2 ($\beta = -0.858$). In the decay 1 sub-phase, provision of public cash assistance was expanded to support the reproductive role of families in response to rising social unrest exposing the contradictions of the post-WWII SSA. However, swollen relief rolls put fiscal pressure on the capitalist welfare state and catalyzed popular backlash against welfare spending. When economic growth slowed, and more families demanded relief, the means of consumption began to shift in the second decay sub-phase through legislation that opened consumer lending to minorities and women, and that promoted low-wage work with the EITC.

Table 2

Models of Family Economic Deterioration

	Full SSA 1948–2007	Consolidation 1948–1966	Decay 1 1967–1973	Decay 2 1974–1979	Prolonged Decay and Initial Exploration 1980–1992	Neoliberalism 1993–2007
Model 1, Total Consumer Credit Outstanding						
Public Cash Assistance	−1.141	7.543+	−7.590*	−5.981*	−2.440	1.369
	(−0.088)	(0.354)	(−0.867)	(−0.837)	(−0.160)	(0.133)
Unassisted Mergers	23.757**	29.055*	−10.855	2.404	22.132	122.357**
	(0.108)	(0.377)	(−0.088)	(0.013)	(0.101)	(0.433)
Unemployment	−11.337**	−4.712+	13.451+	−17.009+	−15.078	−0.869
	(−0.335)	(−0.319)	(0.503)	(−0.414)	(−0.318)	(−0.015)
Constant	107.751**	45.354*	−5.388	149.020+	127.247	10.498
Error	AR(1) MA(1)	MA(1)	WNR	WNR	AR(1)	AR(1) AR(2)
Adj. R^2	0.686	0.498	0.681	0.842	0.273	0.696
Chow LR Test	52.401**					
Model 2, Household Debt Ratio						
Public Cash Assistance	0.000	0.002	−0.003	−0.003*	0.001	0.000
	(−0.050)	(0.181)	(−0.556)	(−0.858)	(0.174)	(−0.067)
Unassisted Mergers	0.006	0.028*	0.006	0.010	0.005	−0.039+
	(0.057)	(0.465)	(0.082)	(0.112)	(−0.065)	(−0.260)
Unemployment	−0.001	0.001	0.007	−0.005	−0.005	0.021*
	(−0.041)	(0.068)	(0.453)	(−0.263)	(−0.296)	(0.695)
Constant	0.020	0.014	−0.028	0.051	0.039	−0.068
Error	AR(1)	WNR	WNR	WNR	AR(1)	AR(1)
Adj. R^2	0.410	0.134	0.000	0.896	0.117	0.585
Chow LR Test	32.273*					

The Economic Deterioration of the Family

Model 3, Income Inequality

Public Cash Assistance	0.000	0.002	0.003	−0.004*	0.001	−0.015*
	(0.011)	(0.058)	(0.269)	(−0.923)	(0.133)	(−0.781)
Unassisted Mergers	0.042+	0.061	0.060	−0.034	0.024	0.180+
	(0.172)	(0.278)	(0.360)	(−0.308)	(0.172)	(0.346)
Unemployment	0.012**	0.021*	0.009	−0.007	0.008	0.104*
	(0.315)	(0.493)	(0.250)	(0.294)	(0.256)	(1.003)
Constant	−0.060*	−0.112*	−0.050	−0.029	−0.036	−0.491+
Error	WNR	WNR	WNR	WNR	WNR	WNR;#
Adj. R^2	0.100	0.242	0.000	0.630	0.000	0.328
Chow LR Test	24.106+					

Model 4, Liabilities-to-Assets Ratio

Public Cash Assistance	0.002*	0.002	−0.001	0.001	0.003+	0.010**
	(0.267)	(0.113)	(−0.273)	(0.229)	(0.540)	(1.096)
Unassisted Mergers	0.013	0.050*	−0.032	0.040	0.003	−0.032
	(0.090)	(0.449)	(−0.519)	(0.419)	(0.040)	(−0.132)
Unemployment	−0.004	0.000	0.007+	−0.012	0.001	−0.037*
	(−0.197)	(−0.017)	(0.502)	(−0.607)	(0.034)	(−0.762)
Constant	0.039+	0.041	−0.044	0.074	−0.003	0.194+
Error	AR(1)	WNR	AR(1)	WNR	WNR	WNR
Adj. R^2	0.267	0.055	0.454	0.356	0.040	0.263
Chow LR Test	30.093+					

Notes: One-tailed significance levels: **$p < 0.01$; *$p < 0.05$; +$p < 0.10$ (constant is two-tailed).
Error Codes: WNR = white noise residuals; AR(1) = autoregressive, order 1; MA(1) = moving average, order 1.
#White's corrected standard errors for heteroskedasticity; standardized coefficients are in parentheses.

In the prolonged decay and initial exploration phase, and amplified in the neoliberalism phase, increased access and use of credit mechanisms sustained the needs of families to access means of consumption, but their expenditures on goods and services brought little in return to their net worth. In Model 4, the expected pattern of effects in the latter two SSA phases ($\beta = 0.540$ and $\beta = 1.096^4$, respectively) demonstrate how, concomitant with continued policy shifts promoting workfare and consumer debt, liabilities outpaced growth in the value of assets, strengthening the correlation between consumption and the economic deterioration of families. Together with the effects in Models 1 and 2, trading public welfare for low-wage tax credits is a strong predictor of increasing consumer debt.

In the consolidation phase, middle-class families covered by the post-WWII SSA accords translated to a positive weak effect of cash assistance on outstanding consumer credit ($\beta = 0.354$). This finding, though not outlined in the empirical expectations, is supported by SSA theory where the use of credit was purposeful in a stable institutional environment conducive for consumer confidence and capital accumulation (Kotz 2009).

The estimates from Model 3 provide support for the second expectation that anticipated that changes in public cash assistance expenditures exacerbate inequalities between families. The negative relationship between public cash assistance and income inequality in the second decay sub-phase ($\beta = -0.923$) and in neoliberalism ($\beta = -0.781$) reinforces the correlation between the promotion of low-wage employment and growing social inequalities. In the first sub-phase of decay, when the balance of public cash assistance expenditures is dominated by publicly financed cash welfare, inequalities between families are unchanged. However, in the following sub-phase, the unstandardized coefficient shows that for an annual decrease of $1 billion in cash assistance, there is an increase of 0.4 percent in income inequality. The widening divide between the top 5 percent and bottom 40 percent of the family income stratification, despite a growing number of dual-income households, accelerated as tax credits were unable to offset low wages. In the neoliberalism phase, this effect is greater, where income inequality is increased by 1.5 percent for each $1 billion decrease in public assistance spending.

Finally, across all four models, the third expected relationship between the rate of change in the number of commercial bank mergers and the deterioration of families is observed during particular historical moments. Expected across all SSA phases, and weakly corroborated in Model 1 ($\beta = 0.108$) and Model 3 ($\beta = 0.172$), significant positive effects are more prevalent in the consolidation period of rapid economic growth from 1948–1966 and in the neoliberalism phase from 1993–2007 as the financial sector responded to rapid economic policy changes. In the consolidation phase, low but significant increases in the rate of bank mergers aided the growth in the use of credit by the middle class (Model 1: $\beta = 0.377$; Model 4: $\beta = 0.449$). For example, still regulated by the post-WWII regime, credit was low risk and relatively safe and offered to families covered by the capital-labor accord; thus, for every proportional increase in bank mergers, total consumer credit outstanding increased by $29.1 billion. In addition, as banks continued to merge in neoliberalism, Model 3 shows that for a proportional change in the rate of bank mergers, the proportion of income going to the top 5 percent and the bottom 40 percent increased by 18.0 percent ($\beta = 0.346$). Model 1 also supports this expectation where, in neoliberalism, outstanding consumer credit increased by $122.36 billion for every proportional change in the rate of bank mergers ($\beta = 0.433$).

However, the significant negative relationship between the rate of mergers and household debt during neoliberalism in Model 2 was unexpected ($\beta = -0.260$). Here, the increased rates of bank mergers promoted access to consumer credit to purchase homes and durable goods, activities that provided capital with funds for reinvestment from interest payments on obligations. As personal savings rates fell, eroding disposable incomes increased debt and slowed merger activities. Another reason for this relationship, illuminated by the nonsignificant effect found in the neoliberalism phase in Model 4, where the rate of mergers promoted consumption, but for goods and services that brought little increase in the net worth of families. The absence of a significant effect may correspond to the need of the financial sector for effective demand, but less on the long-term value of household assets.

Discussion

These time-series models offer patterns of theoretically informed effects conditioned by the macro-institutional analysis of the family as an institution in the post-WWII SSA in the United States. The economic security of families was established through the New Deal by stabilizing working conditions and compensation, the social safety net, and the banking industry. These institutions also linked key family reproduction, socialization, and consumption roles to the capital accumulation as the benefits and wages of middle-class breadwinners and supported a stable circuit of capital.

Over the next four decades, the contradictions of the New Deal between affluence and poverty exposed how families excluded from the post-WWII SSA languished. As the economy stalled in the early 1970s, capital's attempts to maintain profitability to the detriment of the working and middle classes generated a dilemma for the federal government between capital accumulation and the livelihood of citizens. Subsequently, the negative relationship between public cash assistance and family economic deterioration was observed during the decay of the post-WWII SSA, particularly in the second sub-phase from 1974–1979. Here, to support accumulation, barriers to consumer credit fell and public cash assistance began transitioning to private work-based relief.

From the early 1980s through 2007, financial deregulation, social welfare retrenchment, emerging low-wage workfare, and expanding access to consumer credit promoted the new norms of self-sufficiency and personal responsibility. For the capitalist welfare state, economic growth was linked to the consumption role of families, but these became insolvent long before the onset of the "Great Recession." Beginning in 1993, for every billion dollars annually cut from public cash assistance expenditures the gap between the rich and the poor expanded by 1.5 percent; the top 5 percent of families clearly benefited from the financialization of the capitalist welfare state.

The anticipated positive effects for unassisted bank mergers are most prevalent in the consolidation and neoliberalism phases. Increasing socioeconomic inequality reinforced by consumer borrowing meant that families tapped their savings to pay down debts. When banks merged and developed new means to exploit families as consumers, including loans against the value of their only wealth-generating asset, the family home, the proportional rate of mergers created a $122.4 billion increase annually in total consumer credit outstanding. When defaults on these financial obligations increased, overleveraging the family burst the credit and housing markets and the economic deterioration of the family proved detrimental to financial capital.

Limitations and Implications

Though combining multiple modes of inquiry provides provisional and correlational evidence for historically contingent relationships, further research is needed. For example, the institutional analysis discussed the capitalist-state-citizen accord and capital-labor accord, as well as the financial regulatory regime; however, the time-series models focus on the relationships between the family, the state, and capital. The family household provides critical support to capital and labor power (Kotz 1994), but this relationship has traditionally been anchored by SSA theory in the capital-labor accord; these models refocus the family as an institution in the capitalist-state-citizen accord. To strengthen these models, a measure of labor's strength relative to capital that impacts the economic well-being of families, such as the cost of the risk labor takes in escalating conflicts with management or the decline in union membership, could be incorporated (Bowles, Gordon, and Weisskopf 1989).

A second substantive limitation is the impact of taxes on the economic well-being of families. For example, low-wage earners, as a percentage of total income, lose more to taxes both upfront in the form of payroll taxes and through sales tax and federal excise taxes often passed on to consumers by businesses (Hassett and Moore 2006). Moreover, taxes levied on capital gains from the economic investments of affluent families have traditionally redistributed income from the top to the bottom of the income bracket through social spending. However, cuts to capital gains taxes, promoted as a means to stimulate economic growth, redistribute income upward, intensifying income inequalities (Boyer 2010). Future work should incorporate a measure of personal taxes for both the bottom and top of the family income distribution.

Despite these limitations, this analysis details attempts by the capitalist welfare state of the post-WWII United States to negotiate contradictions between the economic conditions for the reproduction of the family and for the reproduction of capital, leading up to the latest capitalist crisis. Through the phases of the post-WWII SSA, the family's primary contribution to the circuit of capital shifted from reproduction to consumption as the strategic balance of welfare for capital and welfare for families defined the conditions of existence. This change, from a publicly provided safety net for social reproduction to private self-sufficient consumption, underscores the economic deterioration of families in the name of capital accumulation.

Data Appendix

Independent Variables

Total public cash assistance expenditures are the sum total payments for Aid to the Aged, Blind, Permanently and Totally Disabled, and General Assistance. Data for 1960–1973 come from Carter et al. (2006: Bf634, Bf635, Bf636, Bf638); 1948–1949, 1951–1954, and 1956–1959 were missing from later estimates; therefore, early estimates were used (Carter et al. 2006: Bf621, Bf622, Bf623, Bf625).

Aid to Dependent Children (ADC) and Aid to Families with Dependent Children (AFDC) expenditure series 1960–1997 come from Carter et al. (2006: Bf634, Bf635, Bf636, Bf638); 1948–1949, 1951–1954, 1956–1959 were missing from the later estimates; therefore, early estimates for 1948–1959 were used (Carter et al. 2006: Bf621, Bf622, Bf623, Bf625).

Temporary Assistance for Needy Families (TANF) expenditures for 1998–2007 were obtained from the Administration for Children and Families (2009: Table F, Line 5 for selected years).

Total Supplemental Security Income (SSI) payments, which replaced earlier Aid to the Aged, Blind, Disabled and General Assistance programs in 1974, were obtained for 1974–1998 from Carter et al.

(2006: Bf600 and Bf601); data for 1999–2007 come from the Social Security Administration (2008: Table 7.A4, 2010: Table 7.A4).

Earned Income Tax Credit (EITC) payments, first implemented in 1975, are reported in the Internal Revenue Service Statistics of Income data (IRS-SOI); data for 1975–1994 come from the Tax Policy Institute (2011) and for 1995–2007 from the IRS-SOI (2010, selected years).

The *total number of unassisted commercial bank mergers* is the annual sum of unassisted voluntary mergers, consolidations, or absorptions of two or more institutions reported by the Federal Deposit Insurance Corporation (2010).

The Bureau of Labor Statistics' (2010) *not seasonally adjusted unemployment rate*, controlling for business cycle effects, is the percentage of the total labor force 16 years and older without jobs but available and actively seeking work, or on temporary layoff even if not actively seeking employment.

Dependent Variables

Total consumer credit outstanding is the annual (calendar year) average of monthly reported levels of not seasonally adjusted outstanding consumer credit at month's end (Federal Reserve Board of Governors 2010b).

Total household liabilities come from the Federal Reserve's Flow of Funds Balance Sheet of Households and Nonprofit Organizations (2010a: Table B. 100) and are the sum of home mortgage (line 33) and consumer credit (line 34) balances outstanding at the end of the calendar year. *Total household assets* are the sum of the value of the household (line 4) and consumer durable goods at current replacement costs (line 7).

Disposable personal income (Bureau of Economic Analysis 2010: Table 2.1, Line 26) is the annual average of seasonally adjusted quarterly income from wage compensation and supplements from employers, and other forms of income, less contributions to governmental insurance programs and taxes. The use of disposable personal income controls for wage levels, changes in population, price fluctuations, and the general volume of economic activity (Teplin 2001).

Together, the *household debt ratio* is the total household liabilities per dollar of disposable personal income. Other measures comparing debt to income exist (Bucks et al. 2009), but not for the earliest years needed for this analysis. The *liabilities-to-assets ratio* is the total household liabilities per dollar of the total household assets.

Family income inequality is the simple division of the proportion of aggregate family income of the bottom two quintiles into the top 5 percent across all families as reported by the U.S. Census Bureau (2009).

Time-Series Analysis Procedures

The form of each univariate series was determined first by examining time-series plots across the entire post-WWII SSA and within each of the identified sub-phases. Next, univariate descriptive statistics, Jarque-Bera tests for normality, examination of correlograms and Ljung-Box Q-statistics to assess autocorrelation and nonstationarity in the mean of each series, and performance of Dickey-Fuller and Augmented Dickey-Fuller unit root tests were conducted (for a description of these tests, see Cromwell, Labys, and Terraza 1994). If the null hypothesis of a unit root was not rejected ($p < 0.05$), the series was differenced appropriately and tests for normality and autocorrelation were repeated until the series was stationary. A final univariate model was estimated with autoregressive and/or moving average parameters to correct for these processes.

Next, a Chow breakpoint stability test examined historical stability by comparing the full post-WWII series model with separate models for each post-WWII SSA phase under the null hypothesis that each does not vary across these theoretically derived phases of economic growth and decline; stability was rejected when the likelihood ratio statistic is significant ($p < 0.10$), supporting the hypothesis of historical contingency. Separate period-specific univariate models were estimated to determine their proper form and tested for normality, stationarity, and independence, and accepted when Q-statistics in the first two lags failed to reject the null hypothesis of stationarity ($p < 0.05$).[5]

Next, each measure of family economic deterioration was regressed separately on each independent variable to determine bivariate relationships across and within SSA phases. Autocorrelation and partial autocorrelation processes were diagnosed in the residuals, correlograms, and Ljung-Box Q-statistics for nonstationarity were consulted, and if independent errors in the residuals were rejected ($p < 0.05$), autoregressive and/or moving average parameters were added to correct for these processes. The bivariate models were then reestimated and accepted when Q-statistics and Jarque-Bera tests signaled stationarity and normality. The final model was tested with the White's test for heteroskedasticity under the null hypothesis of homoskedasticity ($p < 0.05$); if needed, the model was reestimated using White's correction to produce robust standard error estimates and t-test statistics. Finally, a Chow breakpoint test for each bivariate model across phases of the post-WWII SSA rejected the null hypothesis of stability ($p < 0.10$), showing a significant difference between each family economic deterioration variable and each predictor.[6]

Multivariate models were estimated first through a null model of bank mergers and unemployment, then by adding public cash assistance. The residuals of these models were assessed for stationarity through Q-statistics, Jarque-Bera tests for normality, White's tests for heteroskedasticity, and Chow breakpoint tests for stability. Corrections were made until the residuals were stationary, normally distributed, and corrected for any heteroskedasticity.

Additional tests on models with multiple independent variables were conducted to assess the stability of slope coefficients and presence of multicollinearity. While estimates remain robust with multicollinearity and inflated standard errors, it becomes more difficult to reject the null hypothesis of no relationship (Agresti and Finlay 2008). The variance inflation factor (VIF) assessed the impact of highly correlated predictor variables on the variance of the parameter estimates. Collinearity was rejected when the VIF was greater than 2.5 (Allison 1999) and, to determine if estimates were impacted, models were reestimated excluding one collinear variable.

Due to the close historical relationship between public assistance and unemployment (Piven et al. 2002), moderate multicollinearity within the neoliberal phase (VIF values range between 2.85 to 3.81) exists, but does not within other phases or across the full post-WWII SSA.

Second, the condition index is a measure of the numerical stability of slope coefficients affected by collinearity. Unstable slope estimates are not reliable predictors of relationships between the affected independent and dependent variables. All models in this analysis, even those showing moderate VIF values greater than 2.5, possess condition indices less than the cut-off of 30.0 (Belsley 1991), supporting the numerical stability of all estimates.

Finally, each measure of family economic deterioration was regressed on public cash assistance expenditures, the unassisted mergers of commercial banks, and the not seasonally adjusted unemployment rate across the full post-WWII SSA and each sub-phase. Model diagnostics followed the same procedures as above, including rejecting independent errors in the residuals through autocorrelation and partial autocorrelations functions and associated Ljung-Box Q-statistics ($p < 0.05$). In the presence of serial correlation, autoregressive and/or moving average parameters were added to the model until stationarity was achieved. Normality of the residuals was tested using the Jarque-Bera test, and the White's test for heteroskedasticity was performed. Finally, the Chow breakpoint test rejected model stability across the phases of the post-WWII SSA ($p < 0.10$) thus full post-WWII and SSA phase-specific results for the relationships between public assistance and family economic deterioration are provided.

Notes

1. The phases of the post-WWII SSA are provided in Table 1. Theoretical disagreement exists on whether a newly consolidated SSA formed in the early 1990s; this analysis considers the most recent phase a prolonged neoliberal exploration (McDonough 2008).

2. Detailed definitions and sources for each variable are provided in the Data Appendix.

3. Time-series model building procedures are described in detail in the Data Appendix

4. Inflated standard betas are expected due to micronumerocity within short time series (Goldberger 1991) and, shaped by historically contingent shifts in social conditions, enlarged variances and moderate multicollinearity during the decay 2 and neoliberalism phases exist. Strong statistical results in the presence of micronumerocity are favorable, as is the case here. Where traditional practices may outright dismiss such estimates, it is more prudent to interpret effects within historical conditions (Griffin 1992).

5. The final form of each series is as follows: public cash assistance is first-differenced; total consumer credit outstanding is first-differenced except in neoliberalism where it is second-differenced; the household debt ratio is first-differenced; income inequality is first-differenced; the liabilities-to-assets ratio is first-differenced; the total unassisted mergers of commercial banks is the first-difference of the natural log; and unemployment is in levels.

6. A *p*-value of 0.10 is used rather than the customary 0.05 because the number of degrees of freedom in the separate SSA phase models is low relative to the number of predictor variables and likely to result in large standard error estimates. In addition, these are not sample data; significance tests are used to rule out chance findings rather than to draw inferences about a population.

References

Administration for Children and Families. (2009). "TANF Financial Data." U.S. Department of Health and Human Services Washington, DC. http://www.acf.hhs.gov/programs/ofs/data/index.html

Agresti, A., and B. Finlay. (2008). *Statistical Methods for the Social Sciences*, 4th ed. Upper Saddle River, NJ: Prentice-Hall.

Allison, P. D. (1999). *Multiple Regression: A Primer*. Thousand Oaks, CA: Pine Forge Press.

Almond, B. (2006). *The Fragmenting Family*. Oxford, UK: Clarendon.

Barba, A., and M. Pivetti. (2009). "Rising Household Debt: Its Causes and Macroeconomic Implications—A Long-Period Analysis." *Cambridge Journal of Economics* 33(1): 113–137.

Becker, G. S. (1991). *A Treatise on the Family: Enlarged Edition*. Cambridge, MA: Harvard University Press.

Belsley, D. A. (1991). "A Guide to Using the Collinearity Diagnostics." *Computational Science in Economics and Management* 4(1): 33–50.

Blank, R. M., and M. S. Barr, editors. (2009). *Insufficient Funds: Savings, Assets, Credit, and Banking Among Low-Income Households*. New York: Russell Sage Foundation.

Blundell, R., L. Pistaferri, and I. Preston. (2008). "Consumption Inequality and Partial Insurance." *American Economic Review* 98(5): 1887–1921.

Bostic, R. W., and K. O. Lee. (2009). "Homeownership: America's Dream?" In *Insufficient Funds: Savings, Assets, Credit, and Banking Among Low-Income Households*. Eds. R. M. Blank and M. S. Barr, pp. 218–256. New York: Russell Sage Foundation.

Bowles, S., D. M. Gordon, and T. E. Weisskopf. (1989). "Business Ascendancy and Economic Impasse: A Structural Retrospective on Conservative Economics, 1979–1987." *Journal of Economic Perspectives* 3(1): 107–134.

——. (1990). *After the Wasteland: A Democratic Economics for the Year 2000*. Armonk, NY: M.E. Sharpe, Inc.

Boyer, R. (2010). "The Rise of CEO Pay and the Contemporary Social Structure of Accumulation in the United States." In *Contemporary Capitalism and its Crises: Social Structure of Accumulation Theory for the Twenty-First Century*. Eds. T. McDonough, M. Reich, and D. M. Kotz, pp. 215–238. Cambridge: Cambridge University Press.

Bucks, B. K., A. B. Kennickell, T. L. Mach, and K. B. Moore. (2009). "Changes in U.S. Family Finances from 2004 to 2007: Evidence from the Survey of Consumer Finances." *Federal Reserve Bulletin* 95(February): A1–A56.

Bureau of Economic Analysis. (2009). "National Income and Product Accounts Table: Table 1.12. National Income by Type of Income, Line 15." Washington, DC. http://www.bea.gov/national/nipaweb

——. 2010. "National Income and Product Accounts Table: Table 2.1. Personal Income and its Disposition." Washington, DC. http://www.bea.gov/national/nipaweb

Carlson, S. M., M. D. Gillespie, and R. J. Michalowski. (2010). "Social Structures of Accumulation and the Criminal Justice System." In *Contemporary Capitalism and its Crises: Social Structure of Accumulation Theory for the Twenty-First Century*. Eds. T. McDonough, M. Reich, and D. M. Kotz, pp. 239–266. Cambridge: Cambridge University Press.

Carter, S. B., S. S. Gartner, M. R. Haines, A. L. Olmstead, R. Sutch, and G. Wright. (2006). "Historical Statistics of the United States Millennial Edition Online." New York: Cambridge University Press. http://hsus.cambridge.org/HSUSWeb/HSUSEntryServlet

Collins, J. L., and V. Mayer. (2010). *Both Hands Tied: Welfare Reform and the Race to the Bottom in the Low-Wage Labor Market*. Chicago: University of Chicago Press.

Collins, R. (1975). *Conflict Sociology: Toward an Explanatory Science*. New York: Academic Press.

Coontz, S. (1992). *The Way We Never Were: American Families and the Nostalgia Trap*. New York: Basic Books.

Creed, G. W. (2000). "'Family Values' and Domestic Economies." *Annual Review of Anthropology* 29(1): 329–355.

Cromwell, J. B., W. C. Labys, and M. Terraza. (1994). *Univariate Tests for Time Series Models*. Thousand Oaks, CA: Sage Publications.

Danziger, S., and R. H. Haveman. (2001). *Understanding Poverty*. New York: Russell Sage Foundation.

Dickinson, J., and B. Russell, editors. (1986). *Family, Economy and State: The Social Reproduction Process Under Capitalism*. New York: St. Martin's Press.

Engels, F. ([1884] 2001). *Origins of the Family, Private Property and the State*. London: ElecBook.

Federal Deposit Insurance Corporation. (2010). "CB02: Changes in Number of Institutions FDIC-Insured Commercial Banks United States and Other Areas." Washington, DC. http://www2.fdic.gov/hsob/HSOBRpt.asp

Federal Reserve Board of Governors. (2010a). "Statistical Release Z.1 (March 11, 2010): Flow of Funds Accounts of the United States, Table B.100." Washington, DC.

———. (2010b). "Total Consumer Credit Outstanding, Release G-19: Series TOTALNS." Board of Governors of the Federal Reserve System, Washington, DC.

Goldberg, G. S., and S. D. Collins. (2001). *Washington's New Poor Law: Welfare "Reform" and the Roads Not Taken, 1935 to the Present.* New York: Apex Press.

Goldberger, A. S. (1991). *A Course in Econometrics.* Cambridge, MA: Harvard University Press.

Goodman, P. S. (2009). *Past Due: The End of Easy Money and the Renewal of the American Economy.* New York: Henry Holt and Co.

Gordon, D. M., R. Edwards, and M. Reich. (1982). *Segmented Work, Divided Workers: The Historical Transformation of Labor in the United States.* New York: Cambridge University Press.

Gough, I. (1979). *The Political Economy of the Welfare State.* London: MacMillan.

Griffin, L. J. (1992). "Temporality, Events, and Explanation in Historical Sociology: An Introduction." *Sociological Methods Research* 20(4): 403–427.

Harvey, D. (2005). *A Brief History of Neoliberalism.* New York: Oxford University Press.

Hassett, K. A., and A. Moore. (2006). "How Do Tax Policies Affect Low-Income Workers?" In *Working and Poor: How Economic and Policy Changes are Affecting Low-Wage Workers.* Eds. R. M. Blank, S. H. Danziger, and R. F. Schoeni, pp. 265–288. New York: Russell Sage Foundation.

Hays, S. (2003). *Flat Broke with Children: Women in the Age of Welfare Reform.* New York: Oxford University Press.

Howell, B. (2006). "Exploiting Race and Space: Concentrated Subprime Lending as Housing Discrimination." *California Law Review* 94(1): 101–147.

Internal Revenue Service. (2010). "SOI Tax Stats—Individual Income Tax Returns: Table 4." Washington, DC. http://www.irs.gov/taxstats/indtaxstats/article/0,,id=133414,00.html

Jessop, B. (2007). *State Power: A Strategic-Relational Approach.* Malden, MA: Polity.

Katz, M. B. (1996). *In the Shadow of the Poor House: A Social History of Welfare in America*, rev. ed. New York: Basic Books.

Kotz, D. M. (1994). "Household Labor, Wage Labor, and the Transformation of the Family." *Review of Radical Political Economics* 26(2): 24–56.

———. (2009). "The Financial and Economic Crisis of 2008: A Systemic Crisis of Neoliberal Capitalism." *Review of Radical Political Economics* 41(3): 305–317.

Marx, K. (1998). *The German Ideology: Including Theses on Feuerbach and the Introduction to the Critique of Political Economy.* Amherst, NY: Prometheus Books.

McDonough, T. (2008). "Social Structures of Accumulation Theory: The State of the Art." *Review of Radical Political Economics* 40(2): 153–173.

McLean, B., and J. Nocera. (2010). *All the Devils Are Here: The Hidden History of the Financial Crisis.* New York: Portfolio/Penguin.

Mills, C. W. (1959). *The Sociological Imagination.* New York: Oxford University Press.

Morgen, S., J. Acker, J. Weigt, and L. Gonzales. (2006). "Living Economic Restructuring at the Bottom: Welfare Restructuring and Low-Wage Work." In *The Promise of Welfare Reform: Political Rhetoric and the Reality of Poverty in the Twenty-First Century.* Eds. K. M. Kilty and E. A. Segal, pp. 81–94. Binghamton, NY: Hawthorn Press.

Neubeck, K. J. (2006). *When Welfare Disappears: The Case for Economic Human Rights.* New York: Routledge.

Newman, K. S. (2006). *Chutes and Ladders: Navigating the Low-Wage Labor Market.* New York: Russell Sage Foundation.

O'Connor, J. (1973). *The Fiscal Crisis of the State.* New York: St. Martin's Press.

O'Hara, P. A. (1995). "Household Labor, the Family, and Macroeconomic Instability in the United States: 1940s–1990s." *Review of Social Economy* 53(1): 89–120.

Parsons, T., and R. F. Bales. (1955). *Family, Socialization and Interaction Process.* Glencoe, IL: Free Press.

Pattillo-McCoy, M. (1999). *Black Picket Fences: Privilege and Peril Among the Black Middle Class.* Chicago: University of Chicago Press.

Piven, F. F., J. Acker, M. Hallock, and S. Morgen, editors. (2002). *Work, Welfare, and Politics: Confronting Poverty in the Wake of Welfare Reform.* Eugene, OR: University of Oregon Press.

Piven, F. F., and Cloward, R. A. (1997). *The Breaking of the American Social Compact.* New York: New Press.

Pressman, S., and R. Scott. (2009a). "Consumer Debt and the Measurement of Poverty and Inequality in the United States." *Review of Social Economy* 67(2): 127–146.

———. (2009b). "Who are the Debt Poor?" *Journal of Economic Issues* 43(2): 423–432.

Reinhart, C. M., and K. S. Rogoff. (2009). *This Time is Different: Eight Centuries of Financial Folly.* Princeton, NJ: Princeton University Press.

Sidel, R. (2006). *Unsung Heroines: Single Mothers and the American Dream.* Berkeley, CA: University of California Press.

Social Security Administration. (2008). "Statistical Abstract of the United States: 2000." Washington, DC.
——. (2010). "Statistical Abstract of the United States: 2009." Washington, DC.
Sorkin, A. R. (2009). *Too Big to Fail: The Inside Story of How Wall Street and Washington Fought to Save the Financial System—and Themselves.* New York: Viking.
Spiegel, J. W., and A. Gart. (1996). "What Lies Behind the Bank Merger and Acquisition Frenzy?" *Business Economics* 31(2): 47–52.
Swenson, D. (2004). *A Neo-Functionalist Synthesis of Theories in Family Sociology.* Lewiston, NY: Edwin Mellen Press.
Tax Policy Center. (2011). "Earned Income Tax Credit: Number of Recipients and Amount of Credit, 1975–2009." Urban Institute and Brookings Institution Washington, DC. http://www.taxpolicycenter.org/taxfacts/displayafact.cfm?DocID=37&Topic2id=40&Topic3id=42
Teplin, A. M. (2001). "The U.S. Flow of Funds Accounts and Their Uses." *Federal Reserve Bulletin* 87(July): 431–441.
Turner, L. J., S. Danziger, and K. S. Seefeldt. (2006). "Failing the Transition from Welfare to Work: Women Chronically Disconnected from Employment and Cash Welfare." *Social Science Quarterly* 87(2): 227–249.
U.S. Bureau of Labor Statistics. (2010). "(Unadj) Unemployment Rate Series LNU04000000." U.S. Department of Labor Washington, DC. http://data.bls.gov/PDQ/servlet/SurveyOutputServlet?data_tool=latest_numbers&series_id=LNU04000000&years_option=all_years&periods_option=specific_periods&periods=Annual+Data
U.S. Census Bureau. (2009). "Historical Income Table—Families: Table F-2, Share of Aggregate Income Received by Each Fifth and Top 5 Percent of Families, All Races: 1947 to 2007." Washington, DC.
Warren, E., and A. W. Tyagi. (2003). *The Two-Income Trap: Why Middle-Class Mothers and Fathers are Going Broke.* New York: Basic Books.
White, J. M., and D. M. Klein. (2008). *Family Theories*, 3rd ed. Los Angeles: Sage.
Wilson, W. J. (1996). *When Work Disappears: The World of the New Urban Poor.* New York: Vintage Books.
Wolfson, M. H. (1994). *Financial Crises: Understanding the Postwar U.S. Experience*, 2nd ed. Armonk, NY: M.E. Sharpe.
Wolfson, M. H., and D. M. Kotz. (2010). "A Reconceptualization of SSA Theory." In *Contemporary Capitalism and its Crises: Social Structure of Accumulation Theory for the Twenty-First Century.* Eds. T. McDonough, M. Reich, and D. M. Kotz, pp. 72–90. Cambridge: Cambridge University Press.
Zaretsky, E. (1976). *Capitalism, the Family, and Personal Life.* New York: Harper Colophon.

The Market Concept: A Characterization from Institutional and Post-Keynesian Economics

By Eduardo Fernández-Huerga*

ABSTRACT. The neoclassical concept of the market is built on a number of assumptions that lead one to view it as a type of ether, devoid of any institutional content. In opposition to this point of view, this article proposes an alternative characterization of markets based on the fundamental principles of institutional and post-Keynesian economics. After reviewing the main features that characterize the behavior of economic agents, we analyze the set of interrelations between these agents within markets and the role of institutions in the regulation of these interrelations. Finally, we discuss some of the consequences generated by the institutional dimensions of markets with regard to their origins and evolution, the justification for their existence, or the evaluation of their results.

Introduction

The term "market" is used within economics to refer to a variety of diverse phenomena. In fact, its contemporary use is in many cases metaphoric (Rosenbaum 2000: 456) because its meaning is shaped by the context in which the term is used. Nevertheless, this is not to say that this concept does not need to be imbued with specific content. This need is crucial because the term "market" is frequently used in association with properties that demand a particularly specific context that is often different from that in which the term is used. In fact, many of the disputes that arise in economics between the orthodox and heterodox visions are associated with the underlying conception of the market. This is the case for topics such as the assessment of public intervention, the role of money in the economy, or unemployment analysis and its potential solutions. Furthermore, the current economic

*Department of Economics and Statistics, University of León, Spain; E-mail address: eduardo.fernandez@unileon.es

crisis has revived the need to clearly define this concept by placing the financial markets in the spotlight and emphasizing the convenience or inconvenience of market regulation.

Despite the central role of the market within economic theory (especially within the orthodox approach), finding studies that have produced deep and systematic analyses of this concept is difficult (Swedberg 1994: 257). Nevertheless, in the past few years various economists have shown a renewed interest in this topic, most particularly from the standpoint of economic sociology (Fligstein 1996; Tordjman 2004; Coriat and Weinstein 2005; Callon, Millo, and Muniesa 2007; Allaire 2010). Important contributions have also come from other branches of heterodox economics, such as institutionalist economics and, perhaps to a lesser extent, post-Keynesian economics. In this context, the aim of this article is to bring together these latest contributions and try to present, in a structured and coherent manner, a vision of markets that fits within the theoretical framework offered by institutional and post-Keynesian economics (hereafter I/PK).[1] Moreover, we intend to build this characterization on an alternative conception of the behavior of economic agents. This aspect is relevant because the analysis of what happens in markets is substantially conditioned by the conception of agents operating in them.

In this sense, the present study is organized as follows. In the next section a brief review is made of the neoclassical conception of the market, emphasizing its assumptions and those concerning the behavior of agents. Then, an alternative characterization of the market is presented. First, we describe some of the features that define individual and firm behavior from the I/PK point of view. Second, we analyze the set of interrelations that occur between these agents in markets, distinguishing between horizontal relations (between potential sellers and buyers) and vertical relations (between several potential buyers or several potential sellers). In the latter case, we insist on the need to use a different and larger concept of competition than is used in neoclassical economics; this is an aspect that perhaps has not been sufficiently emphasized in the literature. Finally, we expose some of the consequences that are generated by the institutional dimension of markets on various aspects, such as their origins and evolution, the justification for their existence, or the evaluation of their results.

The Neoclassical Conception of the Market and its Basic Assumptions: An Overview

The neoclassical concept of the market is built on a variety of assumptions concerning not only its own content but also the behavior of the agents that operate within it. Hence, it is assumed that individual behavior (particularly that of consumers) is guided by specific rules. First, consumer behavior is assumed to be directed toward a single objective: the maximization of utility. This assumption is possible, among other reasons, as it is assumed that the preferences of individuals are comparable (and measurable) based on their ability to provide utility. Second, human beings are assumed to have cognitive capabilities that make reality known or knowable, as well as reasoning capacities sufficient to process all this information and apply instrumental rationality. All of this suggests that a human being can be reduced to a simple preference function, which is known and determines the individual's actions.

Something similar occurs with the behavior of the firm. In the simplest neoclassical vision, the organizational dimension of the firm is not taken into account or is considered irrelevant. Therefore, a firm's behavior is ultimately similar to that of the individual. The neoclassical model assumes that all of a firm's activities can be compared and reduced to a common valuation scale: its capacity to generate profits. This assumption in turn allows all of a firm's actions to be understood with regard to a single objective: maximizing profits. In this context, a firm is reduced to a technical production function. Added to this is a type of "hidden mind" with some cognitive and rational abilities that allows the firm to develop an optimizing behavior aimed at reaching that objective.

The result of the foregoing is that, in the absence of imperfections, the behavior of agents is not conditioned by the institutional environment. Within this context, the interaction between buyers and sellers takes place solely through prices. In fact, the assumptions adopted in the agents' behavioral model—essentially that agents are rational actors and have perfect information—lead to the conclusion that price is the sole variable relevant to decision making. Any other type of interaction between agents or between agents and the institutional environment becomes an imperfection that causes agents to deviate from behavior directed toward price "competition" (Hodgson 1988; Jackson 2007). In this context, a price adjustment "process" starts in the market and culminates by reaching an equilibrium that clears the market; in the absence of imperfections, this equilibrium simultaneously implies an allocation that is regarded as efficient. The pricing process is assumed to develop *as if* an auctioneer is present yet assumes that one does not exist because this would admit the presence of an institution (Sawyer 1993). It is further assumed that no exchange is developed during the adjustment process. These exchanges instead take place when equilibrium is reached, which in turn supposes that the process develops in logical time (Hodgson 1988; Sawyer 1993).

All of the above features characterize a perfect market concept (and, simultaneously, perfect competition), with the pricing mechanism as a crucial element of this concept. Thanks in part to the impetus of the use of the term "perfect," this characterization has become an ideal (Sawyer 1993: 20) or a totem (Jackson 2007: 237), often invoked as if this ideal was a desirable and attainable outcome. In fact, it is common to ascribe any differences between reality and this characterization to "imperfections" of reality and not to deficiencies in the specifications of the model (Sawyer 1993: 20).

Ultimately, centering the description of the market on the pricing process leads to the identification of one with the other: the price mechanism *is* the market (Ménard 1995: 169; Liljenberg 2005: 1000). In other words, the only thing the market does is establish prices. In addition, the perfect market is assumed to neither require nor present any institutional elements (Ménard 1995: 169): property rights are not defined (nor do they need to be), no regulations are required (not even to ensure contract compliance), and money does not exist (or the situation is the same as if it did not). In short, the market is an ether (Hodgson 1988: 177–178) with hardly any content; this lack of specificity causes the market to be invoked with a certain mysticism, as a "something" that is not clearly defined yet is associated with efficiency. Furthermore, this lack of specificity also permits the application of the analytical tools of the market to other areas of relations such as marriage formation, a fact emphasized by

Lie (1997: 342): "The analytical structure developed for the abstract market... can be used for non-market spheres precisely because there is nothing particular about the institution or the structure of the abstract market."

The elimination of any institutional features in the concept of the market and in decision-making processes of agents has resulted in the conclusion, by way of tautological reasoning, that the market is the preeminent medium for the expression of individual choice (Hodgson 1988: 178). By association, this has led to equating the market with "freedom" and institutions (or "socialization") with "restrictions" that limit this freedom.[2]

Many of these assumptions are clearly questionable, and abandoning them may lead to a radically different understanding of markets and the roles of institutions within them. In fact, the dominance of the neoclassical conceptualization of the market has distracted the attention of economists from the mechanisms that drive the allocation process in the real world, as Ayres (1957: 26) pointed out many years ago. This critique has become one of the central elements of institutional economics (Samuels 1995: 571). Furthermore, the post-Keynesian literature has emphasized that the pricing process that takes place in the real world diverges, in a variety of aspects, from the description in the neoclassical model (Lavoie 1992; Lee 1998; Downward 1999).

Many of the limitations of the neoclassical view of the market are rooted in its ontological conception of reality and in the implementation of the deductive method. As noted by Lawson (1994, 1997), orthodox economics appears linked to the philosophical system of positivism, which holds that reality encompasses the constant conjunction of atomistic events. In short, it is a closed system approach to theorizing. The assumption of constant conjunction of events allows for mathematical modeling and the construction of functional relations, which triggers the application of the deductive method. This, in turn, implies the need to close the system by imposing a series of conditions. The problem arises because the systemic closure often requires the use of false assumptions that are in conflict with reality and that call into question the explanatory power of the theoretical construction (Caldwell 1982; Fleetwood 2006).

In this context, the purpose of this article is, precisely, to present an alternative characterization of how markets function that is consistent with the theoretical framework that offers the I/PK approach.

Toward an Alternative Characterization of Markets

The essence of markets is associated with exchange, even if both concepts cannot be fully defined: not all exchanges take place through a market (Hodgson 1988; Fourie 1991; Rosenbaum 2000; Jackson 2007) and interactions and activities other than exchange take place within a market (Hodgson 1988; Fourie 1991; Jackson 2007). Nevertheless, exchanges in the market presuppose a *relation* between parties (Hodgson 1988; Fourie 1991; Jackson 2007). This allows for a conception of the market as a special type of social structure (Swedberg 1994; Jackson 2007), which, in turn, necessarily allows its institutional features to surface. In fact, Hodgson (2006: 2) defines institutions as "systems of established and prevalent social rules that structure *social interactions*" (italics added). Ultimately, as we will see, markets do not and cannot exist if they are not woven by and with a series of institutions that structure the different relations that occur within them (Hodgson 1988; Fourie 1991; Samuels 1995; Ménard 1995; Allaire 2010).[3]

Obviously, this conception of markets demands for analysis a meta-theoretical apparatus different from the positivist philosophy typical of the neoclassical approach. In this sense, the philosophical framework of critical realism is particularly useful here because it provides a meta-theoretical apparatus specially designed to study social structures and their continuous interaction with human agency (Fleetwood 2006: 79). Critical realism starts from an open-system understanding of reality, and recognizes that reality, which is transmutable, appears to be characterized by the presence of deep social structures that govern the observed phenomena (Lawson 1994, 1997; Fleetwood 1999). In this context, the objective of the theorization is to identify the structures and causal mechanisms underlying the phenomena of interest. Finally, the theorization appears to be directed toward explanation instead of deduction and/or prediction, and the deductive method is replaced by the causal-explanatory method (Fleetwood 1999).

The Behavior of Economic Agents: An Alternative Conception

Before analyzing the set of relations that take place in the markets, it is useful to describe (however briefly) some of the features that characterize the behavior of the agents who maintain these relations (particularly those of individuals and firms). While there is no completely uniform view of this behavior within institutional and post-Keynesian economics, it is possible to find a series of elements that these schools of thought generally share (Fernández-Huerga 2008). Moreover, individual motivation generally seems directed toward the satisfaction of a set of different needs and wants, organized under some type of complex structure that changes over time. The construction and identification of this structure is a cognitive process and, as such, is subject to the influence of the institutional environment and the actions of other agents. This creates the possibility that market institutions will affect the priorities and values of the agents who participate in them and, in short, condition the structure of the agents' needs and wants (Hodgson 1988; Fourie 1991; Bowles 1991, 1998; Bowles and Gintis 1993; Tsakalotos 2005). However, in a world with fundamental uncertainty, knowledge—including the knowledge of what takes place in the market—is imperfect and fallible, easily influenced by other agents, and built to a large degree through the use of habits that reflect the institutional environment (Hodgson 1988, 1997; Loasby 2001). Something similar takes place with the reasoning process, which given the limited rational capacities of individuals, is directed by a type of "procedural rationality"[4] that largely develops through appeals to rules or conventions learned through social participation (Simon 1976; Lavoie 1992; Dequech 2006) in combination with elements of both creativity (Dequech 2006; Loasby 2001) and emotional rationality (Dequech 2003; Elster 1998).[5] The decision-making process in the market is further complicated because the goods that are exchanged frequently exhibit multiple attributes that can affect different needs and wants. This results in the absence of a one-to-one correspondence between needs and wants and the chosen goods and instead produces a more complex structure of interrelations (Georgescu-Roegen 1954).

Firms, in turn, are organizations that perform multiple activities to achieve different objectives; these different sub-goals act to drive the behavior of the firm as a whole (Cyert and March 1963; Simon 1979) and are difficult to reduce to a common valuation scale. Some of these activities occur in markets in which the firms are involved as producers or consumers.[6] Typically, this participation is not "passive" or limited to, for instance, launching a product in a market and hoping that said product finds a price and an allocation, nor is participation "impersonal" (in the sense that interactions with other agents and the environment are only connected through the price). Moreover, the participation of a firm in real-world markets is much more active and focused on acquiring necessary supplies or selling its products in the most favorable conditions, as well as seeking to control what happens in them.

To summarize, the actions of the agents who participate in the markets are necessarily conditioned by the institutional environment (in particular, the owner of the market). In this context, we will attempt to analyze what actually happens in markets[7] and describe the set of relations that occur within them in the paragraphs that follow. To facilitate this presentation, we will distinguish—in the same manner as Fourie (1991)—vertical relations (between potential buyers and sellers) from horizontal relations (between different potential sellers and/or different buyers). In addition, we will attempt to pay special attention to the role of institutions in the regulation of those interrelations.

Vertical Relations Among the Agents Who Operate in the Markets

The primary vertical relation that occurs in the markets, and that in fact gives a meaning to their existence (Fourie 1991; Rosenbaum 2000; Jackson 2007), is the exchange relation. In this regard, we need to ask what is being exchanged and what defines and distinguishes a transaction in the market from other forms of exchange. It seems clear that a market exchange implies a transfer of goods and services. Nevertheless, this assertion alone may hide some significant aspects involved in the exchange. Hence, Hodgson (1988) emphasizes that an exchange also assumes a transfer of property rights, thus adopting an idea that was previously put forth in Commons (1934) and underlined by, among others, Ménard (1995) and Jackson (2007). In this regard, Fourie (1991: 42) has pointed out that many market exchanges do not strictly involve the transfer of property titles, but of rights of access to or usage of a particular good or service. This means that agreeing to a market exchange implies the transfer of not only goods and services but also of rights (and, in some cases, the transfer of obligations) associated with these exchanges.[8] This fact reveals the need for a set of rules or institutions (legal and otherwise) to determine what is being exchanged and to specify and give coverage to the existence and transfer of the rights involved (Hodgson 1988; Fourie 1991; Ménard 1995; Tordjman 2004; Jackson 2007). Although it is true that exchanges often appear to be associated with contractual agreements, a system of exchange cannot be reduced to contracts alone (Hodgson 1988). Contracts and legal systems are by nature incomplete and require the presence of additional regulatory elements arising from customs, the precedents, or cultural elements (Hodgson 1988, 2006).[9] This idea is generally shared by post-Keynesian scholars who emphasizes the fact that fundamental uncertainty prevents the *ex ante* drafting of complete contracts (Williams and Findlay 1986: 37).

Furthermore, conducting market transactions often requires control mechanisms to monitor compliance and enforce the application of the terms governing the exchange (Hodgson 1988; Coriat and Weinstein 2005). This usually involves the appearance of additional institutions in the market to enforce and regulate the application of the terms of exchange.[10] This aspect, among others, is what makes markets not only allocating mechanisms but also disciplinary environments (Bowles 1991, 1998; Bowles and Gintis 1993).

Finally, the presence of agreements and legal institutions that regulate the terms of exchange and their application appear to be ontologically linked to the existence of yet another institution: the state (Hodgson 1988; Dequech 2000). Indeed, the state performs a central role in the establishment of a public legal order in markets—it also affects the establishment and evolution of nonlegal institutions— and participates in markets as a buyer and seller (Fligstein 1996); this is one of the reasons why separating "the sphere of the market" from "the sphere of the state or of politics" is not a sustainable endeavor (Fourie 1991: 50).

In any case, not all transfers of goods and services are associated with market exchange. At least two other requirements must be met: first, a *quid pro quo* must be established, that is, the transfer must take place in exchange for something else (unlike, for instance, the giving of a gift); second, this obligation must assume a *monetary* transfer with a rate of exchange or *price* (Fourie 1991; Rosenbaum 2000; Jackson 2007). In fact, as emphasized by Fourie (1991: 44), "the phenomenon of price is peculiar to economic exchange: it captures and symbolizes the specifics of the *quid pro quo.*" Consequently, an exchange relation not only implies a transfer of goods and services but also includes a relationship associated with the pricing process. In this regard, the market, through the mediation of the legal and nonlegal institutions that comprise it, provides an environment that facilitates the development of the pricing process (Hodgson 1988). This does not mean that it is "the market" that "sets" the prices. In fact, the roles of the different agents and institutions in the pricing process vary according to the market. In some markets, the price is established by way of an auctioning process (in any case, of a different nature than that of the neoclassical model, even if because it only requires the explicit presence of an institutional framework to operate); nevertheless, the role of price setting in the majority of markets is filled by one of the parties to the transaction, usually the seller (Hodgson 1988; Sawyer 1993; Jackson 2007).[11] In any case, institutions of each market perform a key function in the pricing process, establishing the rules that regulate this process (Hodgson 1988). Thus, for example, price determination practices in many labor markets are conditioned by collective negotiation mechanisms and are completely different from those existing in stock markets. In turn, these practices differ from those existing in many goods markets, where the agents seem to accept the legitimacy of the institutionalized price determination rules that are based on adding a margin to unit costs. Formal and informal institutions of each market help to determine the roles of different agents in the pricing process, condition the practices that direct the establishment and publication of prices, and even influence the price adjustment processes, thus conditioning how and when they can occur and which practices are considered legal or legitimate.

Monetary pricing is essentially linked to the existence of money. In this regard, Loasby (2000, 2001) has emphasized that the substitution of money for the use of barter is useful not only in reducing transaction costs but also leads to the establishment of a set of prices that simplifies the comparison of the values of products; in sum, money improves knowledge, frees time and cognitive resources, and eases the consumption process. In a similar manner, post-Keynesian studies have emphasized that money is a way to address uncertainty. Money is a mechanism that makes a connection between the past and the future in a real-time context possible and is a key instrument that permits planning and the organization of production and exchange processes, the execution of which takes time (Davidson 1972, 1988; Kregel 1980). In summary, money is an essential institution within the modern economy and, as any other institution, contributes in multiple ways to diminish uncertainty, generate knowledge, and adopt decisions within a non-ergodic world (Hodgson 1988, 1997; Dequech 2006). In fact, in the Arrow-Debreu model, in which real time does not exist, money does not play an important role—it is as if it did not exist (Friedman 1962)—hence, goods are exchanged, fundamentally, for other goods. Only in the non-ergodic world does the existence of money (and of contracts valued in money) acquire its real meaning and achieve its authentic relevance, which in turn leads to its lack of neutrality in the long term (Davidson 1988).

The relation between money and uncertainty is complex and is not independent of the role of other institutions. This is so, among other reasons, because the existence of money appears linked to the emergence of debt relations or of contracts for deferred payment. In this context, "the existence of institutions which can enforce the discharge of contractual commitments for future action are essential in providing trust in the future of the monetary system" (Davidson 1972: 147). Obviously, the state is one of the institutions that contributes to create the conditions for money to be used as store of value and means of payment—as it is emphasized, in particular, by the chartalist approach (Wray 1998), although also other institutions can play an important role in this process (Rochon and Vernego 2003). In fact, the relevance of these institutions has increased during the last years, in the context of increasing financialization of the economy and confidence in a growth model based on credit money.[12]

At any rate, prices in the real world fail to impart all of the necessary information for exchanges to take place. The characteristics of the pricing process (in particular, the fact that the price-setting role is taken by one of the parties) results in prices performing multiple functions and in the confusion of their messages. Moreover, in a world in which activity takes place in real time, a change in prices may have multiple origins and characteristics (Hodgson 1988; Sawyer 1993). Furthermore, because goods typically have different attributes that are hard to know and value, and even more difficult to reduce to a common and price-independent valuation scale, price is no longer the unique element against which to compare and choose goods; in fact, price becomes in practice yet another attribute of a good (Earl 1983). All of the above makes additional information on a product useful, which allows a "transmission of information" relationship to emerge. While different situations are possible, in the majority of markets the suppliers have the primary role in this process, which is an additional source of asymmetries in the market (Jackson 2007). The market institutions themselves can have an important role in this process when they condition or regulate these transfers of information and when they directly intervene in such transfers (Tordjman 2004; Allaire 2010).

In any case, conceptualizing the cognitive process as a simple accumulation of external information is incorrect; cognition is a social construction process conditioned by the surrounding institutional and cultural framework (Hodgson 1988; Loasby 2001). This implies recognizing that the actors in a market can influence the knowledge and the entire decision-making process of the other agents either directly or by conditioning the institutional framework. This assumes, for instance, that both suppliers and market institutions can influence the knowledge the consumers have about products and even the structures of their needs and wants (Hodgson 1988; Bowles and Gintis 1993; Bowles 1998; Tsakalotos 2005). In addition, in a world with fundamental uncertainty, emotions and the interrelations with other agents perform an important role in any decision-making process and particularly in any choice in a market. Consequently, the advent of relations between buyers and sellers can generate trust or lead to the advent of emotions that effectively contribute to choice, without necessarily being an imperfection. This possibility can be exploited by the parties involved in the transaction for their own interests.

The importance and characteristics of each of the previous relations is not independent of the type of object in the transaction (Prasch 1995). Thus, the greater the complexity of the good, the more important the relations that condition knowledge of the agents and the personal or emotional relationships that influence the confidence associated with that knowledge are (Sawyer 1993; Jackson 2007). Similarly, the less specified are the terms of the exchange, the more relevant the interpersonal relations associated with loyalty or trust become (Prasch 2008; Rosenbaum 2000; Jackson 2007). Furthermore, interpersonal relations and enforcement mechanisms are usually more important in cases where the exchange involves establishing some type of lasting relationship between the parties, as in credit or labor relations (Prasch 2008).

Horizontal Relations Among the Agents Who Operate in the Markets

Because several buyers and/or sellers can operate in one market, an exact characterization of the market demands that careful attention be paid not only to relations between both groups but also to those that exist within each group (Fourie 1991; Jackson 2007). Hence, the market appears as "a structured and interwoven cluster of economically qualified exchange and rivalry relations" (Fourie 1991: 48). Interrelations can be present both among different potential buyers and among potential sellers. Nevertheless, the relations among producers/sellers are more relevant in practice because the lasting character of this type of activity tends to leave a greater margin for planning and the development of more or less organized relations between them (Jackson 2007). Conversely, as the final purpose of a market action is to perform an exchange and this excludes (or may exclude) some of the potential buyers or sellers, horizontal relations always imply a certain degree of rivalry or competition.[13]

In neoclassical economics, the model for horizontal relationships between agents is reduced to the concept of "competition," that is, as we will see, a specific type of competition, and is linked to the ideal of "perfect competition." The only factor that sellers and buyers have to compete is price. There are no horizontal relations between agents, nor are there any institutions to regulate these relations. Further, once "the market" sets a price, the agents have only one viable option: exchange at that price. Consequently, the neoclassical model of perfect competition is quite restrictive (deep down, there are no possibilities to compete[14]), far away from most of the situations that take place in the real world and theoretically unacceptable once the existence of fundamental uncertainty is recognized.

In this context, it seems necessary to propose a model of the horizontal relations between the agents that accept the presence of fundamental uncertainty, that acknowledge the role of institutions in reality, and that, in short, fit the I/PK behavioral model. The first aspect that must be taken into account is that economic agents, particularly firms, develop multiple and diverse activities, both internal and external; this recognizes that there is no single competitive mechanism but rather many, as each of the different fields of action can be a space in which to exert rivalry and attempt to overcome potential opponents. In fact, a firm competes not only through its present but its past decisions because the incorporation of the real dimension of time acknowledges that the past matters and that there is *path dependence* (Teece et al. 1994). In addition, the presence of fundamental uncertainty implies that the decisions made by economic agents in different fields not only consist of *discovering existing* options and choosing among them but that it is necessary to incorporate also the creativity and the possibility for innovation (Sawyer 1990; Dosi and Egidi 1991; Dequech 2000, 2006; Dunn 2002). Furthermore, in a world with fundamental uncertainty, the results of any activity depend not only on the decisions of an individual but also on those undertaken by the rest of agents and on the evolution of the environment, which allows the search for control to acquire meaning and reach its true relevance (Dunn 2002).

In short, economic agents are rivals throughout the entire set of decisions they make, both present and past, seeking good solutions, at times imitating those of others, sometimes innovating and creating new options, and attempting to control what other agents make or can (or want to) make. If we restrict the analysis to the market environment, each one of the vertical relations that we indicate in the previous section comprises a space in which attempts are made (or are not made) to surpass other potential sellers or buyers. This assumes that the agents, particularly the firms, can compete not only through prices,[15] in which determination processes play a more active role than that imposed in orthodox economics, but also by attempting to control the process and terms of trade, offering additional warranties, creating new products, attempting to influence the motivation (the needs and wants) of the buyers, conditioning the knowledge of the agents, creating specific emotions in the buyers (trust, loyalty), among other ways.

This does not imply that horizontal relations are always dominated by the exertion of rivalry in every field. The type of effective relationship and the degree of rivalry that each of these actions incorporates can vary on a case-by-case basis (Sawyer 1990; Fourie 1991). Thus, it may be the case within a sphere of action that no agent attempts to move to surpass the rest, while in others, an intense rivalry may take place; in other cases, several agents may decide to cooperate to reach common objectives or to offer joint options. In fact, not all of the activities of a firm incorporate the potential rivalry to the same degree, as in some cases there may be more or less common interests. Clearly, the number of agents may condition the type of relation and the degree of rivalry produced among them, but this does not necessarily determine them (Sawyer 1990; Dunn 2002). In the same way, the type of good (its complexity, its durable nature or not) also conditions the forms of both relation and rivalry that each sphere of action entails (Prasch 1995, Jackson 2007).

Finally, the rivalry can be exercised as an attempt not only to directly surpass the other sellers or buyers but also to control and modify the institutional environment for the seller's or buyer's own benefit. In fact, we have explicitly differentiated between two types of relations in the markets (horizontal and vertical), but there is also a type of additional relation that has been implicitly present throughout this article: the relationships between the agents and the market institutions themselves. The institutions of the market, like any others, are conditioned by the habits and actions of the agents under their umbrella, although they are not completely reducible to them (Hodgson 2003).

Some Additional Aspects: Justification, Origins, and Evaluation

The institutional dimension that markets present has multiple consequences. For example, it explains why markets tend to exhibit some continuity and stability over time (Fourie 1991), in opposition to the temporary character they present in neoclassical economics (Loasby 2000). This stability helps explain, at least in part, the existence of markets, as they provide an environment that facilitates the development of repeated transactions and that reduces the costs of performing these transactions in isolation (Hodgson 1988; Fourie 1991; Ménard 1995; Loasby 2000, 2001). In short, rather than being a source of transaction costs, markets are the means to reduce these costs in a world of fundamental uncertainty (Hodgson 1988; Fourie 1991; Loasby 2000, 2001). In other words, markets are a means to provide easier and less costly access to specific capacities that economic agents need or want (Langlois 1992; Loasby 1998, 2001); in this regard, markets can also be conceived as a capacity (Loasby 1998). Further, because markets reduce transaction costs and provide capacities that can be used to the advantage of the agents who wish to (or can) make use of them, they present some characteristics of public goods (Loasby 2000).

The institutional content of markets and the benefits they generate for those who use them leads to a question of how they are created and by whom. For orthodox economics, markets are a natural phenomenon, a sort of "mushroom" that grows spontaneously (Meurs 2000). By contrast, the conceptualization advanced in this article is that markets are the result of evolutionary processes, conditioned, at least in part, by human activity. In this evolutionary process, intentional actions play an important part (Dugger 1989; Fourie 1991; Loasby 2000). In this regard, the creation of markets sometimes requires a deliberate application of resources (Loasby 2000). These resources are usually provided by agents who expect to undertake large-scale transactions in one of the two sides of the market; however, it is also necessary to emphasize the role of the "state" in the institutional development of many markets (Fligstein 1996; Meurs 2000). In a word, markets are conditioned by the habits and actions of the economic agents that operate within them. This is not to say that markets will be exactly the result designed by these agents (Loasby 2000). Moreover, the creation and development of market institutions are not independent from the other institutions in a society (Samuels 1995; Loasby 2000; Liljenberg 2005; Jackson 2007). All of this provides an explanation for the historical and geographical specifications that markets typically present (Dugger 1989; Jackson 2007) and fits the explanations for market evolution that are frequently discussed by historians, anthropologists, and sociologists (Lowry 1994).

The fact that markets are, at least in part, a "human" creation and not some form of natural order, implies that their results are changeable and that they should not be accepted unquestioningly (Dugger 1989). If the institutional content of markets is acknowledged, the evaluation of their results undergoes a shift in perspective (in fact, it expands). The explanation for this phenomenon is twofold. First, the institutional content of markets forms part of a power structure; indeed, market institutions (as any institutional framework) create a series of rights, duties, permits, authorizations, and rules, among others (Bowles 1991, 1998; Searle 2005), which need to be accounted for and evaluated. Orthodox economics takes the current power structure as something appropriate and not subject to debate, yet unquestioning acceptance does not necessarily entail a neutral or value-free position (Klein 1987); on the contrary, values are endogenous to institutions (Tsakalotos 2005). Second, acknowledging the institutional content of the markets recognizes that the markets do more than allocate goods or set prices. Consequently, the standard efficiency analysis is clearly insufficient. Any rigorous evaluation of market outcomes must account for the effects of the market's institutional framework on knowledge and on the generation of innovations as well as on the evolution of values, motivations, and the behavior of human beings (Bowles 1991; Kerber 2006; Hahnel 2007).

The need to evaluate market outcomes in all of their dimensions is especially relevant because the institutional framework affects the reproduction of the model and its future evolution. In orthodox economics, in which activity develops in logical time with the possibility of perfect knowledge, and dominated by maximizing behaviors, the selection imposed by the forces of "competition" ensures "long-term efficiency" in the absence of imperfections. However, the perspective we advance accommodates diversity, and existence and survival are not necessarily linked to "efficiency." Finally, a market's institutional framework affects the necessary conditions for success and survival and, therefore, influences the selection environment and the evolution of the market itself (Moati 1995; Kerber 2006).

Notes

1. Although this is not a completely new topic, the compatibility of the two approaches has recently been highlighted by several authors (Hodgson 1989; Lawson 1994; Arestis 1996; Dunn 2000), opening a promising theoretical field that has begun to be exploited to study various concrete themes (Seccareccia 1991; Niggle 2006).

2. There is also a tendency to identify the concept of "market" with that of "capitalism." Although an in-depth analysis of the notion of capitalism is beyond the scope of this study, a brief comment on this subject is relevant. It is well known that there is no clear and commonly accepted definition of capitalism. Most definitions usually insist on the presence of two basic elements: the private ownership of the means of production and allocation of resources through "market mechanisms" (with them, other elements such as the development of wage labor and, therefore, the emergence of inherently conflicting class relations between capitalists and workers). Thus, the standard neoclassical approach has consistently identified capitalism with the "free market," and at the same time, presented a dichotomic vision of economic systems by differentiating those in which coordination is reached through market mechanisms from those in which coordination is based on non-market means. In contrast to this definition, some authors have insisted on analyzing the institutional content of economic systems in their various areas (not only in markets), which has resulted in the identification of various forms of capitalism (Amable 2003; Crouch 2005). From this point of view, the historical transformations of capitalism—and geographical differences—appear linked to changes in market forms and institutions, although are not entirely reducible to it.

3. This implies that the dichotomy between free markets and constraining institutions must be rejected (Hodgson 1988: 178; Fourie 1991: 49), given that markets have an inherent institutional dimension.

4. Procedural rationality consists of using means that permit excessively complex calculations to be avoided and of applying procedures that make it possible to make decisions despite the fact that the information available is not exhaustive or perfect (Simon 1976: 131; Lavoie 1992: 55). In this sense, it seems to be linked to the search for good solutions and the idea of satisfaction. In contrast, the instrumental or substantive rationality of neoclassical economics is associated with optimization and consists of finding the most efficient means to achieve a given objective (Simon 1976: 130).

5. This view of human beings shares many features with the concept of *acting person* developed within the social economics literature (O'Boyle 2011), such as the recognition of their social dimension, of the role of feelings or of their ability to act not only in a passive way, but trying to transform reality.

6. This vision of the firm as an organization continuously involved in different types of transactions and activities evokes the idea that the firm is a special type of *going concern* (Commons 1934).

7. This should not be interpreted as an attempt to provide some sort of empirical evidence (and even less so in terms of quantitative type) for the events or results that are observable in markets. Instead, and consistent with the perspective of critical realism, the objective is to identify semi-regularities, or the "generative structures, powers, mechanisms and necessary relations, and so on, that lie behind and govern the flux of events in an essentially open world" (Lawson 1994: 516).

8. The exchange relation can also be coupled with activities or agreements related to transport and warranties, which can be regulated or mediated by market institutions (Hodgson 1988).

9. Indeed, in most cases the parties involved in an exchange are typically forced to rely on institutional rules, standard patterns of behavior, cultural norms, and other elements that cannot be completely codified in laws or contracts (Hodgson 2006: 12). These elements help define what is really exchanged in the transaction (with regard to rights and duties) and what constitutes the "normal," "acceptable," or "just" content. This occurs, for instance, when hiring the services of a professional or, in general, with employment contracts. See the extensive exhibition held in this regard by Hodgson (1988: ch.7).

10. This role is often played by the state (or by some kind of authority), usually through the creation of monitoring and enforcement mechanisms formally established and accompanied by clearly defined sanctions (Redmon 2010). In other cases, it is possible to find mechanisms of enforcement of a tacit or informal nature, arising from peers or the community, and involving the imposition of different penalties or costs for rule-breakers (for example, signs on their reputation, social isolation, or expulsion of the market).

11. The fact that the role of price setting falls basically on one side of the exchange relation is a source of asymmetries in the market, since it implies that one of the parties takes on an additional role as either the buyer or the seller (Jackson 2007). In a more general sense, this conception of the pricing process provides a potentially useful framework for analyzing some of the phenomena and asymmetries that currently characterize the world economy. In particular, it allows to explain, at least partly, the global patterns of restructuring of production and the fact that the periphery of the economy has become a supplier of cheap products for the core (Amin 2010). In turn, these processes have an impact on various factors, including the global flow of funds and the process of financialization of the economy (Milberg 2008).

12. Indeed, over the past few years the aggregate demand in many countries has been supported by easy access to credit and international monetary flows associated with imbalances in current accounts of nations (Ivanova 2011; Tridico 2012). These phenomena have been accompanied by a process of "deregulation" and financial innovation that has led to the emergence and increased use of a large number of derivative financial instruments. Based on a neoclassical conception of markets, many economists argued that financial innovation would lead not only to an increase in funding but also to a reduction of risks or efficient management thereof. As the current crisis has shown, what has occurred is an increase of instability and uncertainty. Moreover, the absence of a sufficiently developed and balanced institutional framework has led to a blurring effect on obligations and responsibilities associated with transactions in these markets (Sen 2009).

13. The concept of competition used here should be understood in a broad sense and away from its meaning in neoclassical economics. Instead, it is nearer to Weber's vision (1922: 108), for whom competition consists of "a formally peaceful attempt to attain control over opportunities and advantages which are also desired by others," or to Rosenbaum's vision (2000: 472), who considers competition to be "a form of indirect conflict which is not directed at the opponent but consists of a parallel effort, attempting to surpass an opponent by offering opportunities for exchange which are preferred by other buyers or sellers."

14. Ultimately, the model of perfect competition demands perfect information and maximizing behavior from agents. If these two factors are present, it is impossible to find an opportunity to "surpass" the opponent.

15. The idea that firms do not compete solely or directly through prices has traditionally been present in the work of many post-Keynesian authors, but with differences between them and perhaps presenting an excessively restricted vision of interrelations among firms (Sawyer 1990). Surely the most representative view of the post-Keynesian approach in this regard has been associated with the Eichnerian megacorp, which competes through its investment plans (Eichner 1976).

References

Allaire, G. (2010). "Applying Economic Sociology to Understand the Meaning of 'Quality' in Food Markets." *Agricultural Economics* 41(1): 167–180.

Amable, B. (2003). *The Diversity of Modern Capitalisms.* Oxford: Oxford University Press.

Amin, S. (2010). *The Law of Worldwide Value.* New York: Monthly Review Press.

Arestis, P. (1996). "Post-Keynesian Economics: Toward Coherence." *Cambridge Journal of Economics* 20(1): 111–135.

Ayres, C. E. (1957). "Institutional Economics: Discussion." *American Economic Review* 47(2): 26–27.

Bowles, S. (1991). "What Markets Can—and Cannot—Do." *Challenge* 34(4): 11–16.

——. (1998). "Endogenous Preferences: The Cultural Consequences of Markets and Other Economic Institutions." *Journal of Economic Literature* 36(1): 75–111.

Bowles, S., and H. Gintis. (1993). "The Revenge of Homo Economicus: Contested Exchange and the Revival of Political Economy." *Journal of Economic Perspectives* 7(1): 83–112.

Caldwell, B. J. (1982). *Beyond Positivism. Economic Methodology in the Twentieth Century.* London: George Allen & Unwin.

Callon, M., Y. Millo, and F. Muniesa (eds.) (2007). *Market Devices.* Malden., MA: Blackwell Publishing.

Commons, J. R. (1934). *Institutional Economics. Its Place in Political Economy.* New Brunswick, NJ: Transaction Publishers.

Coriat, B., and O. Weinstein. (2005). "The Social Construction of Markets." *Issues in Regulation Theory* 53: 1–4.

Crouch, C. (2005). "Models of Capitalism." *New Political Economy* 10(4): 439–456.

Cyert, R. M., and J. G. March. (1963). *A Behavioral Theory of the Firm.* Englewood Cliffs, NJ: Prentice-Hall.

Davidson, P. (1972). *Money and the Real World.* London: Macmillan.

——. (1988). "A Technical Definition of Uncertainty and the Long-Run Non-Neutrality of Money." *Cambridge Journal of Economics* 12(3): 329–337.

Dequech, D. (2000). "Fundamental Uncertainty and Ambiguity." *Eastern Economic Journal* 26(1): 41–60.

——. (2003). "Conventional and Unconventional Behavior Under Uncertainty." *Journal of Post Keynesian Economics* 26(1): 145–168.

——. (2006). "The New Institutional Economics and the Theory of Behaviour Under Uncertainty." *Journal of Economic Behavior and Organization* 59(1): 109–131.

Dosi, G., and M. Egidi. (1991). "Substantive and Procedural Uncertainty: An Exploration of Economic Behaviours in Complex and Changing Environments." *Journal of Evolutionary Economics* 1(2): 145–168.

Downward, P. (1999). *Post Keynesian Pricing Theory: A Realist Approach.* Aldershot: Edward Elgar.

Dugger, W. M. (1989). "Instituted Process and Enabling Myth: The Two Faces of the Market." *Journal of Economic Issues* 23(2): 607–615.

Dunn, S. P. (2000). "Wither Post Keynesianism?" *Journal of Post Keynesian Economics* 22(3): 343–364.

———. (2002). "A Post Keynesian Approach to the Theory of the Firm." In *Post Keynesian Econometrics, Microeconomics and the Theory of the Firm: Beyond Keynes, Volume One.* Eds. S. C. Dow and J. Hillard, pp. 60–80. Cheltenham-Northampton: Edward Elgar.

Earl, P. E. (1983). *The Economic Imagination: Towards a Behavioural Analysis of Choice.* Brighton: Wheatsheaf Books.

Eichner, A. S. (1976). *The Megacorp and Oligopoly.* Cambridge: Cambridge University Press.

Elster, J. (1998). "Emotions and Economic Theory." *Journal of Economic Literature* 36(1): 47–74.

Fernández-Huerga, E. (2008). "The Economic Behavior of Human Beings: The Institutional/Post-Keynesian Model." *Journal of Economic Issues* 42(3): 709–726.

Fleetwood, S. (1999). *Critical Realism in Economics: Development and Debate.* London: Routledge.

———. (2006). "Re-thinking Labour Markets: A Critical Realist-Socioeconomic Perspective." *Capital & Class* 89: 59–89.

Fligstein, N. (1996). "Markets as Politics: A Political-Cultural Approach to Market Institutions." *American Sociological Review* 61(4): 656–673.

Fourie, F. C. v. N. (1991). "The Nature of the Market: a Structural Analysis." In *Rethinking Economics: Markets, Technology and Economic Evolution.* Eds. G. M. Hodgson and E. Screpanti, pp. 40–57. Aldershot: Edward Elgar.

Friedman, M. (1962). *Capitalism and Freedom.* Chicago: University of Chicago Press.

Georgescu-Roegen, N. (1954). "Choice, Expectations and Measurability." *Quarterly Journal of Economics* 48(4): 503–534.

Hahnel, R. (2007). "The Case Against Markets." *Journal of Economic Issues* 41(4): 1139–1159.

Hodgson, G. M. (1988). *Economics and Institutions. A Manifesto for a Modern Institutional Economics.* Cambridge: Polity Press.

———. (1989). "Post-Keynesianism and Institutionalism: The Missing Link." In *New Directions in Post-Keynesian Economics.* Ed. J. Pheby, pp. 94–123. Aldershot: Edward Elgar.

———. (1997). "The Ubiquity of Habits and Rules." *Cambridge Journal of Economics* 21(6): 663–684.
———. (2003). "The Hidden Persuaders: Institutions and Individuals in Economic Theory." *Cambridge Journal of Economics* 27(2): 159–175.
———. (2006). "What Are Institutions." *Journal of Economic Issues* 40(1): 1–25.
Ivanova, M. N. (2011). "Money, Housing and World Market: The Dialectic of Globalised Production." *Cambridge Journal of Economics* 35(3): 853–871.
Jackson, W. A. (2007). "On the Social Structure of Markets." *Cambridge Journal of Economics* 31(2): 235–253.
Kerber, W. (2006). "Competition, Knowledge, and Institutions." *Journal of Economic Issues* 40(2): 457–463.
Klein, P. (1987). "Power and Economic Performance: The Institutionalist View." *Journal of Economic Issues* 21(3): 1341–1377.
Kregel, J. A. (1980). "Markets and Institutions as Features of a Capitalistic Production System." *Journal of Post Keynesian Economics* 3(1): 32–48.
Langlois, R. N. (1992). "Transaction-Cost Economics in Real Time." *Industrial and Corporate Change* 1(1): 99–127.
Lavoie, M. (1992). *Foundations of Post-Keynesian Economic Analysis*. Aldershot-Brookfield: Edward Elgar.
Lawson, T. (1994). "The Nature of Post Keynesianism and its Links to Other Traditions: A Realist Perspective." *Journal of Post Keynesian Economics* 16(4): 503–538.
———. (1997). *Economics and Reality*. London: Routledge.
Lee, F. S. (1998). *Post Keynesian Price Theory*. Cambridge: Cambridge University Press.
Lie, J. (1997). "Sociology of Markets." *Annual Review of Sociology* 23(1): 341–360.
Liljenberg, A. (2005). "A Socio-Dynamic Understanding of Markets." *American Journal of Economics and Sociology* 64(4): 999–1023.
Loasby, B. J. (1998). "The Organisation of Capabilities." *Journal of Economic Behaviour and Organization* 35(2): 139–160.
———. (2000). "Market Institutions and Economic Evolution." *Journal of Evolutionary Economics* 10(3): 297–309.
———. (2001). "Cognition, Imagination and Institutions in Demand Creation." *Journal of Evolutionary Economics* 11(1): 7–21.
Lowry, S. T. (1994). "The Institutionalist View of the Market." In *The Elgar Companion to Institutional and Evolutionary Economics*. Eds. G. M. Hodgson, W. J. Samuels, and M. R. Tool, pp. 47–53. Aldershot: Edward Elgar.
Ménard, C. (1995). "Markets as Institutions Versus Organizations as Markets? Disentangling Some Fundamental Concepts." *Journal of Economic Behavior and Organization* 28(2): 161–182.

Meurs, M. (2000). "Are Markets Like Mushrooms? And Other Neoliberal Quandries." *Review of Radical Political Economics* 32(3): 461–469.

Milberg, W. (2008). "Shifting Sources and Uses of Profits: Sustaining US Financialization with Global Value Chains." *Economy and Society* 37(3): 420–451.

Moati, P. (1995). "Goals, Rationality Criteria and Market Functioning." *Review of Political Economy* 7(1): 52–71.

Niggle, C. (2006). "Evolutionary Keynesianism: A Synthesis of Institutionalist and Post Keynesian Macroeconomics." *Journal of Economic Issues* 40(2): 405–412.

O'Boyle, E. J. (2011). "The Acting Person: Social Capital and Sustainable Development." *Forum for Social Economics* 40(1): 79–98.

Prasch, R. E. (1995). "Toward a 'General Theory' of Market Exchange." *Journal of Economic Issues* 29(3): 807–828.

———. (2008). *How Markets Work: Supply, Demand and the "Real World."* Cheltenham-Northampton: Edward Elgard.

Redmon, W. H. (2010). "Rules and Roles in the Marketplace: Self-Organization of the Market." *Journal of Economic Issues* 44(2): 337–344.

Rochon, L-P., and M. Vernego. (2003). "State Money and the Real World: Or Chartalism and its Discontents." *Journal of Post Keynesian Economics* 26(1): 57–67.

Rosenbaum, E. F. (2000). "What is a Market? On the Metholodology of a Contested Concept." *Review of Social Economy* 58(4): 455–482.

Samuels, W. J. (1995). "The Present State of Institutional Economics." *Cambridge Journal of Economics* 19(4): 569–590.

Sawyer, M. C. (1990). "On the Post-Keynesian Tradition and Industrial Economics." *Review of Political Economy* 2(1): 43–68.

———. (1993) "The Nature and Role of the Market." In *Transaction Costs, Markets and Hierarchies*. Ed. C. N. Pitelis, pp. 20–40. Basil Blackwell.

Searle, J. (2005). "What is an Institution." *Journal of Institutional Economics* 1(1): 1–22.

Seccareccia, M. (1991). "An Alternative to Labour-Market Orthodoxy: The Post-Keynesian/ Institutionalist Policy View." *Review of Political Economy* 3(1): 43–61.

Sen, A. (2009). "Capitalism Beyond the Crisis." *New York Review of Books* 56(5): 1–8.

Simon, H. A. (1976). "From Substantive to Procedural Rationality." In *Method and Appraisal in Economics*. Ed. S. Latsis, pp. 129–48. Cambridge: Cambridge University Press.

———. (1979). "Rational Decision Making in Business Organizations." *American Economic Review* 69(4): 493–513.

Swedberg, R. (1994). "Markets as Social Structures." In *The Handbook of Economic Sociology*. Eds. N. J. Smelser and R. Swedberg, pp. 255–82. Princeton: Princeton University Press.

Teece, D., R. Rumelt, G. Dosi, and S. Winter. (1994). "Understanding Corporate Coherence. Theory and Evidence." *Journal of Economic Behavior and Organization* 23(1): 1–30.
Tordjman, H. (2004). "How to Study Markets? An Institutionalist Point of View." *Revue d'économie industrielle* 107(3): 19–36.
Tridico, P. (2012). "Financial Crisis and Global Imbalances: Its Labour Market Origins and the Aftermath." *Cambridge Journal of Economics* 36(1): 17–42.
Tsakalotos, E. (2005). "*Homo Economicus* and the Reconstruction of Political Economy: Six Theses on the Role of Values in Economics." *Cambridge Journal of Economics* 29(6): 893–908.
Weber, M. (1922). *Economy and Society: An Outline of Interpretive Sociology.* Berkeley: University of California Press.
Williams, E. E., and M. C. Findlay. (1986). "Risk and the Role of Failed Expectations in an Uncertain World." *Journal of Post Keynesian Economics* 9(1): 32–47.
Wray, L. R. (1998). *Understanding Modern Money: The Key to Full Employment and Price Stability.* Cheltenham: Edward Elgar.

The Organization, Operation, and Outcomes of Actually Existing Markets: A Suggested Approach for Empirical Analysis[1]

By Lynne Chester*

ABSTRACT. Public policies have become embedded with market-based mechanisms to radically transform essential goods and services markets. This article proposes a framework for empirical analysis of these markets. Key theoretical propositions are distilled to 12 distinctive properties of markets. These properties foreshadow a set of questions to interrogate a market's structure, operation, participants, behaviors, rules, and price setting to generate a substantive, realistic picture of outcomes. This "analytical grid" of questions is applied to four Australian essential goods and services markets. The findings unequivocally demonstrate a very different picture of markets from that promulgated by mainstream neoclassical economics and public policies.

Introduction

The market is now considered by the vast majority of mainstream economists, policymakers, the media, and politicians as being the far superior coordinating mechanism for all capitalist economies.

> [B]y century's end, to speak ill of markets narrowed one's access to ears, and progressive economists quickly learned to reformulate criticisms as suggestions about improving market performance. Any hint that one considered markets to be part of the problem rather than the key to the solution to any economic problem was sure to blow one's cover in the economics profession as well as policy circles. (Hahnel 2007: 1140)

Free market fundamentalism has assumed "an almost biblical status" (Giroux 2009).

*Department of Political Economy, The University of Sydney, Australia; E-mail address: lynne.chester@sydney.edu.au

With the market's virtual canonization, public policies have become embedded with market-based mechanisms based on economic concepts derived from the logic of perfect competitive markets. As a consequence there has been a radical transformation of markets that have been a longstanding domain of state intervention over the last 20 years or so. These markets provide goods and services essential to society's well-being such as education, health insurance, public housing, electricity, water, and services for the disabled, aged, and unemployed. Direct provision by government has been supplanted by contractual arrangements with private-sector providers, there have been significant price increases, complex new regulatory regimes have been instituted, and public-sector assets have been privatized. This has been strongly evident in the Anglophone economies of the United States (US), United Kingdom (UK), Canada, Australia, and New Zealand.[2] Within the observed typologies or varieties of capitalism, these economies are commonly categorized as liberal market-based economies given the high reliance placed on market mechanisms (Amable 2003; Crouch 2005; Hall and Soskice 2001).

The rationale for market-based public policies has been couched in terms of the need for greater economic efficiency. Consequently, contemporary public policies are almost exclusively framed in the abstract concepts of competition, efficiency, supply and demand, or the need to address market failures. This is the lexicon of neoclassical economics, which portrays the market as a normative ideal framed around a set of abstract assumptions, where a market is conceived "as a space for carrying out identical transactions which bear on one well-defined product and lead to the determination of one price" (Coriat and Weinstein 2005: 2). But abstract terms, identical transactions, one product, and one price cannot explain the operation and outcomes of these transformed markets for essential services that characterize contemporary liberal market-based economies. Markets are not purely about relationships between inanimate objects, between goods and services, which is the strong impression evoked by any mainstream economics text or government publication. Nor are markets simply the intersection of demand and supply functions. Markets involve people, their preferences (influenced by opinions, values, and advertising), and relationships with others. Market prices also will influence people's accessibility to, and participation in, a market.

Many markets delivering the objectives and priorities of public policies determine—to a very significant measure—the health, standard of living, and social inclusion of the population. The contemporary markets to provide these essential goods and services bear little resemblance to those of the 1980s or 1990s. It is with these markets that I am concerned: markets providing essential goods and services, radically transformed by market-based public policies, as distinct from markets such as those for money, labor, or the environment. These latter markets have also dramatically changed in the last 20 years or so but stand apart from "essential" markets in two key respects. They have not been traditional domains of direct state intervention (such as through direct provision) and thus have not been restructured through the embedding of market-based mechanisms. These markets also form a different, and much more contestable, relationship to society's general well-being. "Essential" markets, on the other hand, are those shaped and directed by government to provide a base or minimum level of goods and services for individual, family, and household purposes to "protect its citizens from misfortune and the random blows of fate by providing the most basic rights and levels of collective security and protection" (Giroux 2009).

How can we understand, and explain the impact on society of, these restructured real-world markets for essential goods and services given that economists have, until recently, shown little interest in the "emergence and real constitution of markets" (Coriat and Weinstein 2005: 1)? How are these actually existing markets organized? What ensures their ongoing functioning? Does the nature of the goods and services provided by these markets differ from previous provision? What issues or barriers do participants encounter when engaging with these markets? To what extent do these markets ensure adequate provision to those on lower incomes? What outcomes are these markets delivering? How can we empirically analyze markets in order to answer these questions?

The discourse about markets has been overwhelmingly skewed towards the theoretical, "concerned more with analyzing how people conceive of market systems than . . . with analyzing the operation of those systems or the activities of market actors" (Carrier 1997: xiii). Empirical markets have attracted few analytical studies to determine the specific pragmatic manifestation or representation of their structure, operation, participants, behaviors, rules, and/or price determination. Notable exceptions have been French strawberry and fish markets, financial and emission trading markets, and the UK's markets for food, housing, water, telecommunications, public transport, financial services, and energy (for example, see Garcia-Parpet 2007; Kirman and Vignes 1992; MacKenzie 2009; Public Services International Research Unit 2008). Similarly, "operationalizing" the theoretical and conceptual into an analytical framework to conduct empirical analyses of real-world markets has received limited attention. This article seeks to address these lacunae not to provide a contribution to the perennial debate about the role of the market vis-à-vis the state or the limits of market organization. The outcomes of markets for essential goods and services, directly determined by contemporary market-based public policies, and the impact on society's well-being need to be understood if that perennial debate is to be progressed. Moreover, "a clearheaded perception of how different institutions actually work . . . from the market to the institutions of the state" (Sen 2009) is needed to establish a credible foundation for the development of options to ameliorate the inequities and disadvantages of market provisioning. Empirical analysis of real-world markets aids the development of those options. It can also inform the development of "progressive" alternative forms of market organization and operation as advocated by Baker (2011).

This article presents a methodological basis for a detailed empirical analysis of essential goods and services markets to explain their structure, operation, interactions, and outcomes. Such an analysis is a critical prerequisite to understanding the socioeconomic impact of these restructured markets and assessing the appropriateness of market-based public policies. The next section discusses differing conceptualizations of the market. The neoclassical conceptualization is examined closely because it is this lexicon that has become embedded in public policies and led to radically different provisioning in essential goods and services markets. This has occurred during the hegemony of neoliberalism so the relationship between the two is examined also before considering alternative conceptions of the market from economic sociology and institutionalists.

Within this context, a third section reviews key theoretical contributions to our understanding of the organization and functioning of markets that encompass a set of propositions about different types of market in space and time, the role of property rights and contract law, the dimensions shaping the organization of exchange, and the embedded behaviors created by rules reflecting political decision. To "operationalize" these theoretical propositions, and thus enable concrete empirical analysis, the core essence of each proposition is distilled to reveal 12 distinctive properties of markets. These properties help us transcend from the abstract to the more concrete by foreshadowing an analytical grid of questions to conduct detailed empirical analyses. The list of properties forms a bridge between the key abstract propositions drawn from the discourse and a grid of questions to interrogate actually existing markets.

The findings from an application of the analytical grid to four restructured essential goods and services markets of the Australian liberal market-based economy are presented in the fourth section. The findings unequivocally demonstrate a very different picture of the structure, functioning, and outcomes of markets from that promulgated by mainstream economics and deeply embedded in public policies. A final section concludes.

How is the Market Conceptualized?

Neoliberalism and Neoclassical Economics

Since the 1970s mainstream economists and policymakers have increasingly advocated "free and unencumbered" markets as the most efficient method to coordinate the activities of contemporary capitalist economies. Nearly all mainstream economists believe—or at least did until the 2008 admission by former Federal Reserve Chairman Greenspan of a "flaw"—that markets are self-correcting (Skidelsky

2009). Moreover, the notion of perfect markets "imprisoned" the thinking of policymakers, being treated as the "fixed element around which policy must be fashioned" (Lindblom 1982: 333) with policy debates framed around the alternatives of a market-state dichotomy and the object of policy becoming one of "efficient market design" (Galbraith 2009: 152). "The government has no role to play . . . this is not policy by analysis, this is essentially policy by assumption" (Stern 2010: 263–264).

Government intervention has been increasingly portrayed as detrimental, not beneficial, to efficient market operations as the ideology of neoliberalism has metamorphosized into the "central guiding principle of economic thought and management" (Harvey 2005: 2). Market discipline, competition, and commodification denote neoliberalism, which has been described as a mix of neoclassical economic fundamentalism, market regulation, redistribution in favor of capital, moral authoritarianism, free trade principles, and total intolerance of trade unionism (Moody 1997: 119–120). Human well-being is considered to be best achieved through private property rights, free markets, and free trade, and the role of the state is to create an institutional framework that promotes such practices. The market has primacy and virtually all economic and social problems are seen as having a market solution. Nation-states and local states have progressively applied the neoliberalism doctrine of market solutions to a widening realm of activity.

The ideology of neoliberalism is underpinned by notions about the free market, market failure, market primacy, and interrelationships of market, state, and politics. A free market is avowed because it provides choice for a world of "free," independent individuals—anything restricting choice is morally bad—and choice entails competition, which will generate innovation and efficiency. Market imperfections, or distortions, threaten the most efficient allocation of economic resources and lead to market failure, requiring action by the state to restore the primacy of the market, that is, the natural order of things. Finally, because of self-interested politicians and bureaucrats, the scope of the state's activities should be scaled back—through privatization and deregulation—and policy discretion eliminated (Carrier 1997; Chang 2002).

Chang (2002) argues that these neoliberal notions about the market are so seriously flawed that they create a biased and incomplete understanding of reality. For example, the definition of the free market, and thus state intervention, is fraught with difficulty because (a) the participants, and terms of participation, in all markets are determined by some form of state regulation, and (b) the same action by the state may be considered an intervention by one society but not another, depending on the legitimacy and hierarchy of the underlying rights-obligations structure for market participants. The definition of market failure is similarly fraught, in Chang's view, because the notion of failure only makes sense in relation to what is considered to be an "ideal" market.

The views of neoclassical economics about the market, and its relationship with the state, are in close harmony with those of neoliberalism. Neoclassical economics presents the market as an abstract aggregate of individual choices and actions exemplified by the simple intersection of demand and supply curves, as "an allocating machine that solves the main problems of ... what to produce, how, and for whom" (Mantzavinos 2001: 162). This paradigm, which dominates mainstream economics, was criticized by the 1991 Bank of Sweden Prize in Economic Sciences recipient for its increasing abstraction of analysis and preoccupation with price determination, resulting in study of "a system that lives in the minds of economists but not on earth ... The firm and market appear by name but they lack any substance" (Coase 1992: 714). Many others have voiced similar criticisms. For example, Keen (2001) and Lee and Keen (2004) have systematically demonstrated the theoretical incoherence of the tools and models of neoclassical microeconomic theory. Nevertheless, neoclassical economics has successfully shaped

> the general understanding of what a "market", a "market economy", and even an "economy" in general is, or should be ... and, thus, a *general theoretical and normative reference and benchmark* for economic analysis, economic systems and policies ... While the "market" is an *ambiguous positive-normative ideal*, it nevertheless is considered not only an adequate reflection of the capitalist-market reality but also serves as a sound policy guideline for its reform. (Elsner 2008: 370, original emphasis)

But what does neoclassical economics tell us about the perfectly competitive market, the lexicon and logic of which now directly shape a vast array of public policies? First, the perfectly competitive market assumes that products are optimally allocated in a perfectly informed, atomistic world. Second, the market is attributed self-equilibrating properties because it is assumed to clear automatically via price adjustments, that is, prices respond to changes in demand or supply, finding equilibrium at the price at which the quantity supplied equals the quantity demanded. Accordingly, these oscillations underpin a systemic stability across markets for all goods and services and ensure an optimal allocation of resources between competing needs. Yet this self-equilibrating nature of the market rests on numerous assumptions such as identical consumers behaving rationally because they are perfectly informed about all the available alternatives, zero transaction costs, no trading at disequilibrium prices, and infinitely rapid velocities of prices and quantities (Blaug 2002: 40–41). It is also assumed that communication between market participants is solely through price signals, market participants are anonymous, interaction in the market is horizontal, virtually all transactions are commensurable, all goods are non-collective, and the market is not place sensitive (Crouch 2005: 115).

These assumptions mean that optimal market equilibrium can only be achieved if multiple conditions are fulfilled such as: numerous traders so that no one can exert market power; a finite number of goods and there is common knowledge about their quality; no public goods or externalities in consumption or production; returns to scale do not increase; equity issues are completely separate from the objective of efficiency; and the preferences of buyers are convex and the production functions of the sellers are convex, with the marginal productivity of a factor declining (Boyer 1997: 72–74). Thus, multiple and quite precise conditions are necessary to guarantee optimal market equilibrium.

This paradigm maintains that the market should be left unfettered, as does neoliberalism, from state interventions to ensure its efficient workings are allowed to determine output and price. Free, competitive markets allocate resources and distribute income most efficiently, it is argued, because they will tend towards a (Pareto) optimal situation, which occurs when no change can improve the position of one individual (as judged by herself) without a negative impact on the position of another individual (as judged by that individual).

However, six sources of market failure that threaten the achievement of "Pareto efficiency" are deemed to warrant government intervention: the existence of market power; a failure to supply public goods such as defense or national security; negative externalities of production or consumption such as pollution; markets that provide incomplete goods and services (for example, insurance); imperfect information to consumers (for example, weather forecasts); and, "macroeconomic disturbances" like high levels of unemployment or inflation (Stiglitz 2000: 76–90).[3] It is only these types of market failure—which jeopardize the holy grail of economic efficiency—that justify any government intervention for mainstream economics.[4] The imposition of economic incentives to create the "correct price" and reduce the negative externalities of market failure, such as environmental problems, will lead to some optimum market outcome. This typifies the neoclassical policy approach.

The neoclassical conception of the market, and its reality-incompatible assumptions, provides little insight for empirical analysis of actually existing markets, including those transformed by public policies embedded with its lexicon. Neoclassical economics assumes a form of market organization—pure competition, duopoly, oligopoly, or monopoly—and then determines output, price, and cost outcomes within the assumed context (Sherman, Hunt et al. 2008). This abstraction from reality is the antithesis of what we are seeking.

Alternative Conceptions of the Market

Many from within the economics discipline have roundly challenged the neoclassical conception of the market (for example, see Akerlof 1984; Blaug 2002; Grossman and Stiglitz 1980; Härdle and Kirman 1995; Nelson 2005; Simon 1991; Stiglitz 1987). This dissatisfaction accounts for some notable extensions to mainstream thinking (for example, see Coase 1988; North 1990; Simon 1992; Williamson 1975). A burgeoning discourse has also developed that demonstrates real-world markets do not emerge in some vacuum, are persistently vulnerable to failure, influence the nature and relationships of individuals, reflect socially habituated behavior, and their operation depends on highly complex non-market institutional arrangements into which they are deeply embedded (for example, see Altvater 1993; Boyer 1997; Coriat and Weinstein 2005; Hodgson 1988; Martinez 2009; Peck and Theodore 2007; Prasch 2008; Tsakalotos 2004). In addition, Polanyi (2001) contends that self-regulating market mechanisms cannot coordinate fictitious commodities (for example, money, labor, the environment) because their supply is not in response to changing relative prices.

These shortcomings of the neoclassical "markets" view have been claimed as a stimulus for economic sociology, a major contributor to the discourse about markets (Allaire 2009; Fligstein 1996; Zelizer 1988). Economic sociology conceptualizes markets as arenas of social interaction, a form of action (exchange) embedded in social relations that cannot exist without rules to regulate exchange. Economic life is embedded in social relations and social structure, and therefore cannot be analyzed as separate, distinct, or isolated from social worlds (Granovetter 1985). Property rights, governance structures, conceptions of control, and rules of exchange are considered the institutions—the preconditions—for markets to exist (Fligstein 1996). Others have stressed the importance of networks, observed behavior, and population ecology to the social structures exerting control over the market (Granovetter 1985; Hannan and Freeman 1986; White 1981).

Sociologists have conducted detailed analyses of the actual creation and functioning of markets, especially financial markets, which have debunked neoclassical economic notions of markets being atomistic and anonymous, showing instead a range of behavioral rules, relationships, and skills required for participation (for example, see Callon 1998; Callon, Millo, and Muniesa 2007; Granovetter and McGuire 1998; MacKenzie 2007a, 2007b, 2009; MacKenzie, Muniesa, and Siu 2007; Yakubovich, Granovetter, and McGuire 2005). Generally, although it is far from a unified whole, this body of work situates the market as one of a multiplicity of formal and informal institutions comprising capitalism. "All institutions, including the market . . . are defined in relation to the structure of the rights and obligations of the relevant actors" (Chang 2007: 7), which in the case of the market includes the institutional arrangements that determine and/or regulate market participants, and the objects and process of market exchange.

As these "rights and obligations" are deemed to be the result of politics, the market—like all institutions—is considered to be a political construct. Property rights, and the entitlements bestowed on market participants, are not free of politics, along with numerous state actions to "protect" market participants. Far from being natural, "markets are the fruit of complex social and historical developments" (Coriat and Weinstein 2005: 1), with politics, and thus the state, being integral to their creation and functioning. This view of the market assigns a far more active role to the state. Market outcomes result from a myriad of institutional arrangements and processes, all of which are influenced by the state and politics.

Developing an Analytical Framework to Determine the Organization, Operation, and Outcomes of an Empirical Market

An analytical framework is inferred by Fligstein's (1996) list of market preconditions—property rights, governance structures, conceptions of control, and rules of exchange. Zeliver (1994) suggests empirical analysis is about concrete spaces, commodities being heterogeneous in time and space, money having many social uses, and the convergence of divergent interests overcoming the anonymity of market participants. For Coriat and Weinstein (2005: 2) "a market should be analyzed like any institution: it is necessary to study the conditions in which it emerges, is stabilized and transformed and possibly goes into crisis." These all signal possible starting points but each requires the theoretical to be "operationalized" for empirical application to be possible.

This task of operationalization is assisted by: Boyer's (1997) typology of market types; Prasch's (2008) legal institutional framework of the exchange process irrespective of market type; Harvey and Randles's (2002) dimensions of the actual exchange process; and Tordjman's (1998, 2004) more concretized form of market processes of organization and exchange. The conjunction of these insights, rather than each contribution per se, allows us to progressively move from the abstract to the concrete, that is, these insights provide building blocks to progress from the theoretical to a framework for empirical analysis.

Boyer (1997: 62–66) distinguishes six different "types" of markets by the space and time horizon in which the market occurs. First, markets may be periodic and/or peripatetic, presenting an embryonic form of those common to contemporary capitalist economies. These markets are authorized to occur at a specific time and location, may be wholesale or retail, and the scope of transactions is limited. A second type of market occurs as a temporary "screening" device to procure the least costly or most "economically advantageous" of proposals. The usual outcomes of this market are bilateral commercial contracts to supply specified goods or services by a particular time and for particular prices. This market type relies on commercial contracts and thus cannot function without a legal system. An aggregation over a geographical area or for one commodity creates a third market type: for example, the European Union single market. This market form does not hold a physical form or locale and may refer to the demand for a particular good, sector, or "the economywide [sic] level, implying the equivalent of effective aggregate demand" (Boyer 1997: 64).

Neoclassical economics provides a fourth market type as an abstraction to make compatible a series of "individual supplies and demands" that adjust and converge to a unique, equilibrium price that clears the market. The market is conceived as a process of rational, impersonal, discrete transactions between buyers and sellers. Boyer's fifth market type extends this abstraction to characterize an economic system dominated by market competition and a set of interdependent markets. Thus, anything that extends aspects of the market to non-market transactions is perceived as "good" whereas anything that departs from the market model is the converse (Carrier 1997: 19). Finally, there is the metaphoric type assumed to exist whenever social actors compete for limited resources, positions, or status such as that applied by the Chicago school of economics to the social issues of marriage, crime, donations to religious orders, justice, and eternal life beliefs.

Location and time differentiate Boyer's six market types. But the nature of these different types also directly point to aspects about the structure and functioning of markets that signal a "bridge" towards empirical analysis. We can derive from the Boyer typology that markets involve not single but repetitive transactions of commodities, there must be some form of regularity to market organization, a monetary system is required by markets to convey nominal prices and pay for transactions, and a legal regime must have the capacity to enforce commercial contracts. This latter aspect has been a specific focus for Prasch (1995, 2008).

The analytical key, for Prasch (2008), to understanding market relations lies in the evolving system of property rights and contract law, which are the "foundational institutional structures" of increasingly complex markets. A market is the organization of exchanges between transactors, a locus of repeated exchanges. Exchange is the fundamental event to take place in a market and is of "some object, promise, service or privilege" (Prasch 2008: 14). But, and this is pivotal for Prasch, not just anything can be exchanged. Before exchange can occur, one's ownership of (or legal authority over) whatever is to be sold must be established. In addition, each party to an exchange must be deemed able or competent to undertake the exchange, although who is deemed a legitimate owner of property has changed over time.

Thus property ownership—and the right to exchange that property—is not simply about the relationship between "a person and a thing" but "an *artifact* of a complex set of social relations" (Prasch 2008: 14, emphasis added). Property ownership and exchange is subject to rules and law that reflect prevailing norms, values, and technology. The law has almost universally recognized a relationship to property where there is no encumbrance to disposal, that is, there is an exclusive right to control of the property that can be legitimately supported by the state's police powers. In addition, the rules or conditions of exchanging (selling) property are governed by contract law. Implicit contracts, which encompass many day-to-day activities, are not negotiated or in writing, with "completion" usually marked by a receipt. On the other hand, explicit contracts—for purchases like housing or other high-cost transactions—can be quite complex documents with the negotiated terms, of a pending exchange, stipulated and, in the event of a disagreement, contract law drawing on precedent and conventional practice will resolve the matter.

Although a highly generalized summary of Prasch's thesis, the significance of this contribution comes from the proposition that the structure and functioning of a real-world market is based on an evolving but longstanding system of legally defined rights, property law, and contract law. This means that exchange, the fundamental event in a market, is subject to the prevailing legal regime as it applies to property and contracts. The right to exchange—and conditions about the exchange transaction—are embedded within implicit and explicit contracts, i.e., market exchanges cannot occur without property rights and a legal regime.

Harvey and Randles (2002) extend this understanding about the exchange transaction established by Prasch. They posit that the organization of economic exchange, both market and non-market in modern capitalist economies, is framed—and thus can be discerned—through two dimensions. The first dimension is the institution of the exchange process, irrespective of the commodity exchanged, which is evident by considering the formation and differentiation of economic agents (that is, buyers and sellers) in relation to the actual exchange process. The second dimension concerns the differences in the specificities of exchange processes for any given organization of exchange. This dimension is represented by the parties to the exchange process, the commodities exchanged, and the spatial and temporal nature of the exchange. These dimensions of the exchange process introduce a different level of specificity and thus start to reveal different complexities embodied in the exchange process, for example, the criteria used to determine who may be a buyer or seller, the multiple dimensions of any exchange process that distinguish it from others.

Tordjman (1998, 2004) develops a more concrete form of these two exchange dimensions while also extending key aspects from Boyer (1997) of repetitive transactions, regularity to market organization, and a monetary system to facilitate transactions. Tordjman (2004: 20) "envision[s] markets as institutions, that is sets of rules and codes of different nature organizing repeated monetary exchanges." To uncover the domain of markets, and understand their functioning as well as how they shape society, she delineates the "rules" that define the objects of exchange, identify market participants, and establish the market processes for exchange to take place.

Tordjman (2004) denotes those rules determining the principles of exchange (for example, the nature of the good exchanged, who are market participants) as "constitutive" and those rules that implement exchange principles as "procedural." These categories also respectively contain transaction and information rules. If a market is a locus of repeated economic exchanges (posited by Boyer and Prasch) governed by property rights and law (posited by Prasch), this suggests to Tordjman that some kind of formal structures and sets of rules exist that bring together buyer-seller interactions and influence these exchanges, that is, rules governing transactions. It also suggests to her some conventions enabling sellers to propose a price and buyers to accept or negotiate another, that is, rules about the provision of information. The *conjunctive operation* of transaction and information rules induces a behavioral pattern that facilitates the continuity of a market's operation (posited by Boyer).

Tordjman argues that transaction rules organize the *interaction* of buyers and sellers. In a decentralized (local) market, bilateral exchange occurs. Participants engage directly with each other and usually negotiate a price. On the other hand, there is no such direct interaction in a centralized market where an institution collects buy and sell orders, and determines the price until demand equals supply. Transaction rules also determine who is eligible to participate as buyers and sellers, reflect political decisions, and are enforced directly through complex regulatory regimes, competition policies, and trade practices legislation.[5] Market participation eligibility is not decided by the individual. Specific behaviors may be prohibited by transaction rules. For example, buyers may not be permitted to be sellers concurrently to reduce the potential for collusion, insider trading, and speculation, leading to "manipulated" not market-driven transaction volumes and prices.

Tordjman's "information rules" similarly influence the organization and operation of exchange within a market. Product guarantees, labels, standards, credit ratings, qualifications, and other types of information all convey details about the quality of product and reduce the extent of uncertainty about its quality. As Akerlof (1984) demonstrated, if the quality of a good is uncertain, incomplete information leads to poor selection and could result in market failure. Thus, information about commodity quality improves market functioning but will depend upon what information is available to whom and when.

In sum, Tordjman demonstrates that rules establishing market participation eligibility, the form of interaction among participants, and information about product quality, as well as the property rights regime that defines what may be exchanged, induce behavioral responses to facilitate the operation of a market and its continuity.

These contributions to our understanding of the organization and functioning of markets (from Boyer, Prasch, Harvey and Randles, and Tordjman) encompass a set of propositions about different types of market in space and time, the role of property rights and contract law, the dimensions shaping the organization of exchange, and the embedded behaviors created by rules reflecting political decision. These propositions can be distilled to their core essence, which illuminates 12 distinctive properties or characteristics attributable to markets. These properties, ranging from the relatively simple to the more complex and not mutually exclusive, are:

1. A market is a location where buyers and sellers interact.
2. A market may be a physical location but does not need to be as evidenced by eBay, an Internet auction, and online payment for goods and services.
3. Goods may be bought and sold on local or global markets.
4. A market requires a monetary system to facilitate transactions and convey prices.
5. Markets may be for intermediate or final goods.
6. The fundamental event in a market is exchange—of some object, promise, service, or privilege.
7. A market is a locus of repeated exchanges.
8. A legal system of property rights determines what may be exchanged in a market.
9. Implicit or explicit contracts govern the conditions under which property is exchanged.
10. Rules about transactions organize how buyers and sellers interact, and who may be a buyer and a seller.
11. Rules about the provision of information (including about the quality of the good) enable sellers to propose a price and enable buyers to accept or negotiate another.

A Suggested Approach for Empirical Analysis of Markets 143

12. Organized behavior, induced by transaction and information rules, provides continuity to a market's operation.

This distillation to 12 distinctive properties foreshadow a far more extensive and concrete expression of Tordjman's (2004) "agenda of questions" that will enable us to transcend abstract notions about the market to their actualization if the object is conduct empirical analyses of real-world markets. The questions that we can pose from the 12 distinctive properties of markets include, but are not limited to:

(a) What is the commodity "bought and sold"? How are these goods or services defined? To what extent have these definitions changed, or are evolving, with the market's "virtual canonization"?

(b) Who are the market participants (individuals, groups, or organizations)? Who transacts with whom? Are intermediaries involved?

(c) What are the "rules" or protocols that determine eligibility or ineligibility for ongoing access to a market? Are there legal and political decisions, or compromises, which determine who participates? What must a participant do to meet eligibility criteria and maintain ongoing market access?

(d) What forms of interaction take place between buyers and sellers, and other market participants? Are particular behaviors forbidden? Are there implicit rules influencing the behavior of market participants? Are penalties imposed for breaches of market behavior?

(e) How, and where, are market transactions performed? Is there a physical or virtual market location and how is this organized? Is the sphere of interaction local or global? Must participants meet any obligations or criteria to perform market transactions?

(f) What are the institutions, organizations, legislation, or associations that organize the functioning of a market? What are their responsibilities? How do they enforce market operations? To what or who are they accountable?

(g) How is price determined? Are prices set outside or within the market? If it is a price-setting market, does this lead to different bilateral prices?

(h) What is the market's form of competition? How many traders? What is the ownership structure in the market? Is there evidence of market power?

(i) What information is available to whom? Where is it available? What technology and skills are needed to access or process market information? What is the impact on market participation if information access is precluded in some way?

(j) Are there interrelationships between a primary commodity market and other markets? How are these relationships organized? What are the implications of these relationships in terms of market operation, market participation, and market outcomes?

(k) What is the role of the state in terms of, but not limited to, the market's organization and operation, and determining the eligibility of participants?

It is my contention that these questions form a cogent analytical grid that can be used to interrogate the structure, operation, participants, behaviors, rules, price setting, and more of a market and thus generate a substantive, realistic picture of actually existing markets. These questions are far more penetrating than neoclassical economic analysis, which assumes a form of market organization—pure competition, duopoly, oligopoly, or monopoly—and then analyzes output, price, and cost outcomes within this context (Gould 1980). These questions are also far more penetrating than the schema suggested by Aspers (2011: 173) for sociological research of existing markets. Although there are some points of commonality, such as price determination, Aspers's schema will not yield the same depth of findings about the institutional underpinnings, behavioral influences, market operation, availability and accessibility of information, forms of interaction between participants, or market interrelationships.

Applying the Analytical Framework to Markets Transformed by Neoliberal Public Policies

This grid of questions formed the basis of the analytical framework applied to four markets of the Australian liberal market-based economy (Chester 2010).[6] Neoliberalism's free market rhetoric, and the lexicon of neoclassical economics, has smothered Australian

A Suggested Approach for Empirical Analysis of Markets 145

public policy since the 1980s with a vast array of policies transformed by market-based mechanisms. Examples include the charging of fees for time spent in immigration detention centers, contracting out of services delivered to the unemployed through competitive tendering, the charging of market rents to public housing tenants, the removal of barriers to free trade such as tariffs and import quotas, the provision of infrastructure through commercial contracts with the private sector, the development of accounting rules to measure greenhouse gas emissions, the framing of universal health insurance as a solution to market failure, and student fees set at levels equivalent to the costs of providing higher education places. This progressive widespread adoption of market-based policy instruments has meant substantial change to markets that have traditionally supplied goods and services essential to well-being, standard of living, and social inclusion such as education, health insurance, public housing, services for the aged and unemployed, electricity, and water. Most noticeably, direct and sole provision by government of these goods and services has been supplanted.

The four Australian markets analyzed were for the essential goods and services of electricity, water, housing for low-income Australians, and services for the unemployed. Each market has a widespread impact on the lives and well-being of the Australian population irrespective of geographic location or stage of life. A brief overview of the findings for each market analyzed is now discussed before drawing some general findings about actually existing markets and the public policy rhetoric that shapes their organization and operation. (Appendix A presents a detailed comparative table of the four markets' structural features, interactions, and outcomes.)

Electricity

The electricity market has mixed ownership, some exposure to competition, and a centralized wholesale trading market. Most Australian households can now choose the company to supply their electricity. If they do so, the electricity prices paid are set by a market contract. Alternatively, a household may choose to remain on a standard contract, which means their electricity prices are set by regulation. The vast majority of Australian households have not changed their supplier, electing to remain on regulated prices. Most electricity generated and consumed is traded through the wholesale National Electricity Market (NEM).[7] The Australian Energy Market Commission and the Australian Energy Regulator are responsible for the oversight and regulation of the NEM. The National Electricity Rules prescribe the NEM's day-to-day operation, six types of market participant, the process to achieve participant status, and the terms under which each will engage in the market. The Rules also set out the process to determine the wholesale price following bids to supply from generation companies. NEM price volatility has been common, with price spikes at levels well below maximum demand as generators exercise their market power and investment in base load capacity has not been stimulated (Chester 2008). Prices paid by households have risen, on average, by more than 50 percent in the most populous states since 2007 and are far in excess of increases in general prices, wages, or electricity prices paid by business (Chester and Morris 2010). Ownership concentration, private ownership dominating distribution and retail activities, and foreign ownership dominating private ownership strongly characterize today's electricity sector despite the rapid increase in the number of NEM participants.

Water

There is little direct competition in the supply of water and wastewater services. Private-sector involvement is skewed towards capital construction, operation, and maintenance through public-private partnerships. Government authorities dominate the urban water market whereas trading markets have become prevalent in the rural water market. Two kinds of water trading markets have developed—temporary (that is, seasonal water allocations) and permanent (that is, access entitlements). Market participants exchange their allocations or entitlements at an agreed price (water property rights have been separated from land title). Temporary trades between individual water users when water availability is low, facilitated by the emergence of water exchanges, has been the most significant activity to date, especially in the southern Murray-Darling Basin, which produces a third of Australia's food supply. Prolonged drought exacerbated water supplies and prompted government buyback of water entitlements, new regulatory arrangements, use restrictions, information campaigns, and application of scarcity pricing. Australia's contemporary urban and rural water markets are characterized by: increasing access and usage charges for urban users; a myriad of complex regulatory and licensing arrangements; uncertainty amongst participants about future supply; poorly defined, and jurisdictionally inconsistent, property rights to access and entitlement; and increasingly direct intervention by the federal government.

Housing for the Low-Income

Housing for low-income Australians is provided in two forms. Government funds the provision of public and community housing stock, and provides cash assistance for those in the private rental market. The total stock of public and community housing has declined since the mid 1990s, coinciding with tighter targeting to those in greatest need, a real terms decline in federal funding of 24 percent from 1998–1999 to 2007–2008, and greater reliance being placed on the private rental market (Productivity Commission 2009). Eligibility criteria for access to public housing varies across each state and territory jurisdiction in terms of income and asset limits, residency requirements, waiting list segmentation (and lengthening), periodic reviews of eligibility, and rent rebates. All housing authorities apply rent affordability benchmarks of around 25 percent of assessable income, that is, a rebate on market rent.

Rent assistance, a demand-side form of housing assistance, is provided by the federal government to those renting in the private housing market and who receive income support payments or the base level of designated family payments. Rent assistance is paid according to minimum thresholds and maximum rates, which vary according to household type and number of dependents. There is no affordability benchmark as for public housing tenants and no differentiation between rural and urban rental markets.

Following the global financial crisis from late 2008, the federal government announced measures to stimulate the supply of low-cost rental housing. If successful, the addition to stock will represent barely a third of applicants on the waiting list for public and community housing (Productivity Commission 2009).

Services for the Unemployed

Private and not-for-profit providers deliver employment services for the unemployed. Historically, the market for employment services had a single public-sector supplier, the Commonwealth Employment Service. Now the federal government purchases, by contract, the specified employment services from multiple non-government suppliers—one buyer, multiple sellers. As sole buyer, the federal government purchases on behalf of multiple recipients of these services—the unemployed—but mandates certain behaviors as criteria to access these services. Those receiving unemployment benefits are eligible to access employment services. To continue receiving unemployment benefits, there are mandatory activity tests or participation requirements, including attendance at all job interviews, acceptance of "suitable" job offers, evidence of searching for "suitable paid work," and not exiting training or a job without valid reason (Centrelink 2009). Ongoing compliance with these requirements is a condition of payment. Once registered for unemployment benefits, you are permitted to register online with an employment services provider. A considerable amount of the unemployed's interaction with Centrelink (the public-sector organization responsible for the delivery of welfare payments) and employment service providers is via the Internet. Apart from the need for computer access, this interaction requires levels of literacy, numeracy, and computer skills so that the unemployed can "navigate" their way through this market, make informed choices about service providers, search for work, and comply with mandatory reporting requirements.

The performance-linked payment structure has resulted in those requiring more intensive assistance (the longer-term and more difficult-to-place job seekers) being "parked" while those with greater chances of gaining employment are targeted or "creamed" (Productivity Commission 2002).

A Suggested Approach for Empirical Analysis of Markets 149

Actually Existing Markets Framed by Neoliberal Public Policies

The Australian market analysis unequivocally demonstrated a very different picture of the organization, operation, and outcomes of markets from that promulgated by mainstream economics and deeply embedded in neoliberal public policies. The following conclusions are readily apparent from this analysis:

1. Eligibility to participate in a market, by both buyers and sellers, requires predetermined criteria—set by regulators—to be met. These criteria are not static, can be quite complex, and may involve a cost or "entry fee" (for example, water connection fee), assessment by a regulator (for example, competitive tender, data provided by participant), or eligibility to be established first by another market (for example, welfare recipients). Payment of the price of a good or service does not determine eligibility to be a market participant.
2. Ongoing market participation is not assured even if eligibility criteria are satisfied. Participants may be required to make a regular payment (for example, annual NEM fees), be limited to a fixed participation term by contract, be subject to regular reassessment of eligibility, or be required to pay for goods and services by supplier-determined time and method. Payment of the price of a good or service is insufficient for buyers to maintain ongoing market access.
3. Government provides measures that influence the demand and supply of the goods and services sold in each of the markets analyzed and hence the interventions of government are directly influencing market outcomes.
4. Regulators actively determine prices in each of the markets analyzed. The rural water trading market was the only market found to have price agreed by buyer and seller but heavily determined by the extent to which property rights are specified. Price is not the co-coordinating mechanism promulgated by mainstream economics.
5. Intermediaries are evident in many markets, most commonly as market operators. Mainstream economics assumes no intermediaries and market participants are anonymous.

6. The overwhelming form of interaction between market participants is via the Internet, requiring buyers to have computer access as well as literacy and numeracy skills. This may well pose barriers to full and ongoing participation by some eligible participants. Mainstream economics would have us believe that market interaction (communication) is solely through price signals.
7. Quite complex and detailed information is available to buyers (generally via the Internet) relating to their participation, obligations, payments terms, penalties, and performance data about providers. There is also increasingly complex product information such as, for electricity, a range of domestic tariffs, green energy deals, and social concessions, as well as incentive and reward deals. Perfectly informed consumers, as assumed by mainstream economics, are not present. Complex information is available if buyers have access to the necessary technology.
8. Each market is underpinned by a very complex legislative and regulatory regime involving multiple regulatory institutions.
9. There is strong evidence of different market types such as contested, managed, monopoly franchise, and oligopoly. Imperfect competition was found only for the electricity retail market. The mainstream assumes one market type.
10. Government is a very dominant participant in all markets, performing multiple roles as regulator, owner of significant supplier assets, manager of stock, manager of contested markets, market operator, and buyer.
11. Despite government interventions, and significant price increases, the key outcomes in the majority of markets analyzed show that supply is not meeting demand and one market (housing for low-income Australians) is evidence of chronic market failure. The mainstream assumes an optimal allocation of products will be achieved at equilibrium prices but prices are not self-equilibrating nor are there infinitely rapid velocities of prices and quantities. Prices in all except one case were found to be set by regulators.
12. Market power and concentration were strongly evident in the majority of markets analyzed.

The analysis also confirmed that there is not one but a spectrum of contemporary market configurations and exceedingly complex governance regimes as observed by Boyer (1997) and Nelson (2005). Each so-called market is comprised of layers of multiple markets somewhat analogous to a set of Russian *babushka* dolls. "Markets are embedded in each other" (Aspers 2011: 126). For example, the electricity market is made up of generation, transmission, distribution, and retail markets, each of different size. The generation market includes markets for wholesale trading, non-scheduled generation, and generation from energy renewables. Energy provides a further example of the complex web of interrelationships between markets. For example, the operation of the electricity retail market is strongly related to the organization and operation of markets for meters, the retailing of gas and credit services, hot water systems, swimming pools, heating and cooling systems, energy efficiency appliances, and lighting. These market interrelationships raise issues warranting closer examination such as the cumulative impact of market outcomes on end-use consumers and the potential flow-on consequences, like a row of falling dominoes, if one market experiences significant disruption.

Concluding Comments

More and more reliance has been placed on markets by government to solve an increasing range of issues notwithstanding the questioning by some mainstream theorists of the proclaimed efficiency of markets. Yet neoclassical economics has very successfully portrayed the normative ideal of the market, framed around a set of abstract assumptions, as synonymous with the economy and capitalism. Moreover, this normative ideal of the perfectly competitive market has become embedded in public policies, transforming markets that have traditionally been the domain of state intervention and that determine, to a large extent, the well-being of society.

Although markets are not the only institutional arrangement for organizing economic and social life, we need to understand the market's contribution to society's well-being to inform the debate about the relative merits of different forms of provisioning. That understanding must be grounded in robust empirical analysis of the outcomes of markets that impact on well-being. Market outcomes reflect the organization and functioning of those markets. The normative ideal of neoclassical economics cannot elucidate the organization, functioning, outcomes, and implications of real-world markets.

The market is a physical or virtual location for repeated exchanges between buyers and sellers, which may involve intermediate or final goods, may be local or global, and is underpinned by property rights, implicit or explicit contracts, rules about transactions, and information creating organized behavior and continuity of operation. It is these distinctive properties of markets that signal a set of questions that must be addressed if the objective is a realistic understanding of the organization, functioning, and outcomes of actually existing markets. This is the analytical framework that this article has sought to develop.

The analytical framework posited explicitly recognizes the different types of markets that can be discerned, the relationship to property rights, and the dimensions and behaviors shaping the organization of exchange. A distillation of these key propositions to their core essence establishes 12 fundamental properties of markets that enable progression from the abstract to the concrete because they indicate a cogent set of detailed questions to frame and guide a cogent empirical analysis. The list of market properties create a "bridge" between key abstract propositions drawn from the discourse and a pragmatic analytical framework. This "operationalization" from the conceptual has been applied to a handful of markets in one liberal market-based economy. Apart from providing a much richer understanding of essential goods and services market organization, operation, and outcomes than mainstream neoclassical economics, the analysis illustrated the disjuncture between actuality and public policy rhetoric—rhetoric grounded in mainstream economics and neoliberalism.

Boyer (1997: 70) has argued that the organization of capitalist economies, which attribute a leading role to "competitive" markets, can only be explained by ascertaining: the institutions, legislation, organizations, or interactions that organize the functioning of various markets; the series of commodities for which the supply and demand of is heavily determined by market institutions, including regulation by the state; and the forms of competition according to the number of traders, ownership distribution, market power, and the mechanisms to resolve capacity issues or structural changes. These are indeed important "keys" to understanding and explaining the *existence* and *operation* of markets in a capitalist economy. But to understand the impact on society's well-being, it is necessary to go to a further level of disaggregation to consider also the *interactions* and *outcomes* of actually existing markets. To understand the relationship to, and impact on, society's well-being, market interactions and outcomes will be a necessary contributor especially for those markets delivering essential goods and services and shaped by public policies. Thus, if our knowledge of real-world markets is to be deepened and extended, further refinement and application of the analytical framework posited here is warranted to test its validity and representativeness in other markets, other liberal market-based economies, and other varieties of capitalism.

In addition, a far more informed understanding of the societal implications of market provisioning will enable the development of alternatives to public policies delivering markets for essential goods and services based on the abstract concepts of perfectly competitive markets provided by neoclassical economics. The foregoing discussion has clearly indicated that the market is such a complex institution that it cannot be distilled or equated to the sum of bilateral relationships as is neoclassical economics' want. A market's "constitution," functioning, and impact on well-being can only be understood within the context of its empirical complexity as well as by reference to other markets given the diversity and specificities of each. The analytical framework posited in this article contributes a basis to do that and may, as a result, help shift the debate, advocated by Lane (1991) nearly two decades ago, from the relative merits of markets and states to one whose axis is the *contribution* of market provisioning to well-being and human development.

Notes

1. Earlier versions of this article were presented to the 8th Annual Conference of the Society of Heterodox Economists, December 7–8, 2009, UNSW, Sydney, Australia and the 12th Annual Conference of the Association of Heterodox Economics, July 7–10, 2010, Bordeaux, France.

2. In the US, privatization of the electricity and water sectors has not occurred to the same extent given the much higher levels of private ownership historically. Notwithstanding, these markets have experienced significant regulatory and pricing changes driven by market-based public policies.

3. Stigltiz (2000: 87) also argues that even if Pareto efficiency is achieved, government intervention may be warranted to achieve greater equality of income distribution and/or if the government "knows what is in the best interests of individuals."

4. Medema (2009) provides a detailed account of the dominant economic discourse, from the mid-19th century to the late 20th century, about the theory of market failure and government intervention.

5. Commons (2007) explicitly recognized the political nature of transaction rules, and the role of the state in the process of exchange, in his 1924 publication *Legal Foundations of Capitalism*.

6. The analysis was conducted in late 2009. There have been some subsequent marginal changes within these markets but these have not altered the fundamental organization, operation, and outcomes of each market that the analysis revealed.

7. The NEM covers southern and eastern Australia (Queensland, New South Wales, the Australian Capital Territory, Victoria, Tasmania, and South Australia). The geographic remoteness of the population centers of Western Australia and the Northern Territory make the cost of transmission interconnection to a national grid prohibitive. Restructuring of the WA electricity sector has essentially mirrored that involving the NEM.

References

Akerlof, G. A. (1984). *An Economic Theorist's Book of Tales*. Cambridge, UK: Cambridge University Press.

Allaire, G. (2009). "Economics of Conventions and the New Economic Sociology and Our Understanding of Food Quality and New Food Markets and Trade Institutions." Paper presented to the 27th International Conference of Agricultural Economists, August 16–22, 2009, Beijing, China. Http://ageconsearch.umn.edu/bitstream/53203/2/Gilles%20Alaire%20IAAE%202009.pdf.

Altvater, E. (1993). *The Future of the Market*. London: Verso.

Amable, B. (2003). *The Diversity of Modern Capitalism*. Oxford: Oxford University Press.

Aspers, P. (2011). *Markets*. Cambridge, UK: Polity.

Baker, D. (2011). *The End of Loser Liberalism: Making Markets Progressive*. Available at: Http://www.cepr.net/index.php/publications/books/the-end-of-loser-liberalism.

Blaug, M. (2002). "Ugly Currents in Economics." In *Fact and Fiction in Economics: Models, Realism, and Social Construction.* Ed. U. Mäki, pp. 35–56. Cambridge, UK: Cambridge University Press.

Boyer, R. (1997). "The Variety and Unequal Performance of Really Existing Markers: Farwell to Doctor Pangloss." In *Contemporary Capitalism: The Embeddedness of Institutions.* Eds. J. R. Hollingsworth and R. Boyer, pp. 55–93. Cambridge: Cambridge University Press.

Callon, M. (ed.) (1998). *The Laws of the Markets.* Oxford: Blackwell Publishers/Sociological Review.

Callon, M., Y. Millo, and F. Muniesa. (eds.) (2007). *Market Devices.* Malden, MA: Blackwell Publishing/Sociological Review.

Carrier, J. G. (ed.) (1997). *Meanings of the Market: The Free Market in Western Culture.* Oxford: Berg.

Centrelink. (2009). "Activity Test and Participation Requirements for Job Seekers." Australian Government. Http://www.centrelink.gov.au/internet/internet.nsf/filestores/lw054_0906/$file/lw054_0906en.pdf.

Chang, H-J. (2002). "Breaking the Mould: An Institutionalist Political Economy Alternative to the Neoliberal Theory of the Market and the State." *Cambridge Journal of Economics* 6(3): 539–560.

———. (2007). "Institutional Change and Economic Development: An Introduction." In *Institutional Change and Economic Development.* Ed. H-J. Chang, pp. 1–14. New York: United Nations University Press.

Chester, L. (2008). "The Parlous Investment Environment for Australian Electricity Generation and Transmission." *IAEE Energy Forum* Second quarter: 29–35.

———. (2010). "Actually Existing Markets: The Case of Neoliberal Australia." *Journal of Economic Issues* 44(2): 313–324.

Chester, L., and A. Morris. (2010). "Energy Poverty: An Escalating Outcome of Liberalised Energy Markets." Refereed papers: 9th Australian Society of Heterodox Economists Conference, December 6–7, 2010, Sydney.

Coase, R. H. (1988). *The Firm, the Market and the Law.* Chicago: University of Chicago Press.

———. (1992). "The Institutional Structure of Production." *American Economic Review* 82(4): 713–719.

Commons, J. R. [1924] (2007). *Legal Foundations of Capitalism.* With a new introduction by J. E. Biddle and W. Samuels. New Brunswick: Transaction Publishers.

Coriat, B., and O. Weinstein. (2005). "The Social Construction of Markets." *Issues in Regulation Theory* 53: 1–4.

Crouch, C. (2005). *Capitalist Diversity and Change: Recombinant Governance and Institutional Entrepreneurs.* Oxford: Oxford University Press.

Elsner, W. (2008). "Market and State." In *International Encyclopaedia of Public Policy—Governance in a Global Age, Volume 3: Public Policy and*

Political Economy. Ed. P. A. O'Hara, pp. 370–389. Available at: Http://pohara.homestead.com/Encyclopedia/Volume-3.pdf.

Fligstein, N. (1996). "Markets as Politics: A Political-Cultural Approach to Market Institutions." *American Sociological Review* 61(4): 656–673.

Galbraith, J. (2009). *The Predator State: How Conservatives Abandoned the Free Market and Why Liberals Should Too.* New York: Free Press.

Garcia-Parpet, M-F. (2007). "The Social Construction of a Perfect Market: The Strawberry Auction at Fontaine-en-Sologne." In *Do Economists Make Markets? On the Performativity of Economics.* Eds. D. MacKenzie, F. Muniesa, and L. Siu, pp. 20–53. Princeton: Princeton University Press.

Giroux, H. (2009). "Market-Driven Hysteria and the Politics of Death." *Truthout.* Http://www.truthout.org/1106095.

Gould, J. P. (1980). "The Economics of Markets: A Simple Model of the Market-Making Process." *Journal of Business* 53(3, Part 2): s167–187.

Granovetter, M. (1985). "Economic Action and Social Structure: The Problem of Embeddedness." *American Journal of Sociology* 91(3): 481–510.

Granovetter, M., and P. McGuire. (1998). "The Making of an Industry: Electricity in the United States. In *The Laws of the Markets.* Ed. M. Callon, pp. 147–173. Oxford: Blackwell Publishers/The Sociological Review.

Grossman, S., and J. Stiglitz. (1980). "On the Impossibility of Informationally Efficient Markets." *American Economic Review* 70(3): 393–408.

Hahnel, R. (2007). "The Case Against Markets." *Journal of Economic Issues* XLI(4): 1139–1159.

Hall, P., and D., Soskice. (eds.) (2001). *Varieties of Capitalism: The Institutional Foundations of Comparative Advantage.* Oxford: Oxford University Press.

Hannan, M., and J. Freeman. (1986). "Where Do Organisations Come From?" *Sociological Forum* 1(1): 50–72.

Härdle, W., and A. Kirman. (1995). "Nonclassical Demand: A Model-Free Examination of Price-Quantity Relations in the Marseille Fish Market." *Journal of Econometrics* 67(1): 227–257.

Harvey, D. (2005). *A Brief History of Neoliberalism.* Oxford: Oxford University Press.

Harvey, M., and S. Randles. (2002). "Markets, the Organisation of Exchanges and 'Instituted Economic Process'—An Analytical Perspective." *Revue d'Économie Industrielle* 101(4): 11–30.

Hodgson, G. (1988). *Economics and Institutions: A Manifesto for a Modern Institutional Economics.* Cambridge: Polity Press.

Keen, S. (2001). *Debunking Economics: The Naked Emperor of the Social Sciences.* Annandale, NSW: Pluto Press.

Kirman, A. P., and A. Vignes. (1992). "Price Dispersion: Theoretical Considerations and Empirical Evidence from the Marseille Fish Market." In *Issues in Contemporary Economics.* Ed. K. Arrow, Vol 1. pp. 160–185. London: MacMillan.

Lane, R. E. (1991). *The Market Experience.* Cambridge: Cambridge University Press.
Lee, F., and S. Keen. (2004). "The Incoherent Emperor: A Heterodox Critique of Neoclassical Microeconomic Theory." *Review of Social Economy* LXII(2): 169–199.
Lindblom, C. E. (1982). "The Market as Prison." *Journal of Politics* 44(2): 324–336.
MacKenzie, D. (2007a). "Zero is a Clenched Fist." *London Review of Books* 29(21). Http://www.lrb.co.uk/v29/n21/mack01_.html.
———. (2007b). "Finding the Ratchet: The Political Economy of Carbon Trading." *Postautistic Economics Review* 42: 8–17.
———. (2009). *Material Markets: How Economic Agents are Constructed.* Oxford: Oxford University Press.
MacKenzie, D., F. Muniesa, and L. Siu. (eds) (2007). *Do Economists Make Markets? On the Performativity of Economics.* Princeton: Princeton University Press.
Mantzavinos, C. (2001). *Individuals, Institutions, and Markets.* Cambridge: Cambridge University Press.
Martinez, M. A. (2009). *The Myth of the Free Market: The Role of the State in a Capitalist Economy.* Sterling, VA: Kumarian Press.
Medema, S. G. (2009). *The Hesitant Hand: Taming Self-interest in the History of Economic Ideas.* Princeton: Princeton University Press.
Moody, K. (1997). *Workers in a Lean World: Unions in the International Economy.* London: Verso.
Nelson, S. (ed.) (2005). *The Limits of Market Organization.* New York: Russell Sage Foundation.
North, D. C. (1990). *Institutions, Institutional Change and Economic Performance.* Cambridge: Cambridge University Press.
Peck, J., and N. Theodore. (2007). "Variegated Capitalism." *Progress in Human Geography* 31(6): 731–732.
Polanyi, K. (2001). *The Great Transformation: The Political and Economic Origins of Our Time.* Foreword by Joseph Stiglitz and Introduction by Fred Block. Boston: Beacon Press.
Prasch, R. E. (1995). "Toward a 'General Theory' of Market Exchange." *Journal of Economic Issues* 29 (3): 807–828.
———. (2008). *How Markets Work: Supply, Demand and the "Real World."* Cheltenham, UK: Edward Elgar.
Productivity Commission. (2002). "Independent Review of the Job Network." Report No. 21. Canberra: AusInfo.
———. (2009). "Report on Government Services 2009." Steering Committee for the Review of Government Service Provision. Productivity Commission Canberra.

Public Services International Research Unit. (2008). "Poor Choices: The Limits of Competitive Markets in the Provision of Essential Services to Low-Income Consumers". Report prepared for UK Energywatch. Http://www.psiru.org/reports/PoorChoices.pdf.

Sen, A. (2009). "Capitalism Beyond the Crisis." *New York Review of Books* 56(5). Http://www.nybooks.com/articles/22490.

Sherman, H. J., E. K. Hunt, R. E. Nesiba, P. A. O'Hara, and B. Wiens-Tuers. (2008). *Economics: An Introduction to Traditional and Progressive Views*. 7th edition. Armonk: M.E. Sharpe

Simon, H. (1991). "Organizations and Markets." *Journal of Economic Perspectives* 5(2): 25–44.

——. (1992). "Bounded Rationality." In *The New Palgrave Dictionary of Money and Finance*. Eds. P. Newman, M. Milgate, and J. Eatwell pp. 226–227. London: Macmillan.

Skidelsky, R. (2009). "Where Do We Go from Here?" *Prospect Magazine* 154. Http://www.prospectmagazine.co.uk/2009/01/wheredowegofromhere/.

Stern, N. (2010). "Presidential Address: Imperfections in the Economics of Public Policy, Imperfections in Markets, and Climate Change." *Journal of the European Economic Association* 8(2–3): 253–288.

Stiglitz, J. E. (1987). "The Causes and Consequences of the Dependence of Quality on Price." *Journal of Economic Literature* 25(1): 1–48.

——. (2000). *Economics of the Public Sector*. 3rd edition. New York: W.W. Norton & Company.

Tordjman, H. (1998). "Some General Questions About Markets." Interim Report IR-98-025/May, International Institute for Applied Systems Analysis, Laxenburg, Austria.

——. (2004). "How to Study Markets? An Institutionalist Point of View." *Revue d'Économie Industrielle* 107(3): 19–36.

Tsakalotos, E. (2004). "Social Norms and Endogenous Preferences: The Political Economy of Market Expansion." In *Neo-Liberal Economic Policy: Critical Essays*. Eds. P. Arestis and M. Sawyer, pp. 5–37. Cheltenham, UK: Edward Elgar.

White, H. C. (1981). "Where Do Markets Come From?" *American Journal of Sociology* 87(3): 517–547.

Williamson, O. (1975). *Markets and Hierarchies: Analysis and Anti-Trust Implications*. New York: Free Press.

Yakubovich, Valery, M. Granovetter, and P. McGuire. (2005). "Electric Charges: The Social Construction of Rate Systems." *Theory and Society* 34(5/6): 579–612.

Zelizer, V. A. (1988). "Beyond the Polemics on the Market: Establishing a Theoretical and Empirical Agenda." *Sociological Forum* 3(4): 614–634.

——. (1994). *The Social Meaning of Money*. New York: Basic Books.

Appendix A: Comparison of the structural features, interactions, and outcomes of four Australian markets

	Electricity	Water	Employment services for the unemployed	Housing for the low-income
What is the commodity?	Electricity supply	Water supply	Job referral, job search training, training/work experience, individual case management	Low-cost housing in private and public markets
What is the ownership pattern?	Mixed	Public	Private	Mixed
Who are eligible buyers (end-users)?	All organizations, companies, and households connected to the grid.	All organizations, companies, and households connected to water supply system.	Federal government on behalf of those receiving unemployment benefits.	Those receiving income support payments and base-level family assistance.
How do buyers (end-users) maintain market access?	Pay connection fee plus access and usage charges by supplier-determined time and method.	Pay usage and access charges by supplier-determined time and method. Pay agreed price for exchange of water rights.	Retain eligibility for unemployment benefits, meet reporting obligations, and register with Job Services Australia.	Retain eligibility for income support, and base-level family assistance. Meet thresholds for rent assistance and eligibility for public housing.
Who are the eligible sellers and how do they maintain market access?	NEM participants must register, meet/maintain strict prudential criteria, and pay annual fees. Retail companies must be licensed by state government regulators to operate in respective jurisdictions.	State and local government authorities. Sellers of water entitlements or allocations.	Providers contracted for fixed 3-year term.	State government authorities provide public housing stock. Federal government provides rent assistance payments and incentives to stimulate construction of new rental stock. Private sector must meet criteria for financial incentives.

Appendix A *Continued*

	Electricity	Water	Employment services for the unemployed	Housing for the low-income
Demand-side measures provided by government?	NEM allows for withdrawal or "load shifting" by large market customers when wholesale price passes a threshold, e.g., aluminium smelters.	Restrictions on use enforced, in part, by financial penalties. Water efficiency information campaigns. Subsidies to install water-efficient appliances. Application of scarcity pricing.		Rent assistance for those in private rental market. Rent rebate for those in public housing.
Supply-side measures provided by government?	Limited augmentation of govt-owned generation capacity. 10-year projections of adequacy of generation and transmission capacity to meet forecast demand	Construction of desalination plants. Limited measures to increase recycling. Trading of entitlements and allocations.	Competitive tender to provide services for a contracted period	Provision of public housing stock. Funding of community housing. Tax rebates/subsidies to private sector to construct new rental dwellings for low-income.
How is price determined?	Half-hourly wholesale price set by market operator but capped at $10,000 per MWh Transmission and distribution: regulated Retail: regulated for majority of households until evidence of "effective competition"	Urban: State regulators set access and usage charges in respective jurisdiction. Trading: price agreed through exchange.	Performance-linked payments set by government as part of competitive tender.	Rate of rent assistance (and eligibility) subject to annual federal budget process. Rent rebate subject to National Affordable Housing Agreement. Other supply-side measures determined within federal budget process.

A Suggested Approach for Empirical Analysis of Markets   161

Does buyer (end-user) pay price?	Yes. NEM customer pays price set by market operator. End-user pays price charged by retailer.	Yes. End-user pays price charged by supplier or established through trading.	Price paid by federal government on behalf of end-users, the unemployed.	No. Federal government sets and pay all "prices" of rent assistance, public housing stock, and subsidies to private sector.
How do buyers (end-users) and sellers interact?	NEM market operator acts as intermediary between generators and distributors. Direct retailer-consumer interface via Internet, billing, or phone.	Urban: Direct retailer-consumer interface via Internet, billing, or phone. Trading: Through water exchanges.	Online tender process. Unemployed persons register online, meet with provider, and maintain contact via Internet and in-person meetings.	Online or direct interface with Centrelink, state housing authorities, community housing providers.
What information is provided to buyers (end-users)?	NEM market operator: forecasts capacity and demand, NEM prices Retailers: consumer obligations, price, billing, payment terms Regulators: performance reports of regulated monopolies, outage investigations, price determinations	Retailers: Consumer obligations and rights, price, billing, payment terms. Water brokers: Price determination, rules for lodging offers, fees, trade eligibility, payment terms. Regulators: Performance reports of regulated monopolies, rules for water brokers, price determinations.	Details of tender and outcomes. Locations of providers and services. Obligations and reporting requirements if unemployed and penalties for breach.	Eligibility rules for rent assistance and scale of payments. Eligibility for public/community housing. Application process and details required. Ongoing reporting requirements.
How is information provided to buyers (end-users)?	Retailers: websites, telephone, direct mail National and state regulators: websites	Retailers: websites, telephone, direct mail National and state regulators: websites Water brokers: websites	Government websites. Centrelink offices. Direct mail.	Government websites. Centrelink offices. Direct mail to income support recipients.

Appendix A *Continued*

	Electricity	Water	Employment services for the unemployed	Housing for the low-income
What are the main features of the regulatory regime?	National Electricity Rules (1,251 pages). Australian Energy Market Operator. Australian Energy Regulator. Australian Energy Market Commission. States: Regulator for each jurisdiction.	National Water Commission. Murray-Darling Basin Authority. COAG Agreements.	Federal Department of Employment, Education and Workplace Relations. Centerlink.	Centrelink. Federal Department of Family, Housing, Community Services and Indigenous Affairs. National Affordable Housing Agreement. National Rental Affordability Scheme. Social Housing Initiative.
What is the extent of the market or form of competition?	NEM: Managed market Generation: Oligopoly Transmission: Monopoly in each state Distribution: Monopoly franchise in each state Retail: Imperfect competition	Urban: Monopoly franchise Rural: Contested market	Contestable managed market. Providers dominated by handful of large private companies.	Public rental: Monopoly Private rental: Contested
What is the role of government	NEM operator and regulator. Price regulator for transmission, distribution, and retail. Owner of substantial generation, transmission, distribution, and retail capacity.	Owner. Regulator. Buyer.	Regulator. Manager of contested market.	Owner/manager public housing stock. Regulator of community housing. Cash provision of rent assistance. Funding of new public housing stock. Provision of tax and financial incentives to stimulate construction of low-cost private rental housing.

What are the key market outcomes?	Wholesale price volatility not reflecting demand or stimulating investment. Electricity derivatives market to manage wholesale price risk. Generators exercise market power. Retail consolidation. Retail and generation reintegrating. Significant price increases for households. Increasing customer complaints and disconnections. Generation capacity inadequate for forecast long-term demand.	Inconsistent definitions of property rights across Australia. Markedly higher charges paid by all water consumers. Desalination plants have required purpose-built energy capacity. Long-term urban and rural supply capacity is under severe threat. Severe deterioration of Murray-Darling Basin.	Less costly than previous sole provider provision. High compliance and administrative requirements for providers following onerous/costly tender process. Performance-based payments have led to "parking" and "creaming." Limited success for many long-term or difficult-to-place job seekers. High reliance on unemployed having Internet access and computer skills	More than 50% of low-income renting households in housing stress. Growing public housing waiting lists. Supply of public and private rental stock not responding to chronic excess demand for cheap rental housing. Stimulus measures yet to generate forecast stock increases in low-cost rental housing that barely represent a third of waiting lists for public and community housing

Three Modes of Competition in the Marketplace

By WILLIAM REDMOND

ABSTRACT. Competition is often thought of a fairly obvious thing, a rivalry. In a market context the meaning of competition is usually taken to be a rivalry among the sellers. The article seeks to broaden this view by considering other competitive relationships in the marketplace. Using the simplifying assumption that there are only two types of market actors, sellers and consumers, there are three possible types of relationships or interdependencies among these actors in a market. In competitive terms this includes the familiar competition among sellers but there is also the possibility of competition between sellers and consumers, as well as competition among consumers. The article outlines essential characteristics of the three modes. Implications of multi-mode competition for market performance and welfare are discussed.

Introduction

The term *competition* can call to mind different thoughts, depending on how an individual thinks about it. A competition can be a test. For some it appears as an opportunity to succeed; for others the threat of failure looms. In markets, it may mean a salubrious contest to better serve customers, or may mean a ruinous bout of cutthroat price wars. However, the tendency to focus only on sellers is a habit of thought, an institutionalized reflex that blocks other perspectives.

The interpretation given to terms and concepts has the effect of framing one's perceptions, hence shaping one's understanding and evaluation of the phenomenon in question. Consequently, different views of competition are attached to different expectations regarding market performance. For example, the questionable policy of limited regulation of financial markets was justified by a belief in the self-regulatory effects of competition. Fundamental beliefs about competition are a part of cognitive structures that relate individuals to markets, and that vary across different times and societies. Galbraith ([1952]1980) felt that for most Americans, the notion of free competition had essentially become more of a political concept than an economic concept.

For these reasons, discourse on competition in markets tends to be grounded in ideology, and thus to simplify and restrict the understanding of how markets operate. For the evaluation of consumer welfare, certain perspectives depict the outcome as being either primarily positive or primarily negative, just as markets are either feared or glorified (Spillman 1999). The reality of markets is more complicated and nuanced. The following will discuss conceptualizations of market competition as falling into three distinctive types or modes, each related to a different focus on the behaviors of market actors and their interactions. Effectively, the three modes are treated as "ideal types" of competition, *a la* Max Weber ([1920]1968), in order to clarify their fundamental properties. An ideal type is a synthesis of essential characteristics of a social phenomenon. Ideal types have been used previously to gain insights into economic phenomena (for example, Commons [1934]1961; Mukerjee 1942). Further, the scope is limited to consumer markets although certain aspects could be extended to business-to-business or business-to-government markets. When the three modes are viewed as being simultaneously operative, the complex richness that characterizes actual market interactions may be more clearly seen. Implications for performance are outlined in the discussion section.

Horizontal Competition, Part I

The notion that consumers can routinely and reliably benefit from market participation depends on a specific perspective about how markets work. Sellers compete with comparable sellers in the horizontal, or seller vs. seller, mode. In the conventional understanding of competition developed by classical and neoclassical economists, markets are simple and abstract. Markets are basically seen as clearinghouses or transaction arenas in which the sellers are not only numerous but faceless, essentially interchangeable entities. In this viewpoint, competition among sellers results in the sellers being price-takers. Competition is seen as beneficial for consumers, and is thus evaluated as a positive state of affairs. Indeed, competition among sellers is widely seen as necessary to secure the benefits of market exchange to consumers.

The concept of seller vs. seller competition is embodied in the neoclassical economics that forms the basic assumption about markets and frames the understanding of many, probably most, market observers and policymakers. Incorporated in this notion is a belief in the self-regulating property of markets. Under this assumption markets are held to be efficient in the allocation of resources and effective in delivering consumer benefits when driven by competition, in contrast to regulation by government or domination by a large firm or cartel.

The concept of rivalry among sellers fits well with Adam Smith's notion that competition was an *independent* striving among sellers for the patronage of customers (Scherer 1980). That is, sellers compete with other sellers, in a non-collusive manner. In seller vs. seller competition, the competitive arena is defined by the simultaneous offering of similar products. This understanding constitutes a basis for the assumption that consumer sovereignty prevails in markets, thus benefitting consumers.

The ideal form is known as perfect or pure competition, in which the sellers are numerous and none is sufficiently large so as to exercise any influence whatsoever on prices. Deviations from the ideal of pure competition are classed as market failures, to one extent or another. In most developed nations, governments take an interest in maintaining a competitive state in markets. A variety of pricing and anti-trust laws are designed to preserve and maintain active competition among sellers. The presence of multiple sellers in a market is regarded as being good, *prima facia*, and evaluated in a positive light, as contrasted with monopolies or cartels.

Aggregate market concentration in the United States rose substantially during the 20th century, reflecting the trend toward fewer and larger firms. Between the 1920s and the 1970s, the share of assets controlled by the 100 largest firms rose from around 35 percent to nearly 50 percent (Scherer and Ross 1990). Note, however, that the criterion of multiple sellers is associated with the structural properties of markets rather than the actual behaviors of the sellers. That is, the connection between numbers of sellers and desirable outcomes for consumers is an *assumption* of this conceptualization of markets and competition. Most real markets deviate from the ideal of pure competition, but under conditions known as workable competition, consumer benefits are thought to be retained (Clark 1940). Workable competition is assessed by criteria applied to the structure, conduct, and performance of the sellers (Scherer and Ross 1990). In workable competition, as with pure competition, the focus remains on the actions of the set of sellers.

Vertical Competition

Other thoughts about market competition provide alternative views, beyond the seller vs. seller mode, to include a generalized sense of contest. Thus contestability in markets may be present in ways that displace conventional assumptions about competition: in particular, there may be contestability between seller and buyer. This less conventional view is based on a different set of assumptions about how markets work and how sellers orient their actions. (Note that the sense in which *contestability* is used here is distinct from Baumol, Panzar, and Willig's 1982 theory of contestable markets although certain aspects are similar, such as multiproduct oligopolists who are not price-takers.)

As noted above, the conventional economics perspective of markets is abstract, being populated by numerous, interchangeable agents. However an alternate view is provided by institutional economists and economic sociologists, who perceive a different mode of market competition and are not sanguine about the benefits for consumers. These researchers view markets as complex social systems, peopled by identifiable and distinctive actors. Here, markets are viewed as being embedded in the larger social system, with resultant influence on the behaviors of all market participants. Competition may play out in ways not envisioned in the conventional view. Consequently, interpretations of the operations and consequences of competition are correspondingly complex and are not uniformly positive.

As Swedberg (1994) notes, in addition to horizontal competition in markets among sellers, there is also vertical competition between buyer and seller. In the latter, an area of contestability is the price to be paid for the object in question. That is, sellers are motivated to obtain higher prices for their offerings and avoid being price-takers. Thus the term *competition* has been used to refer to either of two distinct modes: the conventional seller vs. seller, or the seller vs. consumer mode. While the latter mode is less commonly envisioned when the term competition is used, it occurs quite frequently. It seems to be the case that the strategic interests of sellers are better served by the seller vs. consumer mode because it results in higher prices and profits, whereas seller vs. seller reduces prices and profits. In pursuing the seller vs. consumer mode, sellers necessarily orient their actions differently. Competition in the seller vs. consumer sense represents both a more frequent and less consumer-friendly orientation than the more widely assumed seller vs. seller mode. The notion of a seller vs. consumer mode of competition is by no means a recent one. Despite this, it is not a common mental image among either policymakers or the wider public.

Sellers have long sought to avoid direct price competition, through means such as trade associations and pooling agreements (Burns 1936). A more effective arrangement was found to be a reduction in the number of competitors. In the late 1800s, a wave of mergers occurred and, with fewer competitors, mutually recognized interdependence led to restraint of price-based competition. The consequences of a re-orientation from seller vs. seller competition to seller vs. consumer competition were apparent to early institutionalists. Veblen ([1904]1965) maintained that oligopolies shifted competition from a contest among firms to a contest between firms and consumers, a shift in which the consumers were made worse off. Veblen viewed oligopolies as a means of acquiring market power; such power would then be used for the gain of the firm at the expense of consumers.

A second means of mitigating the effects of seller vs. seller competition is monopolistic competition via product differentiation. The traditional view of seller vs. seller competition was grounded in the assumption of interchangeable offerings by the sellers. Hence the presumption is that in seller vs. seller competition, consumers are able play one seller against another in order to obtain the best price for the commodities being offered. However, sellers, particularly under oligopolistic conditions, are able to modify such a situation to better suit their strategic interests. If products have distinguishing characteristics and consumers do not view the set of offerings as being interchangeable, differential preferences may be formed and price sensitivity diminished for the preferred offering. Thus seller vs. consumer orientation is augmented by product differentiation, as avoidance of intensive price competition is a matter of the first importance to the sellers. Through differentiation, sellers may achieve a degree of control over customer actions in the marketplace. Distinguishing properties of certain brands lead customers to prefer one brand over others, thus minimizing direct competition among sellers. When successful, the seller not only establishes a brand preference, but evokes feelings such as trust and connectedness that are typically associated with social interactions. In consumers' minds, the brand becomes "their" brand and price sensitivity is curtailed.

Behavioral economists have shown that individuals are subject to a number of cognitive biases, many of which can be induced by the way in which information is presented. Advertising and promotion are primary means through which sellers influence consumer perception. Hanson and Kysar (1999a, 1999b) argue that sellers are invariably driven by market pressures to manipulate consumer perceptions. That is, sellers do this in order to survive in a market in which other sellers exercise this capability.

The phenomenon now known as *brand loyalty* was originally termed *brand habit* by Chamberlin ([1933]1962), emphasizing the possibility of unreflective purchasing and routinization of differential preference. "More and more is price competition evaded by turning the buyer's attention towards a trademark, or by competing on the basis of quality or service," (Chamberlin [1933]1962: 73). Somewhat earlier, in *Absentee Ownership*, Veblen ([1923]1964) noted basic changes in sellers' *modus operandi* that shifted emphasis toward marketing tools such as branding and advertising. In other words, it was observable from the 1920s that a shift from horizontal competition to vertical competition was in progress. The success of this strategy resulted in an increasing concentration of market power on the part of sellers. The exercise of these market powers resulted in higher prices and profits, along with barriers to entry (Minsky

[1986]2008). However, it should be noted that differentiation is also a strategy for overcoming barriers and that credible potential entrants can limit pricing power (Andrews 1964; Andrews and Brunner 1975; Baumol, Panzar, and Willig 1982).

Brand loyalty is repetitive behavior that is rooted in consumer information processing or, more precisely, in the difficulty of coping with too much or too little information. Gathering and processing complete information on all product alternatives is costly in terms of both time and mental effort. Consequently, consumers reduce the task by relying on partial information such as aspirational or target levels of selected product attributes (Earl and Wakeley 2010). Another strategy is to distinguish between products whose quality characteristics can be evaluated before purchase (search goods) and those for which quality evaluations are best made by trial (experience goods). The distinction has implications for market structure: markets tend to be more highly concentrated for experience goods (Nelson 1970). For some products, known as credence goods, quality cannot be adequately assessed even after purchase (Darby and Karni 1973). These tend to be services of a technical nature, such as legal or medical or certain types of repair work. Information overload is also a problem for consumers in certain technical services markets, such cell phone contracts. However, market institutions help to transmit information, including information on quality levels (Hodgson 1988). In all cases, reliance on a trusted brand name as an indicator of quality greatly simplifies information processing and reduces perceived risk.

Taken together, fewer competitors and product differentiation create a powerful and effective antidote to the price pressures present in markets characterized by a strict seller vs. seller regime. Chamberlin ([1933]1962) noted that the combination of oligopoly and product differentiation allows for considerable latitude in avoiding price competition. These properties are characteristic of many markets in developed economies, as well as elsewhere, and can be viewed as resulting from sellers' strategic decisions in pursuit of their interests. That is, sellers are able to exercise some degree of control over the type of competition in which they engage. In this mode, sellers become price-makers and consumers become price-takers (Scitovsky 1951, 1986). Non-price competition involves the power to increase profits, but also carries certain benefits for consumers, such as increased variety, availability, and convenience.

Facets of Vertical Competition

The processes that Veblen and Chamberlin noted continue to the present time. Movement away from seller vs. seller toward seller vs. consumer competition is a highly significant development in markets and market behavior, and has been discussed by researchers from at least three different viewpoints. One is focused at the level of markets. Analyzing the phenomenon he termed *domesticated markets*, Arndt saw a widespread pattern of seller vs. seller competition becoming restricted and attenuated by a variety of agreements and understandings among competitors: "the competitive, open market is in the process of being tamed, regulated and closed" (Arndt 1979: 69). Previous researchers tended to look at one means of suppressing competition, such as oligopolies, in isolation from other mechanisms that had a similar effect. In contrast, Arndt (1979) argued that horizontal integration, vertical integration, joint ventures, joint marketing contracts, joint distribution, and labor-management agreements were all stratagems aimed at the same goal: control of the market by the sellers.

Galbraith (1969) was concerned about the social effects of modern marketing techniques. Oligopoly eased downward pressure on prices, while advertising raised demand in a process of creating "synthetic desire." Galbraith did not regard the added production to satisfy these newly stimulated demands as constituting an increase in consumer welfare. Indeed, he was quite skeptical about the effects of monopolistic competition: "But who could be sure that a blending of competition and monopoly would be benign? Would not such oddly assorted parents produce a misshapen progeny?" (Galbraith 1969: 42). The affluent society was, perhaps, not well served by the abundance of its material wealth.

A third way of looking at the situation is from the perspective of the firms that created these changes in the market. The notion of "conception of control" represents beliefs, shared among top executives and board members, about how corporations should be oriented

(Fligstein 1990). Conceptions of control reflect critical contingencies for firms in various industries that are originated by a few innovative firms and later copied by others. The manufacturing conception of control arose out of conditions that included fierce price competition (that is, sharp seller vs. seller competition) in the latter part of the 19th century. The manufacturing conception emphasized the attainment and maintenance of oligopolistic market structures, generally through vertical and horizontal integration. This became widespread in the early 20th century. Starting in the 1920s, firms began switching to a new orientation: the sales and marketing conception of control. The focus here was stimulation of demand through product differentiation and advertising. The adoption of oligopolistic structures and monopolistic competition strategies are seen to be successive adjustments to the most pressing corporate issues of the day (Fligstein 1990).

In general, markets characterized by oligopoly and monopolistic competition raise serious concerns about the status of consumer sovereignty. The situation is exacerbated by consumers' failure to search out alternative suppliers or to switch suppliers (Waterson 2003). In addition, such failures can act as a barrier to new competitive entry. Advertising and other persuasive tactics by marketers undermine sovereignty. That is, consumers lose the objective mental stance that lets them play one seller against another. The persuasiveness of marketers is thought to affect some consumers more than others (Redmond 2000).

Vertical Outcomes

If many markets are characterized by a competition between sellers and consumers, it is reasonable to inquire as to who is winning. Indicators are indirect, and somewhat mixed. One indicator is consumer demand for non-brands: it is clear that the demand for private label products has grown and is substantial. This indicates that a portion of consumers is able to resist the lure of heavy promotion and focus on price when making market choices. Retailers have done much to increase the appeal of house brands vis-à-vis national brands. Demand for private labels is highly variable by category, indicating consumers do not find them uniformly appealing. The global market share for private label aluminum foil, for example, is 49 percent while that for baby food is 1 percent (Nielsen 2005). The median share of private label products in 80 categories is 13 percent, indicating that the majority of consumers find the advertised national brands more appealing than private labels.

From the seller's perspective, the point of seller vs. consumer competition is not simply sales, but sales and profits. A rough proxy for success in this endeavor may be found in the calculation of the financial worth of individual brands. This indicates the brand's value as a profit-making asset, and is known as brand equity. In the conventional view of seller vs. seller competition, brand equity would necessarily be nil. The increasing emphasis on brand equity at many firms is an indicator of the strategic importance of success in the seller vs. consumer contest. Estimates of brand equity for the top 100 brands worldwide in 2009 range from $3 billion to $68 billion, with a median of $7 billion (Interbrand 2010). That marketers can develop this level of equity in their brands indicates a considerable measure of success in the seller vs. consumer contest. It may also be seen as a rough indicator of the magnitude of consumer vs. consumer competition.

Horizontal Competition, Part II

If seller vs. consumer is less commonly found as a mental image of marketplace competition than seller vs. seller, the third mode is even less so. This competitive dynamic involves the set of buyers: consumer vs. consumer competition. This is another form of horizontal competition, symmetrical with the seller vs. seller mode (Swedberg 1994). It is also a recognition that consumers react to one another, as in the case of consumers discriminating against other consumers (for example, Crofton 2003). Here, contestability is among consumers, and the striving involves something that is not in sufficient supply. Consumer vs. consumer competition can arise in two fundamental ways.

One way this can occur is when some marketed item is in limited supply and buyers compete for the available offerings on the market, bidding up the price. Ordinary commodities, if sufficiently scarce, involve contestability to satisfy basic needs. Natural disasters may occasion temporary shortages of supply, and are sometimes accompanied by price gouging. Anti-gouging laws are enacted to protect consumers in such situations. Man-made disasters, such as wars, may also be accompanied by shortages and are usually longer in duration. When this occurs, governments frequently seek to limit the effects of consumer vs. consumer competition via price controls or rationing schemes. Other forms of consumer contestability are considered more or less benign and consequently do not attract governmental intervention. Art auctions and eBay sales are examples of this type of consumer vs. consumer contestability. In art auctions, well-known auction houses and well-known artists act like brands to build trust on the part of bidders (Thompson 2008). Here, the articles in question may be of very limited supply, perhaps even unique, but the higher prices obtained through auction markets are voluntarily paid and not considered harmful.

The second basic way that consumers compete via the marketplace is a competition for social status. Prestige is in limited supply, and the ownership and display of certain marketed objects is a means of competing for status. Such a competition would apply to positional or symbolic goods, that is, goods that are instrumental in signaling an individual's identity (Aspers 2007). Positional goods are those that involve social scarcity and are therefore instrumental in the positional competition to maintain or improve one's social status (Hirsch 1976). Some buyers may see certain brands as highly distinctive and desirable. Indeed, these brands may appear so desirable that the functionality of the product can be a secondary consideration as compared to public display of ownership. Competition for social status is a market-mediated type of contestability. Increasingly sophisticated advertising and marketing techniques are linked to competitive levels of consumption.

Ostentatious display is thought to date back millennia and has been the subject of comment, condemnation, and attempted regulation for centuries (Mason 1998). In *The Theory of the Leisure Class*, Veblen ([1899]1979) examined the role of costly products and symbolic activities in the competition for social status and termed its pursuit conspicuous consumption. Galbraith (1969) also noted the ratchet-like effect of competitive consumption—it is a contest with no end for the competitors. Objects for sale in the marketplace are continuously assessed for their potential to enhance the status evaluations made by others. Context is important for such assessments; visibility, for example, is an obviously salient factor (Frank 2007).

While status is not sold directly in the market, the presence of a market is essential for the requisite widespread recognition of the brand, along with its price and the promotion of its symbolic meanings. In an instrumental sense, consumers use markets to establish meaning and status (Fligstein and Dauter 2007). A Rolex watch would have no status-enhancing value whatever if no one else had ever heard of it. This is competition through the market rather than competition in the market.

Consumer vs. consumer competition exhibits several characteristics usually associated with the neoclassical ideal of pure competition in the seller vs. seller mode. First, the actors are numerous. Second, when viewed as a group they are basically anonymous and interchangeable (a condition that conspicuous consumption is meant to remedy). Third, just as sellers are price-takers, consumers are takers of symbolic meaning. That is, consumers take as given the power of certain objects to confer or enhance social status. The symbols and meanings that are created by firms in seller vs. consumer competition become the coin of the realm in consumer vs. consumer competition.

Social hierarchies have a role in this competitive dynamic: Veblen noted that each class emulates the one above it. Other authors take a somewhat more nuanced perspective and point out that while class is related to occupation and production, status is related to consumption (for example, Weber [1920]1968, Mills 1956). However, Veblen's basic point remains valid: emulation of those higher in the status hierarchy is pervasive and contagious (Shi 1985). Consumer vs. consumer competition of this sort is widespread. There may be a self-reinforcement effect to the extent that some consumers display positional goods in order to join an aspirational group, which improves career prospects, which in turn improves consumption opportunities. However, success in this competition does require some degree of discernment, as choice of an inappropriate item rather sets one back (for example, Parsons 1967).

Lifestyle choices are a form of competing social expression (Bogenhold 2001). Consumer vs. consumer competition need not be as deliberate or self-aware as the seller vs. seller mode: engagement in the contest may be an unreflective habit as often as conscious strategy. Use of specific objects and consumption patterns is related to expressions of taste and participation in lifestyle choices (Zukin and Maguire 2004). Consumption generates the symbolic display that is essential in the competition for status. What Weber ([1920]1968) referred to as "stylization of life" is an integrating principle of consumption that is visible to others and is meant to be distinctive. In this way, consumers attempt to differentiate themselves from other consumers.

Horizontal Outcomes

In *The Overspent American*, Schor (1998) emphasized the competitive nature of status consumption. Using survey data, Schor established a significant association between positional consumption and overspending. In particular, the variables of interest involved an individual's financial status relative to his or her reference group, and that individual's spending/saving pattern. The lower one's income relative to the reference group, the higher one's spending and the lower one's savings. This "keeping up with the Joneses," however, has an interesting mental aspect: few people engaged in it are aware of it.

> American consumers are often not conscious of being motivated by social status and are far more likely to attribute such motives to others than to themselves. We live with high levels of psychological denial about the connection between our buying habits and the social statements they make. (Schor 1998: 19)

Such a phenomenon is not unique in market-oriented psychology. Like brand loyalty, status competition may also become internalized and routinized. Veblen regarded emulation as a largely *unconscious* drive to keep up with standards (Trigg 2001). In a competitive society, competitiveness may become a natural reaction in many spheres of life.

Importantly for the present discussion, this phenomenon helps to explain why consumer vs. consumer competition rarely springs to mind when market competition is discussed. Most of us have self-protective mental blinders on when it comes to status-seeking behaviors. However, the phenomenon of consumer competitiveness is none the less real for that.

The Marketplace

Beliefs about competition tend to be one-dimensional and the assumptions associated with the beliefs often overshadow a realistic evaluation of market outcomes. Realism in the evaluation of markets requires realism in the understanding of market participants. Market participants are social beings, who act and interact in complex ways. The preceding has outlined three modes of competition; these modes are not exclusive of one another but are, at least potentially, simultaneously in operation in a given market. That is, competition is not a one-dimensional phenomenon but is, rather, a complex interaction among and between market actors. This section discusses various aspects of this complex interaction.

As noted above, an individual's perspective on markets is anchored by assumptions, beliefs, and ideologies concerning market behaviors. Thus one may come to see markets in quite narrow and abstracted terms, exemplified by intersecting supply and demand curves. The first question is how to frame a more realistic and complex conceptualization of markets and market competition. Complexity arises from the reality that markets are as much political and cultural institutions as economic (Bowles 1991). The image of the ancient Greek agora has been used to represent the dual economic and social nature of markets (Slater and Tonkiss 2001; Mittelstaedt, Kilbourne, and Mittelstaedt 2006). The market is not an isolated economic arena, but rather is conditioned by and integrated with the civic and social life of the group. Thus the focus is shifted from individual transactions to systems and patterns of exchanges. This view encompasses the meanings of exchanges to the actors who plan, engage in, and interpret them. Consequently, a market can be seen as a nexus of economic, political, cultural, and ideological factors (Beckert 2009).

Integration of these various elements is the essence of markets. Leaders in ancient Athens recognized the need to integrate economic activity with other social activities. The agora is a locus of interdependence. In this sense, market actors should not be viewed as atomistic entities, but rather as being involved in networks of economic and social relationships. Competitive plans and actions do not maximize profits or maximize utilities, which, in any event, are illusory outcomes of a dubious set of assumptions. Rather, competition involves an appreciation by the actors of the possibilities offered in a complex, dynamic, and on-going interaction. Shopping malls well illustrate the nature of the agora as they can, for example, be both the source of a status-enhancing garment and a place to be seen wearing same.

The various actors in the marketplace use markets to attain important interests and goals. As outlined above, firms use markets to achieve sales and profit goals while consumers use markets to reach various consumption goals. Tilman (2007) has characterized Veblen's notion of status rivalry as a sociology of control. Consumers seek control in their sphere of endeavor just as sellers seek control in theirs. Markets are instrumental in the sense that both sellers and buyers use markets as means to ends. The ends are derived from and legitimated by the society and culture in which they are embedded; competition serves to allocate the market-mediated rewards among the various actors.

The relationship between the social sphere and the economic sphere is grounded in the concept of embeddedness (Granovetter 1985). Markets are embedded in a larger social system, which exercises a strong influence on the particular characteristics of markets. The United States, as noted above, can be said to be a relatively competitive society. Competition is valued not just in markets, but in political elections and corporate hiring and promotions, among other areas of life. Economic exchanges in societies that seek to limit or curtail competition generally would be less oriented to competition in markets. As has been noted in the anthropological literature, some groups have established one set of rules for exchanges with in-group members and another, less benign, set of rules for exchanges with out-group members. The present discussion is oriented to societies and economies that emphasize competition.

An Example of Embeddedness and Interactivity

A growing taste for sport utility vehicles (SUVs) first became apparent among the more affluent members of society in the United States. The spreading popularity of SUVs in the United States resulted in widespread adoption, resulting in a large and growing fleet of vehicles with poor fuel efficiency. As more and more consumers bought the vehicles, the original models retained little power to distinguish the buyers, so larger models were subsequently sought by the more affluent. The auto-makers in their turn were motivated to supply larger and more expensive models, and to draw attention through advertising to their model's distinguishing characteristics. Side effects of this escalating cycle of conspicuous consumption and product development include an overconsumption of natural resources and overproduction of pollutants. The former result contributed to increased trade deficits and higher fuel prices, while the latter contributed to environmental degradation. As a negative externality, these effects were felt by non-SUV consumers as well as SUV buyers. In addition to the consumer vs. consumer competition for prestige, a vertical (seller vs. consumer) competition was underway. SUV prices were relatively high and costs low due to the use of existing truck-based components, resulting in a comparatively unsophisticated product. Profits were substantial for the manufacturers who were, first and foremost, the Detroit auto-makers. This was a nice business for the sellers until escalating gasoline prices and the economic downturn sharply curtailed demand. Compounding that loss, the manufacturers who benefitted most from sales of SUVs seem to have lapsed into inattention with respect to the development of more economical and energy-efficient vehicles in their product lines and were thus ill positioned for the shift in demand. The resultant consequences for shareholders, employees, suppliers, and dealers are well known.

Here, consumers' and sellers' responses reflect the highly interrelated and interdependent nature of the marketplace. In this example, conspicuous consumption and product differentiation entered a reciprocal dynamic with significant negative externalities. Not all, or perhaps even most, externality examples are of the negative type. Markets for more beneficial goods and services can also be subject to bandwagon effects. The market for solar cells, for example, is growing, prices are falling, and increased use of solar power diverts electricity demand from coal-fired plants. It could become a competition among consumers to appear more eco-friendly than the neighbors.

Discussion

Taken together the three modes of competition outlined above make for a more complex perspective on markets. The industrial organization literature addresses structural conditions that deviate from pure competition, and therefore represents a more complex and realistic picture. Much of that learning is applicable to the present article, since IO studies find conditions of oligopoly and monopolistic competition to be commonplace. Industrial organization studies are frequently conducted under the structure-conduct-performance rubric. The present article, however, contemplates an additional element of structure in the form of consumer interactions. This section outlines some implications for performance.

Markets are populated by real people, whether in their roles as sellers or consumers, who are actuated by real interests. Since these interests are varied, markets are correspondingly a nexus of varied interactions among the participants. The market is used by its various participants in an instrumental way; that is, as a means to an end. This is obvious in the sense that sellers seek revenues in the market while consumers seek products and services. This provisioning function is clearly a socially beneficial activity. Firms may compete by developing innovative products or by creating logistical efficiencies and these too are socially beneficial. On the other hand, competition based on superficial styling changes and planned obsolescence is questionable from a social standpoint. Status rivalry via the market is not a clearly beneficial activity.

Regulation

While laws affecting market conduct apply to all firms, certain types of legislation were designed to correct particular types of competition problems. As noted above, seller vs. seller competition is affected by legislation dealing with anti-trust and price fixing. Also as noted above, some forms of consumer vs. consumer competition are affected by anti-gouging laws. In both cases, the object of regulation is pricing and the intent is to hold prices down for consumers. In other words, both modes of horizontal competition attract regulatory attention with respect to pricing. With vertical competition, however, governmental interest is drawn to information. Truth-in-advertising laws, for instance, address information asymmetries between sellers and consumers.

The existence of regulatory remedies means that these are all examples of market failures: both horizontal modes involve imperfect competition, while the vertical mode involves imperfect information. One inference that might be drawn is that the horizontal modes of competition are fundamentally different from the vertical in the sense that they are subject to different market failure symptoms and thus elicit different types of remedies. In the seller vs. seller mode, regulations promote active competition and the resulting prices are simply assumed to be low. In the vertical mode, prices are contestable and are thus not an important object of regulation. That consumers voluntarily pay higher prices when they are loyal to a brand seems to be of less regulatory concern than the availability of complete information on which to base their choices. Forms of X-inefficiency that affect consumers include limited knowledge of offerings and incomplete specification wants (Earl 2007).

Efforts to restrain consumer vs. consumer competition, as exemplified by sumptuary laws, have long since faded from the scene. Since consumer vs. consumer competition is more nearly of the pure kind, governments have largely lost interest in regulating it. Nevertheless, regulatory approaches to remediating some of the unwelcome side effects of consumer vs. consumer competition are viable. In the instance of SUVs, for example, regulations can reduce pollution and improve safety by requiring improved fuel economy, better rollover protection, and lower collision impact on smaller vehicles.

Simultaneity of Modes

Sellers' preference for the seller vs. consumer mode of competition is grounded in expectations of higher sales and profits through differential preference, brand loyalty, and reduced price sensitivity. Considerable evidence from the industrial organization literature supports a connection between differentiation and higher prices. While some consumers form a preference for a particular brand, others may not. For those who do not, structural conditions closer to seller vs. seller competition may obtain. That is, non-loyal consumers focus on price and do attempt to play one seller against another, as assumed in the seller vs. seller mode. At the same time, those consumers who are brand conscious may engage in consumer vs. consumer competition. In this way a given market may be a mixed regime of both modes of horizontal competitions and vertical competition simultaneously. Since the non-loyal buyers are contestable in a seller vs. seller mode, they may exercise some downward pressure on price levels in the market. The more price-sensitive consumers in a market the more low-price sellers there will be, creating a positive externality for some of the less price-sensitive consumers (Waterson 2003).

Advertising and Competition

Advertising involves the creation (or borrowing) and transmission of cultural meanings (Slater and Tonkiss 2001). Sellers spend billions annually on marketing research in order to understand consumer beliefs and thus more effectively manipulate the market (Hanson and Kysar 1999b). In one form of marketing research, known as "cool hunting," researchers seek to observe the hippest consumers in restaurants and clubs, and make note of their styles and choice of products. Using these data as a basis for styling and advertisement creation, sellers find cultural meanings among elite consumers and recycle them back to the mass market.

Consumers are thought to increasingly rely on symbolic value in making purchasing decisions (Venkatesh, Penaloya, and Firat 2006). The advertisements that are essential to seller vs. consumer competition also serve to make known to a wide audience the salience and meaning of the offerings (Shipman 2004). This effect may be enhanced when the advertisements are situated in a complementary editorial framework (Starr 2004). In this sense, sellers are seen to create symbolic resources and to use markets to convert those symbolic resources into economic resources. In other words, they use the market to exchange meanings for money. Similarly, consumers accumulate economic resources and use markets to convert economic resources into symbolic resources. In this sense, they use the market to exchange money for meanings.

Competition among consumers is not merely a reflection of a materialistic society; it becomes an institutionalized component of such a society (Kilbourne, Dorsch, McDonagh, and Urien 2009). That is, advanced economies encourage and facilitate economic dimensions of competition among individuals. As noted above, sellers seek to bring about a state of seller vs. consumer competition to replace seller vs. seller, for reasons of profitability and stability. Transition from seller vs. seller competition to seller vs. consumer competition requires vastly increased levels of advertising and promotion; these high levels must be maintained indefinitely. There is ample evidence from the industrial organization literature that advertising expenditures by oligopolists exceed levels necessary for informational purposes (Scherer and Ross 1990). While the strategic intent may be barriers to entry, the effect on consumers may be to reinforce a materialistic orientation. When the messages appeal to status considerations, the result is higher levels of social competitiveness (Pollay 1986). Thus, there is a cycle of mutual reinforcement of competitiveness between the seller vs. consumer mode and the consumer vs. consumer mode.

Because it is a voluntary behavior, status competition could be appraised as being beneficial to those so engaged. However, as Veblen pointed out, there are significant social pressures to keep up, so that conspicuous consumption may not be as voluntary as it might appear: "In the rare cases where it occurs, a failure to increase one's visible consumption when the means for an increase are at hand is felt in popular apprehension to call for explanation, and unworthy motives of miserliness are imputed to those who fall short in this respect" ([1899]1979: 103). Indeed, it may represent a treadmill of continuous consumption and wastefulness. It is also a source of self-depreciation for those who compete less successfully.

Conclusion

This article has argued that there are three forms of competition enacted in markets, not just one. In addition to the most general interpretation (seller vs. seller), there are two others of significance (seller vs. consumer and consumer vs. consumer). While seller vs. seller is seen as beneficial for consumers, the other two are less favorably assessed. Seller vs. consumer competition offers product variety. But the seller vs. consumer mode also has been found to result in higher prices for consumers and higher profits for sellers. The consumer vs. consumer mode uses markets in an attempt to distinguish oneself. But the consumer vs. consumer form is also thought to foster envy, covetousness, and wastefulness. Competition, per se, is not inherently good or inherently bad: to view it as only one or the other is ideological rather than pragmatic.

Viewing markets as a type of social system, market participants are seen as being embedded in the larger social system. Further, these actors are seen as using markets to achieve goals derived from that larger system. However, being embedded in a larger social system, the sellers must be attentive to the beliefs and perceptions of others. That the sellers have fostered a seller vs. consumer mode of competition makes for poor publicity, and is likely to generate unwelcome political attention. It thus behooves the sellers to sustain the belief that they are operating in the conventionally expected seller vs. seller fashion. "The riskiness of modern corporate life is, in fact, the harmless conceit of the modern corporate executive, and that is why it is vigorously proclaimed" (Galbraith 1969: 100). To maintain and spread the identification of the concept of competition solely with the seller vs. seller mode seems to be the aim of the CEO as well as the ECON 101 teacher.

References

Andrews, P. W. S. (1964). *On Competition in Economic Theory*. London: Macmillan.
Andrews, P. W. S., and Elisabeth Brunner. (1975). *Studies in Pricing*. London: Macmillan.
Arndt, J. (1979). "Toward a Concept of Domesticated Markets." *Journal of Marketing* 43(Fall): 69–75.
Aspers, P. (2007). "Theory, Reality, and Performativity in Markets." *American Journal of Economics and Sociology* 66(April): 379–398.
Baumol, W., J. Panzar, and R. Willig. (1982). *Contestable Markets and the Theory of Industry Structure*. New York: Harcourt Brace Jovanovich.
Beckert, J. (2009). "The Social Order of Markets." *Theory and Society* 38(May): 245–269.

Bogenhold, D. (2001). "Social Inequality and the Sociology of Life Style." *American Journal of Economics and Sociology* 60(October): 829–847.

Bowles, S. (1991). "What Markets Can—and Cannot—Do." *Challenge* July–August: 11–16.

Burns, A. (1936). *The Decline of Competition: A Study of the Evolution of American Industry.* New York: McGraw-Hill.

Chamberlin, E. ([1933]1962). *The Theory of Monopolistic Competition: A Reorientation of the Theory of Value* (8th edition). Cambridge, MA: Harvard University Press.

Clark, J. M. (1940). "Toward a Concept of Workable Competition." *American Economic Review* 30: 241–256.

Commons, J. ([1934]1961). *Institutional Economics: Its Place in Political Economy.* Madison WI: University of Wisconsin Press.

Crofton, S. (2003). "An Extension on the Traditional Theory of Customer Discrimination: Customers vs Customers." *American Journal of Economics and Sociology* 62(April): 319–343.

Darby, M., and E. Karni. (1973). "Free Competition and the Optimal Amount of Fraud." *Journal of Law and Economics* 16(1): 67–88.

Earl, P. (2007). "Consumer X-Inefficiency and the Problem of Market Regulation." In *Renaissance in Behavioral Economics.* Ed. Roger Frantz. London: Routledge.

Earl, P., and T. Wakeley. (2010). "Economic Perspectives on the Development of Complex Products for Increasingly Demanding Customers." *Research Policy* 39: 1122–1132.

Fligstein, N. (1990). *The Transformation of Corporate Control.* Cambridge, MA: Harvard University Press.

Fligstein, N., and L. Dauter. (2007). "The Sociology of Markets." *Annual Review of Sociology* 33: 105–128.

Frank, R. (2007). "Does Context Matter More for Some Goods Than Others?" *Advances in Austrian Economics* 10: 231–248.

Galbraith, J. K. ([1952]1980). *American Capitalism: The Concept of Countervailing Power.* White Plains, NY: M. E. Sharpe.

——. (1969). *The Affluent Society* (2nd edition). New York: Houghton Mifflin.

Granovetter, M. (1985). "Economic Action and Social Structure: The Problem of Embeddedness." *American Journal of Sociology* 91(November): 481–510.

Hanson, J., and D. Kysar. (1999a). "Taking Behavioralism Seriously: The Problem of Market Manipulation." *New York University Law Review* 74: 101–217.

——. (1999b). "Taking Behavioralism Seriously: Some Evidence of Market Manipulation." *Harvard Law Review* 112: 1422–1569.

Hirsch, F. (1976). *Social Limits to Growth*. Cambridge, MA: Harvard University Press.

Hodgson, G. (1988). *Economics and Institutions*. Philadelphia: University of Pennsylvania Press.

Interbrand (2010). "Best Global Brands List." July 2 (http://www.interbrand.com/best_global_brands.aspx?langid=1000)

Kilbourne, W., M. Dorsch, P. McDonagh, and B. Urien. (2009). "The Institutional Foundations of Materialism in Western Societies." *Journal of Macromarketing* 29(September): 259–278.

Mason, R. (1998). *The Economics of Conspicuous Consumption: Theory and Thought Since 1700*. Cheltenham, UK: Edward Elgar.

Mills, C. W. (1956). *White Collar: The American Middle Classes*. New York: Oxford University Press.

Minsky, H. ([1986]2008). *Stabilizing an Unstable Economy*. New York: McGraw Hill.

Mittelstaedt, J., W. Kilbourne, and R. Mittelstaedt. (2006). "Macromarketing as Agorology: Macromarketing and the Study of the Agora." *Journal of Macromarketing* 26(December): 131–142.

Mukerjee, R. (1942). *The Institutional Theory of Economics*. London: Macmillan.

Nelson, P. (1970). "Information and Consumer Behavior." *Journal of Political Economy* 78(2): 311–329.

Nielsen, A. C. (2005). *The Power of Private Label*.

Parsons, W. (1967). "The Wrong Status Symbol." In *Foundations for a Theory of Consumer Behavior*. Ed. William Tucker. New York: Holt, Rinehart and Winston, 81–87.

Pollay, R. (1986). "The Distorted Mirror: Reflections on the Unintended Consequences of Advertising." *Journal of Marketing* 50(April): 18–36.

Redmond, W. (2000). "Consumer Rationality and Consumer Sovereignty." *Review of Social Economy* 58(June): 177–196.

Scherer, F. M. (1980). *Industrial Market Structure and Economic Performance* (2nd edition). Boston: Houghton Mifflin.

Scherer, F. M., and David Ross. (1990). *Industrial Market Structure and Economic Performance* (3rd edition). Boston: Houghton Mifflin.

Schor, J. (1998). *The Overspent American*. New York: Basic Books.

Scitovsky, T. (1951). *Welfare and Competition: The Economics of a Fully Employed Economy*. Chicago: Irwin.

——. (1986). *Human Desire and Economic Satisfaction*. New York: New York University Press.

Shi, D. (1985). *The Simple Life: Plain Living and High Thinking in American Culture*. New York: Oxford University Press.

Shipman, A. (2004). "Lauding the Leisure Class: Symbolic Content and Conspicuous Consumption." *Review of Social Economy* 62(September): 277–289.

Slater, D., and F. Tonkiss. (2001). *Market Society: Markets and Modern Social Theory.* Cambridge: Polity Press.

Spillman, L. (1999). "Enriching Exchange: Cultural Dimensions of Markets." *American Journal of Economics and Sociology* 58(October): 1047–1071.

Starr, M. (2004). "Consumption, Identity, and the Sociocultural Constitution of 'Preferences': Reading Women's Magazines." *Review of Social Economy* 62(September): 291–305.

Swedberg, R. (1994). "Markets as Social Structures." In *The Handbook of Economic Sociology.* Eds. N. Smelser and R. Swedberg, pp. 255–282. Princeton, NJ: Princeton University.

Thompson, D. (2008). *The $12 Million Stuffed Shark: The Curious Economics of Contemporary Art.* New York: Palgrave Macmillan.

Tilman, R. (2007). *Thorstein Veblen and the Enrichment of Evolutionary Naturalism.* Columbia, MO: University of Missouri Press.

Trigg, A. (2001). "Veblen, Bourdieu, and Conspicuous Consumption." *Journal of Economic Issues* 35(March): 99–116.

Veblen, T. ([1899]1979). *The Theory of the Leisure Class.* Franklin Center, PA: Franklin Library.

———. ([1904]1965). *The Theory of Business Enterprise.* New York: Augustus Kelley.

———. ([1923]1964). *Absentee Ownership and Business Enterprise in Recent Times.* New York: Kelley.

Venkatesh, A., L. Penaloya, and A. F. Firat. (2006). "The Market as a Sign System and the Logic of the Market." In *The Service-Dominant Logic of Marketing.* Eds. Robert Lusch and Steven Vargo, pp. 251–265. Armonk, NY: M E Sharpe.

Waterson, M. (2003). "The Role Consumers Play in Competition and Competition Policy." *International Journal of Industrial Organization* 21: 129–150.

Weber, M. (1920/1968). *Economy and Society: An Outline of Interpretive Sociology.* New York: Bedminster Press.

Zukin, S., and J. Maguire. (2004). "Consumers and Consumption." *Annual Review of Sociology* 30: 173–197.

Saving Private Business Enterprises

A Heterodox Microeconomic Approach to Market Governance and Market Regulation

By Tae-Hee Jo*

Abstract. This article develops an argument from a heterodox microeconomic perspective that the business enterprise and the state have to control market institutions in order to protect the vested interests of the ruling class. Market governance by the business enterprise and market regulation by the state are in this regard purposeful and necessary actions to save private business enterprises vis-à-vis fundamental instability inherent in the capitalist system.

Introduction

Heterodox economic analyses in various traditions begin with the historical reality of a society and end up with challenging the vested interests and status quo that are inimical to the development of society in a more humanistic and egalitarian manner. In this regard, heterodox economists reject neoclassical qua mainstream economics outright since it propagates manufactured reality (through their theory) in order to protect and reproduce the existing socioeconomic order.

The difference between heterodox economics and mainstream economics is prominent in the account of the instability of capitalism.

---

*Assistant Professor, Economics and Finance Department, SUNY Buffalo State College, 1300 Elmwood Avenue, Buffalo, NY 14222 USA; E-mail address:: taeheejo@gmail.com. Telephone: (716) 878-6933. Tae-Hee Jo is a heterodox microeconomist who has been working on heterodox microfoundations of macroeconomics. An earlier version of the article was presented at the Association for Institutional Thought Annual Conference in conjunction with Western Social Science Association, Reno, NV, USA, April 14–16, 2010. Tae-Hee Jo is grateful to Frederic S. Lee and two anonymous referees for their critical and helpful comments that led to the significant improvement of the article. He also thanks Nicola R. Matthews for editorial assistance. All remaining errors rest with the author.

American Journal of Economics and Sociology, Vol. 72, No. 2 (April 2013).
DOI: 10.1111/ajes.12009
© 2013 American Journal of Economics and Sociology, Inc.

With the antagonistic class relations and evolving social institutions at the heart of their analysis, many heterodox economists view that instability or crisis is driven by the normal activities of the capitalist class and the state that control the social provisioning process in the capitalist system. Therefore, the cause of instability is to be found in the present institutions and social relations, rather than blaming inexplicable shocks as in neoclassical theory (Marx 1990; Veblen 1904, 1964; Baran and Sweezy 1966).

While the instability of the capitalist system as a whole is well analyzed, how such instability is controlled at the microeconomic level is rarely discussed among heterodox economists.[1] With the absence of microeconomic analysis of macroeconomic outcomes it is hard to advance understanding of socioeconomic system that evolves in the course of interaction between social structures and social agency. In order to fill the lacuna between macro-instability and micro-instability, therefore, this article takes a heterodox microeconomic approach to market governance and market regulation as a vantage point.

The article is structured as follows. The concept of instability vis-à-vis increasing dependence on market institutions is examined in the second section. The argument made in this section is that instability is inextricably associated with both economic and social foundations. The following section advances the argument that market governance and market regulation are institutional arrangements deliberately designed to save private business enterprises by stabilizing inherently unstable market institutions. The final section concludes the article.

Increasing Dependence on Market Institutions and the Instability of Capitalism

Financial Instability

Heterodox economists of many colors see that the capitalist economic system is inherently unstable. Perhaps the most widely received concept of instability among heterodox economists is represented by Hyman Minsky's financial instability hypothesis. In brief, Minsky holds that due to volatile entrepreneurial expectations associated with fundamental uncertainty, investment demand and, consequently, effective demand are unstable; such an instability is unavoidable in a decentralized capitalist economy unless the state exercises its political power to stabilize investment (Minsky 1982: vii–viii).

In spite of its relevance to the macroeconomic instability of a capitalist economy, Minsky's hypothesis is weak in explaining microeconomic instability. Such is due largely to underlying assumptions that the capitalist state is benevolent and class-neutral, and that (industrial) enterprises are highly dependent upon the financial sector. Basing the hypothesis on these assumptions, Minsky was not successful in explaining enterprises' strategic internal decision-making mechanisms or their deliberate actions to make favorable market institutions.

Alternatively, drawing upon heterodox theories of the business enterprise and the state, we consider the following to better understand the nature of instability. Firstly, financial instability appears to be only a part of the intrinsic problems found in capitalism. Secondly, the capitalist economic system is unstable as long as the provisioning process is controlled by the private business enterprises and the capitalist state. Thirdly, the state via its political power and the business enterprise via its market power are able to contain economic instability and to maintain the economic system and the social order (Marx 1990; Marx and Engels 1848; Veblen 1904; Baran and Sweezy 1966; Kalecki 1971). This argument can be evidenced by a series of actions undertaken by the coalition between business enterprises and the state, which have contributed to the more unstable debt-dependent economy (see Meyer 1986; Fligstein 1990; Prechel 2000; Soederberg 2010).

Debt-Dependent Monetary Production Economy

The capitalist economic system, especially the U.S. economy, is highly debt-dependent. Demand is financed and driven largely by debts that are to be paid back at a specified point in time. Such an economy is inherently unstable owing to fluctuations in cash flows. Debts are therefore either productive or destructive for private individual agents and for the economy as a whole.

In the debt-dependent monetary production economy[2] in which households, business enterprises, and the state are organically connected, increasing indebtedness of business enterprises leads not only to the increase in business instability (Kalecki 1971: 105–109), but also to the increase in household instability since the latter is dependent upon the former through the employment-wage relationship. Furthermore, households' dependence on the business enterprise and the market institutions has been amplified by four notable factors: privatization, financialization, deregulation, and the "scaled-back welfare system."[3] Tracing the historical changes in the institutional arrangements in the United States, one would easily observe that those factors interact with each other on the basis of the interests of the business enterprise and the state.

For instance, since the 1960s pension and mutual funds contributed by U.S. households and their share of corporate stocks (0.3 percent in 1945 and 24 percent in 1997) have been growing dramatically. Unlike other OECD countries, the majority of U.S. private pension funds are invested in corporate equities (see Figure 1). Another aspect of financialization of the economy is an increasing share of dividends out of corporate profits from 40 percent (1960–1980) to 70 percent (1982–2003) in the United States. Moreover, the Bush II administration (in 2005) privatized Social Security capital by creating the "Voluntary Personal Retirement Account" (The White House 2005; Lazonick and O'Sullivan 2000; Dallery 2009; Soederberg 2010: 23).

What is evident in the above-mentioned trend is that financial innovations (for example, creating new forms of financial instruments and increasing speculations), deregulating financial markets, negative corporation taxation rates (for example, depreciation allowances, tax credits), downscaling welfare programs, and privatizing the management of pension funds have together helped the expansion of private corporations in money terms, not necessarily in real terms. This means that changes in institutional arrangements lend themselves to the growth of business and absentee ownership rather than that of industry and of material welfare of the public (Veblen 1904, 1921, 1964). In particular, the "Voluntary" Personal Retirement Account is not voluntary per se; workers are forced to invest their funds in riskier assets because the state, private employers, and market institutions do not

Figure 1

Allocation of Private Pension Funds (2007)

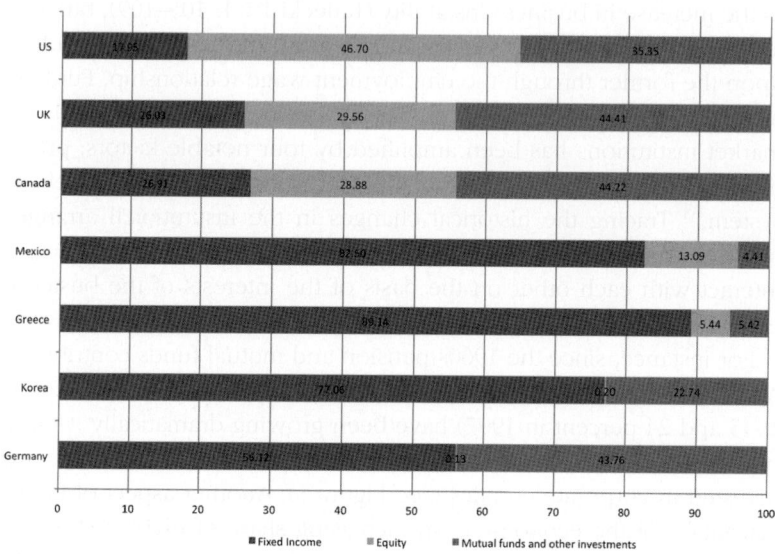

Note: Author's calculations based on OECD Global Pension Statistics (http://www.oecd.org/daf/pensions/gps). All numbers are in percent.

guarantee their well-being after (even before) retirement. Contrary to what state administrators and legislators proclaim, this Account does not "provide ownership and control" for workers. Rather, it is a token of the ownership society that is controlled by the business enterprise and the state through market institutions. Therefore, the increasing dependence of the working-class households on market institutions should be translated into the increasing instability of households as well as the business enterprise. That is, "workers' future lifestyles depend on the profitability of corporate America" (Soederberg 2010: 44) and

> [f]or the first time in US history, the returns to the savings of American households are directly dependent on the sustainability of high yields on corporate stock. What will happen to US consumption, and to the US (and world) economy, if the US stock market should turn down, and stay down? (Lazonick and O'Sullivan 2000: 32)

Saving Private Business Enterprises 193

In a nutshell, the instability of the capitalist economy is not merely a matter of volatile expectations and business investment controlled by private money managers. Instability is inherent to the monetary production economy in an expanded sense that debt-dependent unsustainable economic activities are promoted by the ruling class for the sake of financial gains. Corollary to this, instability has been increased vis-à-vis the market-oriented institutional changes driven by both private business enterprises and the state. As a result, on the one hand, the reproduction of business enterprises and the security of working-class households are not protected or guaranteed under the current institutional set-up. On the other hand, as a response to the serious instability of the capitalist system, dominant actors in the market have exercised their power to stabilize market institutions.

Social Foundations of Instability

Heterodox economists should not be surprised at the argument that instability is produced by the business enterprise and the state. It is clear in Marx (1990) and Marx and Engels (1848) that the class-based capitalist system is its own gravedigger. In a similar vein, Veblen (1904,1921) anticipated that a society dominated by business institutions was prone to disturbances in a chronic manner; Steindl (1952) and Baran and Sweezy (1966) held that normal functioning of the capitalist system (especially, competition between business enterprises) led to a secular stagnation through monopolization and decreasing effective demand. Not to mention, Kalecki noted that

> [a]bove all, we must realize that an increase in the consumption of the working masses is never the basis for a business upswing, but merely its side-effect. The creation of purchasing power for investment purposes always lies at the heart of a business upswing; with a "natural" upswing this additional purchasing power is generated by private entrepreneurs, who build new industrial plants; with a "synthetic" upswing it is generated by the government, which runs public works of one kind or another. (Kalecki 1990: 174)

Keynes and Minsky, for example, would not totally agree with the aforementioned viewpoint. For them, instability arises from volatile entrepreneurial expectations being dependent upon the financial institutions (Crotty 1990). Instability can thus be overcome if "the institutions and interventions that can contain the thrust to financial collapse and deep depression" (Minsky 1982: viii).

Such a viewpoint is not quite congruent with the concept of instability held by more radical heterodox thinkers such as Marx and Veblen. The latter group finds instability more fundamental than capricious investment behaviors. That is, Keynes's and Minsky's instability is basically "financial," whereas Marx's and Veblen's instability is "social" in its nature—that is, social unrest and class conflict underlie the instability of capitalist system.

Central to such a difference is the notion of class and the capitalist state. For Keynes and Minsky, antagonistic class relations virtually have no place in their theory; the capitalist state is viewed as a benevolent administrator who represents the vast majority of the population and whose primary role is reducing uncertainty in economic activities (Hargreaves Heap 1989; Pressman 2006).[4] For Marx and Veblen, albeit differences do exist in details, the capitalist society is in essence viewed through the class relations. Thereby, class conflict is the motor force of socioeconomic changes; and the state, as a capitalist class segment, is an institutional arrangement that represents the vested interests of the ruling class at a given point in time (Marx and Engels 1848; Veblen 1904: 285; Sweezy 1958: 188–192; Dowd 1966: 20–21, 133–134; Waller 2006: 14–15).

When the state is conceived as a benevolent administrator, the primary concern is implementing a "good" policy that would reduce uncertainty, raise employment and income, and improve the welfare of the public. But little is said about the politics of a policy and, more importantly, social foundations upon which a policy is drawn. What this implies is that, without having the concept of antagonistic class relations underlying the capitalist mode of reproduction, it is hardly possible to analyze whose (vested) interests are served. In reality, when the vested interests of the ruling class are promoted, the interests of the ruled class are necessarily sacrificed under the capitalist social structure (Kalecki 1943; Henry 1986; Samuels 1994; Eichner 1987: 702). A good policy, if any, may save capitalism, but it is insufficient to remove fundamental instability that lies at the heart of the capitalist social order. In this regard,

[w]hat is not required for those economists interested in salvaging the economics system, and in redeeming the human misery brought by economic malfunctioning, is a thorough restructuring of theory based, initially, on an objective examination of the underlying economic system itself. For a social science to advance the course of human welfare through correct policy formulation, it must first criticize that which exists. And it must consider the possibilities that observed problems are endemic to the economic system and cannot be eliminated within that system's constraints. To solve social problems may require the elimination of the social order which create them. (Henry 1986: 385)

Given that instability is the outcome of normal functioning of the capitalist system, even wise business decisions and strategic coalitions between enterprises cannot avoid unexpected losses or bankruptcies. Disturbances in the provisioning process have grave repercussions for the entire economic system through interdependence between actors (through social relations) and between industries (through the social system of production and transactions). Obviously, those who are dependent upon business enterprises to access the social provisioning process would have worse effects of such disturbances than those who control the system and determine their own access to the provisioning process. Due to its economy-wide negative impacts, therefore, troubled business enterprises are saved, rather than their wrongdoings punished. Moreover, because of fundamental uncertainty in doing business, enterprises require themselves to be regulated. Otherwise, constantly changing market institutions following emergence, prosperity, and crisis phases do not secure the survival and reproduction of business enterprises (Fligstein 2001: 75–77).

To summarize, what is meant by instability is not merely the irregularity in economic variables. Instead, it is to be perceived as the insecurity in people's lives that results from the normal operation of the capitalist market system. If it is the ruling class that brings about instability and if the interests of the ruling class are served more than any other interests in the society, we must explain how the market system is organized and controlled in the capitalist economic system. This is the issue dealt with in the following section.

Control of Market Institutions by Business Enterprises and the State

A market is a social institution in the sense that it is created and controlled by social agents, and that market activities are legitimized by laws and rules. To ensure the survival and reproduction of agents, a market requires continuous provision of a specific product as well as the rules of exchange and competition. Due to conflicting interests between agents, they must have some sort of power[5] to control themselves and others to achieve their objectives. And it is the agents representing the ruling class who control the markets through the economic, political, and cultural processes (Veblen 1904; Polanyi 1968; Weber 1978: 93; Gruchy 1987: 21; Fligstein 2001; Bourdieu 2005: 81; Swedberg 2005; Lee 2005, 2010).

In support of public interests, some heterodox economists tend to believe that society as a whole is able to achieve "optimal social results" by means of social control of market institutions (see, for example, Miller 1996, 2003). In light of the social foundations delineated above, it should be noted that such a belief falsely assumes 1) a neutralized image of the capitalist state that is willing and able to control private business enterprises in order to protect public interests, and 2) a passive business enterprise that follows the rules set by the state as well as the market. Such a view is an illusion rather than a reality; perhaps as erroneous as the neoclassical view that the Pareto optimal arrangement of resources (including the arrangement of best contracts in new Institutional economics) can be achieved through establishing competitive market institutions. In a structured capitalist society founded on conflicting interests, there is no such thing as the socially optimal outcome.[6] The capitalist society is organized in the way that the vested interests of the ruling class are served most. The primary interest of the capitalist class is making monetary gains as much as possible by, more often than not, destabilizing the economic system, whereas the basic interest of the public is improving welfare (Veblen 1904: 20, 157–158). The history of capitalist society does not show that two contradictory interests can be reconciled harmoniously; rather, the former interests are served, with the help of the state, at the expense of the latter (Fligstein 1990, 2001: 56–59; Prechel 2000). Even social control driven by the state intervention mainly served business interests (Meyer 1986: 67).

If achieving optimal social results is not viable under the capitalist social order, then a more relevant question to be answered is: How is the social provisioning process organized to meet the vested interests of the ruling class? Focusing on the instability inherent in the capitalist market provisioning process, the means of controlling market institutions by the business enterprise and the state, respectively, are delineated in the following section.

Market Governance

In a structurally unstable market, the business enterprise[7] as a going concern has to control itself and surrounding institutions individually and collectively so as to reproduce itself. Such a control takes various forms of actions. Firstly, it involves organizing the internal structure of the enterprise; for example, establishing of a set of rules directing the behaviors of participating actors—managers, owners, and workers—and making of the decision-making process with respect to production, price, finance, and investment, and the like. By doing this, the enterprise is able to stabilize its own business activities. This type of action is commonly called corporate governance (Fligstein 2001: 36, 170; Dixit 2008). Secondly, the business enterprise exercises its market power to control horizontal market transactions. Such an activity or market governance includes, but is not limited to, managing market prices and quantity, organizing the network between competitors, and making market rules (Lee 2005: 35–36; Fligstein 1990).[8]

Conceptualizing corporate control in this way is useful to explain how business enterprises gain access to and control of the social provisioning process and how market institutions are organized and controlled so as to ensure the interest of a dominant agent in the social provisioning process. Indeed, such an approach is blurred by the asocial, apolitical demand-supply framework (Polanyi 1968: 171; Larner 1997: 373).

Corporate control grounded in social agency and social relationship also implies that business activities and corporate structures are in evolution with the response to the changes in the structure of industries, technology, and market institutions. In this context, the optimal choice of inputs and outputs (that is, cost minimization and profit maximization given resource constraints) has no meaning; instead, only strategic and deliberate actions are taken to achieve goals specific to individual enterprises. Even strategic actions do not always lead to intended outcomes on account of changing institutions and behaviors of other agents. That the corporate enterprise involves various relationships with owners, managers, workers, the state, and communities implies that CG (corporate governance) and MG (market governance) are social, economic, and political processes taking place in a specific market, industry, and community.[9]

Instability and Market Governance

From a heterodox economic perspective, fundamental instability vis-à-vis fundamental uncertainty is a matter of fact that figures in every aspect of business activities. That business activities are double-edged (that is, resulting in both monetary gains and instability) implies that business enterprises require CG, MG, and MR (market regulation) in order to protect profitability and reproducibility. In addition, the nexus of privatization–financialization–deregulation has contributed to the increasing instability (Glyn 2006; Dallery 2009; Orhangazi 2009; Wray 2009; Soederberg 2010). In this context, what is relevant to the present discussion is how the corporate enterprise manages itself and market institutions in order to reduce instability.

At the enterprise level, for instance, holding reserved capacity is to be seen as a means to reduce instability. Reserved capacity refers to unused plant segments with an array of fixed investment goods. To increase or decrease the flow rate of outputs in accordance with changing market demand, the enterprise brings on additional plant segments or closes down already-running plant segments. Such a control of production depends upon a given set of techniques (both production and managerial), various inputs costs,[10] and effective demand (Lee 1986).

However, product prices play no significant role in determining production. Disconnection between production and price implies that product prices are controlled in a different manner. That is, business enterprises strategically set the product price given the normal flow rate of output in order to generate cash flow that is sufficient to cover production costs and to finance a planned investment project. Since every enterprise uses a particular set of material inputs and manpower, a conventional cost accounting system, and a pricing principle, the resulting price for a particular product is not necessarily identical even for those enterprises that produce qualitatively similar goods or services. The reason we observe a common price for similar products in the actual market is due mainly to the implicit or explicit price coordination among those enterprises competing with each other in the same market. Otherwise, frequent price variations lead to ruinous price wars and hence the variations in cash flows. Thus product prices are to be stabilized for the sake of enterprise's survival and expansion, but not necessarily for the sake of consumers.[11] Moreover, price control has nothing to do with market clearing; rather, it is a critical means to reproduce business enterprises operating in historical time (Eichner 1976: 196–200; Lavoie 1992: 141–144; Lee 1998: 227–229; Downward 1999: 7–8). As is now well evidenced, prices are stabilized in such a manner that they are altered only few times per year in most industries (for empirical evidence, see Lee 1998: 210; Blinder et al. 1998: Ch. 5; Fabiani et al. 2007; Melmies 2010).

At the industry level, many visible hands appear in a routine manner. Trade associations, cartels, trusts, and joint-ventures, for example, engage in price fixing, restriction of the supply of goods, collective boycott, restriction of association membership, and the like. Such activities are concerted among the member enterprises in order to attain the target profitability, reduce instability in price, quantity, and profits, and thereby to reproduce themselves (see, for example, Veblen 1921: 45–46; Howe 1972–1973; Prechel 2000: Ch.7).

By establishing such organizations, business enterprises together are able to control the entire market in question, often at the expense of public needs and interests. This is not to simply say that business enterprises restrict the quantity of goods or services they offer in the market, but to say that the means to improve workers' welfare are highly dependent on the decisions made by business enterprises. That is, the well-being, not to mention survival and reproduction, of workers and their households are not guaranteed by the market provisioning process as long as it is controlled by the business enterprises. In this regard, "[b]asically, one class—capitalists—organizes to restrict the economic well-being of the community as a whole in order to advantage itself" (Henry 1990: 178).

Therefore, in terms of social foundations coupled with institutional arrangements driven by the ruling class, the welfare of the working class is in conflict with the profitability and reproducibility of the business enterprise. The stronger control of market institutions by the business enterprise implies the higher (perhaps excessive) profits rates and, thereby ironically, slower capital accumulation and increasing instability of the entire system (Baran and Sweezy 1966; Mott 1992; Cornehls 2004; Dallery 2009).

Market Regulation

Since MG always exists, so does MR. Business enterprises and the state stand side by side under the goal of controlling market institutions so as to stabilize the economic system. It is virtually impossible for the business enterprise alone to secure its profitability and growth; nor is it possible for the state alone to maintain the social order without material and political support from the dominant agent in the society. In this context, the foremost concern of the modern democratic state is to protect the existing social order, property rights, and the vested interests of the ruling class, and then the interests of those being ruled, but only incidentally (Veblen 1904: 286, 1964: 37; O'Hara and Sherman 2004: 979). Ample historical evidence indicates that business enterprises require MR to survive and reproduce themselves (see Prechel 2000; Meyer 1986; Fligstein 1990; Soederberg 2010).

It should also be noted that the degree of interdependence between the business enterprise and the state changes over time. Notably, it is in the period of soaring instability (that is, economic recession and crisis) that the business enterprises' dependence on the state through market regulation increases, since the state's immediate market intervention is critical to the survival of troubled business enterprises; and when the crisis is over and economic prosperity has returned, they agitate to reduce that dependency. Thus, there appears an irrefutable pattern in terms of the interdependence before and after the major economic crises in U.S. history (such as 1907, 1929, 1980–1982, 2008): deregulation before the crisis and (re)gulation after the crisis (Meyer 1986; Prechel 2000; Soederberg 2010). Some notable institutional changes are establishing the Federal Reserve Bank (in 1913) after the panic of 1907, the Glass-Steagall Act of 1933, the creation of the Federal Deposit Insurance Corporation and the New Deal after the crash of 1929, the Economic Recovery Act of 1981 after the severe recession, and the call for "sound regulations" by both the state authority and private business enterprises after the crisis of 2008.

Obviously, those changes in regulatory institutions are geared toward stabilizing the economy by saving private business enterprises that contributed to the outbreak of crises. If market regulations distort private market activities and hence restrict profitability, private business enterprises must resist regulations. If enterprises believe that only market principles would make them and the society as a whole flourishing, they must take whatever consequences of their "free market activities." But that is not the case. Free market is empty rhetoric to obscure the reality. One may argue that capitalist economy is free for those business corporations in the sense that they can freely buy privileged access to the state (Levine 2008: 88). At the same time capitalist economy is not free for the working class in that workers' participation in the social provisioning process depends upon the capitalist class and the state.

Likewise, the theory of market failure and government failure makes no sense. Market institutions are not like broken machines that are to be fixed to run again. Market institutions do not work without market governance and market regulation. Markets fail frequently not because of wrong management, but because of their normal operation. The capitalist state exists because of its essential role of protecting the market system from collapsing. Even state welfare policy is designed to placate class tensions, which is expected to help the capital accumulation of private business enterprises (Meyer 1986: 69; Prechel 2000: 98; Soederberg 2010: 30).

In the face of severe economic recession, we expect that there will be increasing demands for market regulations, especially on financial markets. At the same time, according to our lessons from history, we expect that market regulations will not remove fundamental instability, although they may reduce instability to a certain degree, since most problem makers were saved and potential problem makers are still (and will be) operating and controlling the social provisioning process, and thereby the unstable social order remains intact.

Conclusion

The objective of this article is to develop an argument from a heterodox microeconomic perspective that 1) the instability of capitalism is grounded in social foundations, and that 2) market governance by the business enterprise and market regulation by the state are designed to reduce the fundamental instability and to protect the vested interests of the ruling class.

With regard to the first argument, the widely received notion of instability represented by the Minsky's financial instability appears to be limited to dealing with increasing dependence on market institutions as well as increasing instability driven by the business enterprise. Looking from the social foundations perspective, I argue that what is meant by instability, insofar as heterodox theory is concerned, is not merely the irregularity in economic variables. Rather, instability is to be perceived as the insecurity of people's life that results from the normal operation of the capitalist market system.

By putting the business enterprise in the context of social agency and social relationship, I discussed that profit-seeking and instability-generating business activities require market governance and market regulation in order to protect profitability and reproducibility. This argument is supported by deliberate business actions at the enterprise and industry level as well as the state's actions as a response to the instability of the economic system.

In short, market governance and market regulations always exist, regardless of market failure or government failure. Especially, the interdependence between the business enterprise and the state changes through business cycles. During depressions, recessions, and crises, the business enterprise and the state together exercise their power to stabilize the economic system and to protect the existing social order, often at the expense of the interests of the public. Therefore, the so-called optimal social result cannot be attainable through the state or the business enterprise, as long as they are controlling the social provisioning process.

Notes

1. It should be noted that many heterodox economists have made significant contributions to the analysis of the instability of the capitalist system. Regulation theory, for example, extensively examines a set of socioeconomic institutions (including government regulation) that constitute a particular accumulation "regime" in the process of capitalist development. A regime transforms into another regime as a result of changing institutional arrangements. Instability thus is structural and endogenous (see Boyer 2008; Chester 2010). The theory of social structure of accumulation (SSA) also provides the salient explanation of structural macro-instability focusing on the class conflicts and competition among capitals (see McDonough 2010; Kotz 1987). The present article differs from those approaches in that active social agency and micro-instability are located at the center of the analysis. Although those approaches are not dealt with, some of relevant arguments by regulation and SSA theorists are incorporated in due course.

2. The theory of monetary production economy, as opposed to real exchange economy in neoclassical economics, is originated from Marx, Veblen, and Keynes and developed by heterodox economists (especially, Post Keynesians). This theory manifests that the access to the money capital is essential for actors to engage in the social provisioning process. Therefore, the monetary production economy is radically different from the neoclassical real exchange economy in which money does not contribute to the production of real goods and services.

3. One may rightly add the liberalization of commodity/financial markets and the flexibilization of labor markets to the causes of increasing instability. These are, however, not dealt with in the present discussion.

4. Indeed, this view of the state differs from the neoclassical view that the state is a natural, neutral, inefficient entity existing outside the economic domain.

5. It should be noted that such a notion of power is nonexistent in the mainstream qua neoclassical theory of markets that assumes that markets are self-adjusting and market participants are equally sovereign.

6. Optimality, or equilibrium, has no meaning in the context of ever-changing historical time. See Robinson (1980) and Hodgson (1994) for a detailed discussion on this point.

7. The focus is put on the corporation due to its dominant economic power that directs and governs the social provisioning process. This point is extensively discussed by Veblen (1904, 1964), Galbraith (1967), and Berle and Means (1968).

8. Merger and acquisition can be considered as both corporate governance and market governance in the sense that it changes the structure of a corporate enterprise either vertically or horizontally and market structure in the case of a horizontal merger and acquisition.

9. Although CG is an important issue to understand how corporate enterprises are managed, MG and MR (market regulation) are stressed in the article since corporate organizational structure is virtually durable and it changes as a reaction to changes in outer institutions. CG thus is discussed in the context of MG and MR with an emphasis on the latter.

10. Input costs are composed of direct inputs costs (material and labor input costs), shop expenses (depreciation, production management and supervision expenses), and enterprise expenses (management and sales expenses) for a production or accounting period.

11. Consumers qua workers may benefit from stable prices if nominal wage incomes constantly increase. Such a benefit, however, can always be taken away since business enterprises are also able to control employment, wage rates, and profit markups (and hence prices). That is, a certain level of price is maintained in a specific market only if the going price enables participating enterprises to generate target cash flows.

References

Baran, P., and P. M. Sweezy. (1966). *Monopoly Capital: An Essay on the American Economic and Social Order.* New York: Monthly Review Press.

Berle, A. A., and G. C. Means. ([1932]1968). *The Modern Corporation and Private Property.* New York: Harcourt, Brace & World, Inc.

Blinder, A. S., E. R. D. Canetti, D. E. Lebow, and J. B. Rudd. (1998). *Asking About Prices: A New Approach to Understanding Price Stickiness.* New York: Russell Sage Foundation.

Bourdieu, P. (2005). "Principles of an Economic Anthropology." In *The Handbook of Economic Sociology.* Eds. N. J. Smelser and R. Swedberg, pp. 75–89. New York: Russell Sage Foundation.

Boyer, R. (2008). "Regulation." In *The New Palgrave Dictionary of Economics,* 2nd edition. Eds. S. N. Durlauf and L. E. Blume. London: Palgrave Macmillan.

Chester, L. (2010). "Actually Existing Markets: The Case of Neoliberal Australia." *Journal of Economics Issues* 44(2): 313–323.

Cornehls, J. V. (2004). "Veblen's Theory of Finance Capitalism and Contemporary Corporate America." *Journal of Economic Issues* 38(1): 29–57.

Crotty, J. R. (1990). "Owner-Manager Conflict and Financial Theories of Investment Instability: A Critical Assessment of Keynes, Tobin, and Minsky." *Journal of Post Keynesian Economics* 12(4): 519–542.

Dallery, T. (2009). "Post-Keynesian Theories of the Firm Under Financialization." *Review of Radical Political Economics* 41(4): 492–515.
Dixit, A. K. (2008). "Economic Governance." In *The New Palgrave Dictionary of Economics*, 2nd edition. Eds. S. N. Durlauf and L. E. Blume. London: Palgrave Macmillan.
Dowd, D. F. (1966). *Thorstein Veblen*. New York: Washington Square Press.
Downward, P. M. (1999). *Pricing Theory in Post Keynesian Economics*. Cheltenham, UK: Edward Elgar.
Eichner, A. S. (1976). *The Megacorp and Oligopoly: Micro Foundations of Macro Dynamics*. Cambridge, UK: Cambridge University Press.
——. (1987). *The Macrodynamics of Advanced Market Economies*. Armonk, NY: M. E. Sharpe.
Fabiani, S., A. Gattulli, and R. Sabbatini. (2007). "The Pricing Behavior of Italian Firms: New Survey Evidence on Price Stickiness." In *Pricing Decisions in the Euro Area: How Firms Set Prices and Why*. Eds. S. Fabiani, C. S. Loupias, F. M. M. Martins, and R. Sabbatini, pp. 110–123. Oxford, UK: Oxford University Press.
Fligstein, N. (1990). *The Transformation of Corporate Control*. Cambridge, MA: Harvard University Press.
——. (2001). *The Architecture of Markets*. Princeton and Oxford: Princeton University Press.
Galbraith, J. K. (1967). *The New Industrial State*. Boston: Houghton Mifflin.
Glyn, A. (2006). *Capitalism Unleashed: Finance Globalization and Welfare*. Oxford: Oxford University Press.
Gruchy, A. G. (1987). *The Reconstruction of Economics: An Analysis of the Fundamentals of Institutional Economics*. New York: Greenwood Press.
Hargreaves Heap, S. P. (1989). "Towards a Post-Keynesian Welfare Economics." *Review of Political Economy* 1(2): 144–162.
Henry, J. F. (1986). "On Economic Theory and the Question of Solvability." *Journal of Post Keynesian Economics* 8(3): 371–386.
——. (1990). *The Making of Neoclassical Economics*. Boston: Unwin Hyman.
Hodgson, G. M. (1994). "Evolution and Optimality." In *The Elgar Companion to Institutional and Evolutionary Economics*. Eds. G. M. Hodgson, W. J. Samuels, and M. R. Tools, pp. 207–212. Aldershot, UK: Edward Elgar.
Howe, M. (1972–1973). "A Study of Trade Association Price Fixing." *Journal of Industrial Economics* 21: 236–256.
Kalecki, M. (1943). "Political Aspects of Full Employment." *Political Quarterly* 4: 322–331.
——. (1971). *Selected Essays on the Dynamics of the Capitalist Economy 1933–1970*. Cambridge, UK: Cambridge University Press.
——. (1990). "The Business Cycle and Welfare." In *Collected Works of Michal Kalecki*, Volume 1. Ed. J. Osiatyński, pp. 174–181. New York: Oxford University Press.

Kotz, D. M. (1987). "Long Waves and Social Structure of Accumulation: A Critique and Reinterpretation." *Review of Radical Political Economics* 19(4): 16–38.

Larner, W. (1997). "The Legacy of the Social: Market Governance and the Consumer." *Economy and Society* 26(3): 373–399.

Lavoie, M. (1992). *Foundations of Post-Keynesian Economic Analysis*. Brookfield: Edward Elgar.

Lazonick, W., and M. O'Sullivan. (2000). "Maximizing Shareholder Value: A New Ideology for Corporate Governance." *Economy and Society* 29(1): 13–35.

Lee, F. S. (1986). "Post Keynesian View of Average Direct Costs: A Critical Evaluation of the Theory and the Empirical Evidence." *Journal of Post Keynesian Economics* 8(3): 400–424.

——. (1998). *Post Keynesian Price Theory*. Cambridge, UK: Cambridge University Press.

——. (2005). "Teaching Heterodox Microeconomics." *Post-Autistic Economics Review* 31: 26–39

——. (2010). "Alfred Eichner's Missing 'Complete Model': A Heterodox Micro-Macro Model of a Monetary Production Economy." In *Money and Macrodynamics: Alfred Eichner and Post-Keynesian Economics*. Eds. M. Lavoie, L.-P. Rochon, and M. Seccareccia, pp. 22–42. Armonk, NY: M.E. Sharpe.

Levine, D. P. (2008). *Welfare, Right, and the State*. London: Routledge.

Marx, K. (1990). *Capital: A Critique of Political Economy*, Volume II. New York: Penguin Books.

Marx, K., and F. Engels. (1848). "Manifesto of the Communist Party." Marx & Engels Internet Archive. Available at http://marxists.org/archive/marx/works/1848/communist-manifesto

McDonough, T. (2010). "The State of the Art of Social Structure of Accumulation Theory." In *Contemporary Capitalism and its Crises*. Eds. T. McDonough, M. Reich, and D. M. Kotz, pp. 23–44. Cambridge, UK: Cambridge University Press.

Melmies, J. (2010). "New-Keynesians Versus Post-Keynesians on the Theory of Prices." *Journal of Post Keynesian Economics* 32(3): 445–466.

Meyer, P. B. (1986). "The Corporate Person and Social Control: Responding to Deregulation." *Review of Radical Political Economics* 18(3): 65–84.

Miller, E. S. (1996). "Economic Regulation and New Technology in the Telecommunications Industry." *Journal of Economic Issues* 30(3): 719–733.

——. (2003). "Evolution and Statis: The Institutional Economics of David Hamilton." *Journal of Economic Issues* 37(1): 51–63.

Minsky, H. P. (1982). *Can "It" Happen Again?: Essays on Instability and Finance*. Armonk, NY: M. E. Sharpe.

———. (1986). *Stabilizing an Unstable Economy.* New Haven, CT: Yale University Press.

Mott, T. (1992). "In What Sense Does Monopoly Capital Require Monopoly? An Essay on the Contribution of Kalecki and Steindl." In *The Economic Surplus in Advanced Economies.* Ed. J. B. Davis, pp. 114–129. Aldershot, UK: Edward Elgar.

O'Hara, P. A., and H. J. Sherman. (2004). "Veblen and Sweezy on Monopoly Capital, Crises, Conflict, and the State." *Journal of Economic Issues* 38(4): 969–987.

Orhangazi, Ö. (2009). *Financialization and the US Economy.* Northampton, MA: Edward Elgar.

Polanyi, K. (1968). "The Economy as Instituted Process." In *Primitive, Archaic and Modern Economies: Essays of Karl Polanyi.* Ed. G. Dalton, pp. 139–174. Garden City, NY: Doubleday Anchor.

Prechel, H. (2000). *Big Business and the State: Historical Transactions and Corporate Transformation, 1880s–1990s.* Albany, NY: State University of New York Press.

Pressman, S. (2006). "A Post Keynesian Theory of the State." In *Alternative Theories of the State*, pp. 113–138. New York: Palgrave Macmillan.

Robinson, J. V. (1980). "History Versus Equilibrium." In *Collected Economic Papers*, Volume V, pp. 49–58. Cambridge, MA: MIT Press.

Samuels, W. J. (1994). "On Macroeconomic Politics." *Journal of Post Keynesian Economics* 16(4): 661–671.

Soederberg, S. (2010). *Corporate Power and Ownership in Contemporary Capitalism: The Politics of Resistance and Domination.* London and New York: Routledge.

Steindl, J. (1952). *Maturity and Stagnation in American Capitalism*, 2nd edition. Oxford: Basil Blackwell.

Swedberg, R. (2005). "Markets in Society." In *The Handbook of Economic Sociology*, 2nd edition. Eds. N. J. Smelser and R. Swedberg, pp. 233–253. New York: Russell Sage Foundation.

Sweezy, P. M. (1958). "Veblen on American Capitalism." In *Thorstein Veblen: A Critical Reappraisal.* Ed. D. Dowd, pp. 177–197. Ithaca, NY: Cornell University Press.

The White House (2005). "Personal Retirement Account." Available at http://georgewbush-whitehouse.archives.gov/infocus/social-security/200501/socialsecurity3.pdf

Veblen, T. B. (1904). *The Theory of Business Enterprise.* New York: Charles Scribner's Sons.

———. (1921). *The Engineers and the Price System.* New York: Viking Press.

———. ([1923]1964). *Absentee Ownership and Business Enterprise in Recent Times: The Case of America.* New York: Sentry Press.

Waller, W. (2006). "The Pragmatic State: Institutionalist Perspectives on the State." In *Alternative Theories of the State*. Ed. S. Pressman, pp. 13–33. New York: Palgrave Macmillan.

Weber, M. ([1922]1978). *Economy and Society: An Outline of Interpretive Sociology*. Eds. G. Roth and C. Wittich. Berkeley: University of California Press.

Wray, L. R. (2009). "The Rise and Fall of Money Manager Capitalism: A Minskyan Approach." *Cambridge Journal of Economics* 33: 807–828.

Market Cycles: Bicycles, Riders, Industries, and Environments in France and the United States, 1865–1914

By THOMAS BURR*

ABSTRACT. Issues of supply and demand are basic to markets, but economic sociologists ignore consumers, while sociologists of consumption rarely treat consumption as demand. I conceptualize markets as cyclic interactions of producers and consumers around a product, each group embedded in different types of macrosocial patterns, with different purposes and structures. I apply this conceptualization to the French and U.S. bicycle markets from 1865 to 1914. The model helps explain differing market trajectories in these cases.

Introduction

Economists and sociologists usually ignore how supply and demand interact in markets, instead analyzing markets either as collections of producers or of consumers. Furthermore, purchase and use among consumers is often studied separately, although use drives purchase. This fragmentation limits our understanding of consumer markets. In this article I conceptualize a market as the ongoing interaction between producers and consumers about a product. They interact within macrosocial institutions and macroeconomic performance. Differing national institutions and performance influence market actors' choices; these choices, and the resulting market interaction, lead to different product markets in different countries.

The article comprises four sections. First, I argue that economists and sociologists mostly have one-sided models of markets, but need two-sided models. Second, I conceptualize consumer product markets institutionally. The third and largest section illustrates the conceptualization by comparing the early American and French bicycle markets. They were similar in their early years (1875–1892), but

*Sociology and Anthropology, Illinois State University; E-mail address: tburr@ilstu.edu

increasingly dissimilar during and after the "golden age" of cycling in the 1890s. Market-level and macrosocial factors interacted to create these similar, then different, market trajectories. Finally, I discuss the wider applicability of this conceptualization of markets.

Markets: One Side or Two?

Many definitions of markets exist, but most empirical work examines markets as industries or as consumers, thus omitting factors that affect market outcomes. Attempts to relate producers to consumers rarely discuss them as markets, but provide ways to conceptualize markets as such interactions.

Although economists complain about how little they examine markets as institutions (Callon 1998; Hodgson 1988), they have developed many definitions of markets (Callon 1998; Hodgson 1988; Liljenberg 2005; Rosenbaum 2000). All define markets minimally as sellers and buyers and an institutional structure facilitating exchange. Relations between buyers and sellers take many forms, producing many typologies. Some define markets by structure—the number and size of market actors (Swedberg 1994). Some define markets by product, including supplier and consumer markets (Hamilton, Senauer, and Petrovic 2011), labor markets (Granovetter 1973), and financial markets (Baker 1984). Finally, some define them by geographic size—small marketplaces or national and international markets (Rosenbaum 2000).

In economics, one-sided markets are common. For instance, while "market structure" implies the number and size of both buyers and sellers, in practice scholars treat it as industry structure, or the structure of producers (Sawyer 1999: 687; Swedberg 1994). The economics of consumption are generally separate from industry studies (Fine and Leopold 1993; Pietrykowski 2009). Also, with few exceptions (see Lancaster 1966), economists ignore how people use products, focusing exclusively on purchase, despite use driving purchase (Pietrykowski 2009).

One-sided markets are also common in sociology. Using market structure concepts (Swedberg 1994), White (1981) defines a market as a set of networked, competing firms, attending to each other, not to consumers. Other sociologists follow White, mentioning but not examining consumers (Fligstein 2001; Burt 1988). Economic sociologists acknowledge that consumers are under-researched (Zelizer 2005). In contrast to consumption economists, consumption sociologists only occasionally study purchase (DiMaggio and Louch 1998), mostly showing how people use goods and services materially and symbolically to define group membership. Such memberships are usually rooted in social class (Bourdieu 1984; Holt 1998), gender (Auslander 1996), race or ethnicity, or age (Bryson 1996).

Scholars also address institutional environments of markets, or market economies as institutional systems, again in one-sided ways. "Varieties of capitalism" scholars in sociology, political science, and economics (Streeck 2011) examine how national economies vary institutionally, mostly analyzing production. Economists and political scientists pay explicit attention to issues of economic growth and institutional patterns (Hall and Soskice 2001), but sociologists rarely address institutions and economic growth (though see Evans and Rausch 1999).

Systemic accounts of consumers are relatively old, but rarely related to production. Veblen (1953) and Simmel (1971) analyzed patterns of emulation between classes. Bourdieu (1984) examined consumption "regimes," systems of tastes between hierarchically arranged and interacting groups. Taste patterns vary nationally, whether considering use (Bourdieu 1984; Holt 1998) or purchase, even when incomes converge (de Mooij 2004), but comparative studies of consumption are still rare. Pietrykowski (2009) also takes a systemic approach, discussing consumer practices within the "social relations of consumption."

These one-sided market accounts fail to analyze factors that affect either industries or consumers. Producers need revenue, and thus buyers of their goods and services, while buyers need products. Other scholars recognize this interdependence, developing accounts of interactions between producers and consumers, but rarely treat such interactions as "markets." Marketing scholars are keenly aware of firms' revenue sources—consumers—and study consumer-producer relations closely, but only between individual firms and consumer "segments," not as entire markets (Araujo, Finch, and

Kjellberg 2010; Meldrum and McDonald 2007). Fine and Leopold (1993) examine the interrelation between production, distribution, and consumption as "systems of provision," not as markets. Cowan (1987) and Bijker (1995) examine consumers and producers, but neither analyzes "markets"; Cowan analyzes consumer costs, then producer capabilities, and Bijker interprets product meanings among different groups. Gottdiener (1985) and Johnson ([1986]1987) also posited cycles of producer-consumer relations around the meanings of products.

These separate literatures exhibit two consistent tendencies. First, they analyze interaction between producers and consumers around products over time; this fits with dynamic approaches to market interaction (Langlois and Robertson 1995; Liljenberg 2005). Many historical studies examine such interaction (for example, Fischer 1992; Mintz 1986), but none theorize markets. The "product life-cycle" metaphor of a product market's origin, growth, maturity, and decline is also time-based (Meldrum and McDonald 2007). Second, all accounts acknowledge that producers and consumers have different orientations. Both buyers and sellers in supplier, financial, and labor markets prioritize costs and profits; buyers buy to re-sell goods or to produce salable goods or services. However, "the use of material goods rather than the transaction itself is what matters to most consumers" (Pietrykowski 2009: 4). Although innovative consumers often become producers in early markets (Shah and Tripsas 2007), these markets are usually "fixed-role" markets (Aspers 2007); sellers are profit-oriented, while buyers are use-oriented.

Thus, economists and sociologists have produced many one-sided accounts of markets, and many scholars recognize how incomplete these accounts are, but as yet there is no model of markets as interacting sets of producers and consumers.

Markets as Producers and Consumers: A Conceptual Model

Drawing on the previous discussion, I offer such a conceptualization. I define a consumer market as an ongoing interaction between a set of producers making and selling a product to a set of consumers buying and using it. Product markets exist in socioeconomic environments; individuals and groups are affected by and draw on these environments to structure any market.

Rosenbaum (2000) argues that market definitions are not true or false, but are useful for a purpose. My purpose follows the varieties of capitalism literature: to understand how modern markets operate. They operate within modern economies, defined by states that control bounded territories (Streeck 2011). This produces a variant definition: a national market is an ongoing interaction between producers and consumers across a national state, requiring intermediaries such as wholesalers or retailers (Hamilton, Senauer, and Petrovic 2011).

Socioeconomic environments consist of macrosocial regimes and macroeconomic performance. Regimes are institutional environments for markets. The production-distribution regime includes the state's laws regulating organizational forms and commercial behaviors; the state's institutional support for commerce, including banking and money; common informal organizational patterns, including employment; technology for physically producing and distributing products; and practices for influencing consumers (Fligstein 2001; Hamilton, Senauer, and Petrovic 2011; Meldrum and McDonald 2007; Streeck 2011). The consumption regime includes the hierarchical organization of groups within societies (or states); group tastes and practices in using products, including emulation or avoidance of other groups (Bourdieu 1984; Bryson 1996; Pietrykowski 2009; Simmel 1971; Veblen 1953); patterns of moving products into or out of the regime, or "fashion" (Auslander 1996); forms of consumer organization; and physical conditions of product use. The business cycle, or macroeconomic growth and contraction (Szostak 2009), constitutes the economic environment for markets. Firms change their behaviors to handle profits or losses, and consumers respond to rising or falling incomes.

As Hodgson argues (1988), markets are sets of social institutions that facilitate exchange. However, no single market involves all social institutions. Instead, producers and consumers co-construct markets where the product intersects regimes. They draw on institutions to organize themselves (in, for example, firms or clubs) and the sociotechnical environment—production-distribution technologies and techniques, or social and material conditions of use—constrains their choices.

Market actors have only four basic choices. Producers who make and sell a product may attempt to initiate a market, but only when consumers buy and use it does the market exist. When other firms make and sell it, and other consumers buy and use it, they "enter" the existing market. Once in the market, firms and consumers have three more options (Hirschman 1970). One is market exit—stop making and selling or buying and using. Another is loyalty, or continuing previous behavior. The most variable option is voice: staying in the market, but changing influence flows. Consumers offer feedback to producers, or try to change conditions of use; producers change prices, production quantities, product design, or promotion to influence consumers.

The obvious objection—that consumers are in "the market" only while purchasing, not while using—applies individually but not collectively. Bass (1980) shows that saturation levels of consumer durable sales fall only slightly from their peak, due to replacement over time. Thus, any product user is a latent buyer from forced or chosen replacement. This is even truer for non-durables and services. Product use is therefore part of consumer markets.

Producer and consumer choices create market structures. Analyzing the number and size of firms is traditional (Sawyer 1999), but one can also include product variations by firm. The consumer side is better analyzed as market segments than as individuals (Meldrum and McDonald 2007), either by purchase price, by category of person (gender, race, occupation), or by purpose of use (leisure or utilitarian).

Markets change through a combination of these factors. Firms and consumers choose strategies in response to three basic groups. Non-producers and non-consumers alter production and sales or conditions of use with substitutes or disapproval. Producers compete or cooperate with other producers, and consumers influence each other through imitation and avoidance. Ultimately, producers and consumers influence each other through new offers and feedback.

This conceptualization implies interaction (Liljenberg 2005) in consumer markets; the fundamental dynamic is a back-and-forth between an industry and its consumer base over time. Producers act; consumers respond; producers respond to this response; and so on. This back-and-forth leads to two sociohistorical cycles: the product development cycle and the product life-cycle. Producers' offerings and consumers' feedback shape product design, so markets alternate in cycles of product-oriented "design ferment" and production-process-oriented "dominant design" (Anderson and Tushman 1990), dependent upon learning. Consumers learn about product use during design ferment, and producers learn during periods of dominant (or standardized) designs; product standardization and organizational learning changes inter-firm relations and industry structure (Langlois and Robertson 1995). Sales depend upon entries and exits of producers and consumers over time, and product "lives" or sales histories vary greatly (Meldrum and McDonald 2007).

I illustrate this conceptual model with comparative historical cases. The French and American bicycle markets remained similar from the 1860s through 1892; after 1893 they diverged, and were dissimilar by 1914. Historians argue that consumers shifted purchase and use from bicycles to automobiles in America but not in Europe (Smith 1972). I believe that consumers substituting automobiles for bicycles cannot explain the difference; rather, the intersection of product cycles in bicycle and automobile markets occurred within macrosocial and macroeconomic conditions to reduce bicycle use in America, and increase it in France.

In this study I used comparative historical methods from sociology and history. Systematically comparing two or more cases helps sociologists understand change by analyzing causation. Researchers usually approach cases inductively, applying "a tool-kit of theoretical ideas" to an empirical base (Dobbin 2005: 45; Mahoney and Rueschemeyer 2003). Comparative historical sociologists often examine macrosocial phenomena, using many different specific methods. I used primary sources (contemporary publications and archives), supplemented by secondary sources, carefully "evaluating the reliability and usefulness" of sources (Rampolla 2010: 9), comparing different sources, looking for biases and internal contradictions, and questioning sources' purposes. I conducted most research in Washington, DC, at the Smithsonian Institution and the Library of Congress, and in Paris, France, at the Bibliothèque Nationale de France; I did supplementary research in Minneapolis, Minnesota, Hartford, Connecticut, and Saint-Étienne, France.

French and American Bicycle Markets, 1865–1914

Early Markets, 1867–1875

Bicycles originated in France in the 1860s, and diffused to Britain and America. War nearly destroyed the French market, while the American market disappeared under adverse conditions of use. The English market lasted, fostering product re-design.

National production regimes were changing in the 1860s. France and the United States had been agrarian societies with high transport costs and predominantly local markets; craft production dominated manufactures (Atack 1993; Mathias and Postan 1978). Most distribution was regional or local; only bulk and luxury goods shipped nationally (Blackford and Kerr 1986; Braudel and Labrousse 1976: III). Both countries were shifting to steam-driven factories organized as partnerships or limited liability corporations, and were constructing geographically national markets (Atack 1993; Blackford and Kerr 1986; Mathias and Postan 1978; Price 1981).

Consumption regimes were also changing. Titled French elites had long dominated tastes (Auslander 1996), a tradition continuing through the 19th century (Price 1987; Sorlin 1969). The middle classes still copied noble styles, while urban working classes and peasantry could not afford much imitation (Price 1987). In the United States, southern landowners and northern merchants historically influenced tastes, and middle-class imitation of elites was even stronger (Blumin 1989; Klein and Kantor 1976).

Europeans developed the bicycle over decades. In 1817, a German baron invented a walking machine; the rider straddled a frame over two in-line wheels. This "velocipede" (*velox*, fast, and *pede*, foot) enjoyed brief popularity in Europe and America before 1820, and faded. A French inventor (of disputed identity) attached pedaled cranks to the front wheel in the 1860s (Herlihy 2004). The first producer was so successful that by 1869 over 100 competitors had entered the market, including makers of carriages, toys, and steel products (Herlihy 2004; Firmin-Didot 1867–1870). One possible inventor emigrated to America in 1865, patented the machine, started manufacture, and soon saw competitors. In both markets, makers sold to retailers or directly to consumers. The machines were expensive; only young, upper-middle-class men bought them, mostly for leisure (Herlihy 2004).

Both markets ended quickly. Americans rode indoors in the winter of 1868, but abandoned the machine after riding on wretched American streets and roads in the spring of 1869 and after new legal proscriptions (Dunham 1956; Kron 1887). After the cataclysmic Franco-Prussian War, only a small French market remained.

The English market started in 1869 (sources mentioned "the English," never "the British"). The machines quickly became popular, and manufacturers and racers together modified the design. They expanded the front wheel and reduced the rear one; added solid rubber tires; and used hollow metal frame tubes and tensioned spokes. This new, high-wheeled "bicycle" was faster and more comfortable than the velocipede, but much more unstable (Dunham 1956; Baudry de Saunier 1891); falls and injuries were common. This danger, and customary full-length skirts for women, greatly limited the market (Bijker 1995). Still, by 1875 England had scores of producers, hundreds of retailers, and thousands of riders (Poyer 2003). Manufacturers developed tricycles—pedaled carriages—for women, with two large side wheels and a small central wheel. Pedaled cranks drove a chain, which drove the wheels (Ritchie 1975). Again, consumers were mostly leisure-oriented.

The bicycle's early history had repeated brief, failed markets. In one lasting market, producer-consumer interaction resulted in two new products, the bicycle and tricycle. This enabled new French and American markets.

Market Revival, 1875–1885

These markets revived in the mid-1870s. The tiny French market expanded, and American entrepreneurs started over. By 1885 both markets were numerically small, but geographically national and growing.

By the mid-1870s, state and entrepreneurial efforts to create truly national markets had matured, organizationally and physically, in France and America. Banking systems and fast freight companies complemented new national rail and telegraph systems. Industries continued moving to factory production (Hounshell 1984; Price 1981), the Americans more quickly than the French. Producers competed with each other nationally, replacing wholesale distribution with retail (Blackford and Kerr 1986; Braudel and Labrousse 1976: III; Segal 1995; Strasser 1989). French industrial growth slowed after 1870, while agricultural output declined (Caron 1979). The U.S. economy grew quickly, experiencing short, severe cycles of growth and recession.

Entrepreneurs developed national bicycle markets in these environments. By 1876 only 15 Parisian firms made velocipedes (Firmin-Didot 1873–1879). One, Clément, acquired key patents, and became the leading producer. By 1880, more than 11 English firms exported to France, thanks to proximity and low tariffs (Baudry de Saunier 1891). Two Boston businessmen, Pope and Weston, separately imported bicycles in 1877. Pope bought most bicycle patents, then started manufacturing, becoming the leading producer and licensing competitors. Soon the industry had seven importing firms and three manufacturers (*Bicycling World* May 5, 1882).

These industries responded to their environments. By 1886, Clément built a steam-driven factory (*Sport Vélocipédique* May 21, 1886). Pope started steam-driven production in a sewing machine factory with a firearms tradition (Hounshell 1984). Marketing also used contemporary customs. English, French, and American firms sponsored racing teams, sold to consumers through catalogs, and advertised in consumer cycling magazines. Pope and Weston portrayed bicycles as big improvements over velocipedes (*Bicycling World* April 17, 1880, May 15, 1880). Pope sent out traveling salesmen, a new practice (Burgwardt 1996; Strasser 1989). English firms established wholesale-retail networks, while Clément and Pope distributed nationally through small retailers (Baudry de Saunier 1891; *Bicycling World* June 13, 1884; Clément 1897; Pope 1880; *Sport Vélocipédique* September 15, 1883).

The consumer environment also evolved. The number of large industrialists in both countries kept growing, and intermarried with "old-money" elites (Steele 1998; Tiersten 2001; Klein and Kantor 1976). Both middle classes—professionals, managers, clerks, and bureaucrats—continued imitating elites, and grew as industrialization proceeded. Elites and middle classes comprised less than 20 percent of the population; most people farmed, but many moved to cities for wage work (Blumin 1989; Bruchey 1990; Price 1987; Wright 1995; Spahr 1896).

Price, age, and gender limited these markets. Pope's bicycle prices ranged from $105 to $145, Clément's from $75 to $200 (350 to 1,000 francs). Most American working-class families made under $1,000 a year, equivalent French families even less (Price 1987; Spahr 1896). Therefore, most riders were middle-class men in their 20s and 30s (Kron 1887; *Sport Vélocipédique* June 22, 1882; Baudry de Saunier 1891). Tricycles cost even more, and norms required modest public behavior of women; expense and public disapproval severely limited tricycle purchase (Cott 2000; Kron 1887; McMillan 2000; *Sport Vélocipédique* November 1, 1883). Few riders raced; more commuted; and most rode for leisure (Kron 1887; *Revue Vélocipédique* April 23, 1885). However, elites in both countries disdained bicycles (*Scribner's Monthly* June 1895; *Sport Vélocipédique* December 22, 1883).

French conditions of use were much better than U.S. conditions. Due to state support, French roads were excellent (Price 1981), and the government gave cyclists road rights in 1874 (Baudry de Saunier 1891). American police enforced anti-velocipede laws as the market revived (Dunham 1956), while the comfortable high-wheeler handled bad American roads well.

Consumers organized to ride together and to improve use conditions (Poyer 2003). American clubs formed the national League of American Wheelmen (L.A.W.) in 1880 to fight restrictions and improve roads (Dunham 1956; Mason 1957). Industry leaders worked closely with the League (*Harper's Weekly* June 9, 1883). French clubs combined to form the Union Vélocipédique de France (U.V.F.) in 1881 (Poyer 2003).

The two markets grew over the 1870s and 1880s, but remained small. By 1885 U.S. firms produced 10,000 bicycles (Epperson 2001); many more were imported. French production estimates do not exist, but there were 52 bicycle clubs in 1882 and 80 clubs in 1885 (Poyer 2003; *Revue du Sport Vélocipédique* January 15, 1885).

Design Ferment, 1885–1892

Safety issues limited these markets. English firms offered new designs over the 1880s, which consumers rode and discussed; subsequent purchases provided feedback to producers, a process that developed the modern bicycle. Markets grew, but experienced other limitations.

Producers had many paths for consumer feedback. They read consumer cycling magazines (*Bicycling World* April 8, 1881; *Sport Vélocipédique* June 28, 1884); belonged to clubs and national associations (*Harper's Weekly* June 9, 1883; *Sport Vélocipédique* October 28, 1880); owned retail stores (*American Bicycling Journal* May 11, 1878; Clément 1880); and had traveling salesmen. They knew the high-wheeler was dangerous.

English firms also followed consumers, and responded first. Before 1884, they developed high-wheeled "safety" bicycles; that year they marketed chain-driven bicycles with separate cranks and equal-sized wheels (Bijker 1995). By 1890, French and American consumers had replaced high-wheelers and tricycles with chain-driven safeties (Dunham 1956; Baudry de Saunier 1891). Despite social disapproval, women increasingly rode (*The Wheel* February 15, 1889; *Revue du Sport Vélocipédique* January 3, 1890). This machine was uncomfortable; designers used springs throughout the frame. The development of air-filled, pressurized rubber tires in 1889 helped manufacturers to develop the simple diamond frame we now know (Bijker 1995), which dominated all bicycle markets, and thus produced a "dominant design."

Design changes transformed these markets. Estimated American production grew from 10,000 in 1885 to 54,000 in 1893 (Epperson 2001), plus imports, and the number of French clubs grew from 80 in 1885 to 271 in 1891 (Poyer 2003). Another national consumer association, the Touring-Club de France, formed in 1890. Clément's and Pope's patents expired mid-decade, and firms making sewing machines, firearms, and metal goods entered both industries, as they faced low capital requirements (Hounshell 1984; *Journal des Machines à Coudre* May 31, 1890). In 1885 the U.S. bicycle industry had six large firms and many small ones; by 1891 there were 52 factories and 40 to 50 importers (*Bicycling World* February 20, 1885; *The Wheel* September 4, 1891). In France, over 100 firms produced bicycles by

1891 (*L'Industrie Vélocipédique* Jan-Feb 1891). French production centered in Paris and Saint-Étienne (Vant 1993; Thévin and Houry 1892), while American production concentrated in the Northeast and Midwest. Both countries raised tariffs (*Véloce-Sport* December 3, 1891; Hounshell 1984), and English imports declined (Harrison 1969). Producers created national networks of retailers, established regional wholesalers, and owned branch stores (*Véloce-Sport* April 16, 1891; *The Wheel* February 8, 1889). Trade journals developed in both countries, and a Parisian trade association formed (*Revue du Sport Vélocipédique* May 2, 1890).

Three factors still limited markets. Disapproval of female riding lessened but continued; cyclists remained mostly male. Prices for new bicycles still excluded workers. Finally, only a small proportion of middle-class people owned bicycles. Despite increasing bourgeois power in the Third Republic, nobles retained fashion power (Steele 1998; Wright 1995), and continued ridiculing cyclists (*La Vie Parisienne* August 22, 1891; *Revue du Sport Vélocipédique* August 16, 1889). American elites imitated Parisian fashions, so they also excluded cyclists (Klein and Kantor 1976; *The Wheel* October 5, 1894). Since middle-class imitation continued, markets remained small.

Product re-design involved repeated producer offerings and consumer feedback about use. This interaction developed the modern bicycle, greatly expanding the two markets. Still, price, gender, and tastes limited sales. In the 1890s, tastes changed, and the two markets were transformed.

Popularity, 1893–1898

Sales usually rise after producers settle on a dominant design (Anderson and Tushman 1990) and bicycle sales rose after 1892. Extra-market efforts in France catalyzed this growth, but the two markets grew differently. The French consumer base grew quickly during steady economic growth, and the industry flourished; the U.S. consumer base grew explosively during a severe depression, forcing harsh industry competition.

Outside intervention started the bicycle "craze" (*vélocipédomanie*) of the 1890s. In 1891, a French cycling magazine and France's leading newspaper, *Le Petit Journal*, sponsored inter-city road races, the Bordeaux-Paris and Paris-Brest-Paris, respectively. *La Petit Journal* heavily publicized these spectacles. French bicycle historians credit its coverage with sparking popularity (Durry 1973). In 1892, some nobles and industrialists rode bicycles; many more rode the next season (*Véloce-Sport* July 14, 1892, April 27, 1893). Elite Americans visiting Paris copied the new fashion back home in 1894, just when French middle-class bicycle riding sharply increased (*Revue Mensuelle* Nov 1894; *The Wheel* August 10, 1894). In 1895, American production doubled, and grew rapidly through 1898 (Epperson 2001).

Industries did not start the mania. The number of bicycle ads increased neither in *Le Petit Journal* nor in *Harper's Weekly* before demand spiked. Instead, contemporaries attributed the craze to consumer changes. As one American said, many "who might have hesitated between desire and dread in the uncertainty as to whether it was the proper thing" were reassured by elite riding (*Harper's Weekly* August 17, 1895). People knew that the product was useful ("desire") but worried about social repercussions ("dread"). Once taste leaders legitimated cycling, demand soared.

Many firms entered each industry. By 1898 there were 316 large and 2,500 small American producers (*Bicycling World* May 27, 1898). The French industry also grew three times in the same period (Thévin and Houry 1892–1893, 1897). By 1897, six French companies produced as much as the next 150 did, not counting small producers (*Journal des Machines à Coudre* March 31, 1897). Trade presses and exhibitions flourished, and the American industry formed an association.

However, these industries followed different paths, influenced by production regimes. In this period, French courts increasingly allowed industrial cartels (Kemp 1971). Getting rich and retiring was still prestigious; the pool of potential entrepreneurs was small; and demographic stagnation limited economic growth (Beltran and Griset 1994; Cameron and Freedeman 1983; Levy-Léboyer 1976). In the United States, entrepreneurship was prestigious, failure was not stigmatized, and local elites adopted business-friendly policies (Galambos and Pratt 1988). The federal government formally forbade cartels, but allowed holding companies (Bruchey 1990; Fligstein 1990). American industries were more productive than French ones, but American overproduction, endemic by the 1870s, intensified in the 1890s (Braudel and Labrousse 1976: III; Fligstein 1990).

Macroeconomic performance shaped bicycle industry experience during popularity. It started as the American economy entered a four-year depression and the French economy ended a two-decade depression (Bruchey 1990; Caron 1979). Many American industries suffered severe price competition and decreasing demand (Lamoreaux 1985). The bicycle industry was one of the few experiencing increasing demand, so many existing and new firms entered the industry. Entries and exits matched the macroeconomic pattern of crash, weak recovery, further contraction, and full recovery (Dowell and Swaminathan 2000; Engerman and Gallman 1996). Over-entry led to overproduction (*The Wheel* June 25, 1897), overwhelming normal interfirm coordination (Richardson 1990). The American industry exported the excess—23 percent of production by 1899 (Epperson 2001). French exports remained steady over the decade, while the French industry could not quite meet demand, probably made up by English imports (*Cycle et Automobile Industriels* December 10, 1899; *Journal des Machines à Coudre* February 15, 1898). Competition squeezed American profits, but French profits remained high until 1899, when American imports caused a brief recession (*Cycle et Automobile Industriels* August 13, 1899, August 20, 1899).

Other factors also reduced profits. Once a dominant design appears, firms innovate in the production process (Anderson and Tushman 1990). Overall product standardization helped (Langlois and Robertson 1995), though parts sizes were not yet standardized (*Cycle Age* August 25, 1898; *L'Industrie Vélocipédique* December 9, 1905). Re-using the previous season's tools, previously rare, became common (*The Wheel* December 18, 1896, May 19, 1898; *Journal des Machines à Coudre* February 29, 1896, February 28, 1899). Other process innovations, such as sheet-metal stamping, also reduced costs (Hounshell 1984). In turn, bicycle prices fell. Soon $25 was a typical mid-level price in both countries (*Cycle et Automobile Industriels* September 24, 1899; *Cycle and Automobile Trade Journal* Nov 1903).

In 1893, the two industries prospered. Extra-market intervention led to French taste-leader approval and increasing demand; trans-Atlantic elite imitation diffused the increase. French demand grew in a stable production regime and economic prosperity, and the industry flourished. American demand mushroomed during a depression, leading to massive entry, overproduction, and severe price competition.

Diverging Markets, 1899–1905

These changes initiated a divergence in use and demand. The French bicycle market continued expanding after 1898, but American demand fell drastically. This divergence resulted from differing middle-class responses to elite exit, worker entry, and infrastructural patterns.

French and U.S. middle-class practices diverged after 1900. Leisure cycling disappeared in New York, Washington, DC, Texas, and Minneapolis (*Bicycling World* August 29, 1901; City Engineer [Minneapolis] 1904; *Cycle Age* April 25, 1900; *New York Times* September 13, 1900). Cycling in urban parks vanished (City of Detroit 1898–1904). The League of American Wheelmen lost 94 percent of its 103,000 members from 1898 to 1902 (*Bicycling World* October 23, 1902), and nearly all local clubs disbanded (*Bicycling World* April 27, 1912). The number of French bicycles registrations, however, increased every year from 1893 to 1914 (Ministère de commerce 1914–1915). Commuting and racing both grew (*Revue Mensuelle* April 1908), and the number of cycling clubs increased (Poyer 2003).

Automobile sales did not cause this divergence. While both countries had over a million cyclists, American makers produced only a few thousand automobiles to 1903 (Flink 1975), when only 13,000 French autos were registered (Ministère de commerce 1914–1915). Instead, market changes intersected with consumption regimes to create divergent markets.

First, consumption regimes kept evolving. American middle classes continued close imitation of elites (Matt 2003), while the French middle classes slowly developed independent tastes (Sorlin 1969; Tiersten 2001). Middle-class attitudes toward workers also differed. Local French middle classes faced culturally similar local workers. In 1906, 79.9 percent of people lived in their *département* of birth (Ogden and White 1989). In 1911, only 3.3 percent of the population was foreign (Mathias and Postan 1978). Lower-middle-class people shared tastes with skilled workers (Berlanstein 1984). Conversely, the English Protestant American middle classes faced foreign, often Catholic, workers; over 75 percent of laborers were immigrants or their children (Gutman 1987). Middle-class Americans found immigrants threatening, moved to outer-ring suburbs to avoid them (Monkkonen 1988), and disdained their consumption patterns (Altschuler 1982; Matt 2003).

Second, two market changes occurred. First, *automobilisme* became fashionable among Parisian elites in 1897 and 1898 (*La Vie Parisienne* September 4, 1897). In July 1899, elite Americans returning from Paris introduced the fashion, which spread quickly (*Harper's Weekly* August 19, 1899). Both national elites replaced leisure bicycling with leisure driving (*Cycle Age* January 4, 1900; McShane 1994; *Revue Mensuelle* April 1902). Second, price reductions allowed many workers in both countries to buy bicycles (*Bicycling World* March 28, 1901; *Cycle Age* February 1, 1900; Thompson 1997; Weber 1986).

The two middle classes responded differently to these changes. Many argued American cycling ended due to imitation of elites (*New York Times* March 31, 1902; *Bicycling World* February 24, 1906). In 1904, consumers "satisf[ied] . . . cravings for an 'auto' by patronizing street cars" (City Engineer [Minneapolis] 1904: 461) and middle-class desires for auto ownership increased over the decade (McShane 1994). When urban workers or poor blacks started riding in large numbers, middle-class people quit cycling (*Bicycling World* September 13, 1900, December 25, 1902, March 26, 1904, February 24, 1906; *Cycle Age* November 23, 1899). However, French workers constituted 10 percent of cycling club memberships after 1900, while local elites remained around 20 percent of members (Poyer 2003). French elites commonly fraternized with workers in cycling clubs to control them (Thompson 1997).

Infrastructure intensified these differences. Some argue that the U.S. trolley-building craze in the 1890s ended cycling's popularity (Berto 2006). Although American cities had eight times as many miles of trolley track as French cities (16,645 to 2,601 miles) in 1902 and 1900, respectively (U.S. Census 1910; Ministère du Commerce 1901), American track mileage had to be longer to achieve the same goals. The largest 20 U.S. cities had a combined square area 3.6 times as large as the equivalent area of the largest 20 French cities, and the U.S. population was double the French population (U.S. Census 1910; Ministère de commerce 1885, 1914–1915). French middle classes mostly lived inside cities, while American middle classes increasingly moved to outer-ring suburbs (Monkkonen 1988). Finally, most leisure riding was rural, not urban. In 1891, France had 328,000 miles of paved roads (Price 1981), but the United States had only 154,000 miles in 1904 (*Bicycling World* October 12, 1907) and 2 million miles of dirt (often mud) roads. Per capita, France had almost five times as many miles of paved roads as Americans did. Once bicycles became *déclassé*, American rural infrastructure made bicycle riding even less attractive.

The American use collapse reduced demand drastically, decimating the industry. From 1900 to 1905, the number of bicycle establishments fell by two-thirds; capital invested dropped by 80 percent; wages fell by 75 percent; and the value of sales fell by 83 percent (*Wall Street Journal* March 2, 1907). Most small firms disappeared (*Bicycling World* February 12, 1903), while large firms exited to their home industries (*New York Times* Jan 1903). As mentioned, the French bicycle industry suffered only from American imports. The number of manufacturers around Paris and Saint-Étienne dropped by 20 percent in one year (Thévin and Houry 1898, 1899); after 1900, when American exporting ended, industry expansion resumed (*Cycle et Automobile Industriels* January 27, 1901, May 11, 1902).

A contemporary transformation of the American production regime—the merger movement of 1895–1904 (Lamoreaux 1985)—did not save the bicycle industry. Many firms combined in the American Bicycle Company in 1899 to reduce competition, but the merger saddled the A.B.C. with crushing debt (Epperson 1999). The company sold factories to service it. However, nothing stemmed the demand decline. The A.B.C. failed in 1902 and reorganized under Pope, the former industry leader (*Bicycling World* May 2, 1903).

Bicycle consumers continued the divergence bicycle producers started. Automobile fashionability coincided with expanded working-class riding. In response, almost all middle-class Americans exited the market, but middle-class French cycling increased. Consequently, the French industry grew, while the American industry withered.

Different Markets, 1903–1914

The divergence widened over time. Since French demand kept expanding, continuing the same path was the obvious option for that industry. American firms collectively faced new conditions, and thus a new choice.

Demand increasingly diverged. American bicycle production remained constant through 1914, averaging 300,000 units a year, except during the Panic of 1907 (Epperson 2001), much higher than the 1880s, but small compared to the 1890s. However, steady sales within population expansion meant that per-capita sales declined (U.S. Census 1910). In 1900, French bicycles registrations numbered around a million; in 1914, they were 3.5 million (Ministère de commerce 1914–1915). Since population growth stagnated, per-capita registrations, and therefore sales, were growing.

Thus, the American industry survived; however, the French industry thrived. Over 80 American firms, including parts manufacturers, made bicycles in 1903 (*Cycle and Automobile Trade Journal* Nov 1903). The new industry association stayed active, successfully maintained prices, and even amicably split into two associations (*Bicycling World* August 10, 1907). Department stores and mail-order houses sold most bicycles by 1907, a trend common in American distribution (*Bicycling World* February 15, 1908; Hamilton, Senauer, and Petrovic 2011). One parts manufacturer, New Departure, and the large retailers increasingly controlled the industry (Schwinn 1993), which started to approximate vertical quasi-integration (Blois 1972). In France, however, hundreds of manufacturers made bicycles and parts (*L'Industrie Vélocipédique* Feb 1906; *L'Industrie des Cycles* Feb 1902). Local industry associations remained, growing in number and size, and federated in 1907 (*L'Industrie Vélocipédique* March 16, 1907). Most firms distributed to small, not large, retailers, some of whom assembled bicycles from parts.

The two industries rested upon dissimilar consumer bases. While French track racing declined, road racing became popular (Durry 1973; Poyer 2003). Middle-class and working-class riders both rode for leisure and commuting (*L'Industrie des Cycles* Jan 1907). A new middle-class, multi-day practice developed, called "cyclotourism." American riding became mostly utilitarian, including farmer, working-class, and middle-class commuting; deliveries; and police use. Leisure riding barely existed (*Bicycling World* March 30, 1907, December 14, 1907). Track racing decreased, but continued (*Bicycling World* May 6, 1911).

The industries responded differently to their consumer bases. The American industry became cautious, the French expansive. Speakers at the American industry association meeting of 1907 warned against overproduction and overmarketing, citing the recent crash (*Bicycling World* August 10, 1907). Thus, American advertising languished, while many French firms used road races to advertise (*Bicycling World* February 1, 1908; Thompson 1997). Inventors developed freewheels and coaster brakes by 1900, but American firms made them standard very slowly (*Bicycling World* February 8, 1908); they offered a specifically utilitarian bicycle only in 1909 (Herlihy 2004). French firms responded eagerly to cyclotourist associations' design competitions for multi-speed designs (*L'Industrie des Cycles* Aug 1905).

By being cautious, American firms ignored an opportunity. Trolleys became increasingly unpopular in the United States (McKay 1976), while bicycles were faster, cheaper over time, and more route-flexible (*Bicycling World* March 24, 1906), their only disadvantage being winter weather. Nevertheless, bicycling declined in the United States, but increased in France. Why?

Conditions of use changed for American cyclists, but not for French cyclists. First, American automobile registrations increased quickly after 1910 (McShane 1994), while French driving grew very slowly (Ministère de commerce 1914–1915). Americans had economic advantages—higher productivity, high wages, and cheap gasoline—but institutional differences also mattered; the French taxed gasoline heavily, regulated driving more strictly, and encouraged public transit more (Flink 1975; McShane 1994). American middle classes increasingly moved to distant suburbs (Monkkonen 1988), while the French lived close to their employment. French firms emphasized large, expensive autos while Americans made small, cheap ones.

Second, transportation scholars argue that mixing bicycles and automobiles in traffic endangers cyclists (Stinson and Bhat 2003). In both countries rural cyclists increasingly worried about automobiles (*Revue Mensuelle* Dec 1907; *Bicycling World* November 10, 1906). The problem was worse in American cities. From 1906 to

1910, the number of bicycles in downtown Minneapolis declined, while the number of autos increased. In 1910, finally automobiles outnumbered bicycles; in 1911 bicycle traffic dropped almost two-thirds (City Engineer [Minneapolis] 1906–1911). Automobiles also increasingly endangered New York City cyclists (*Bicycling World* February 4, 1911). Affluent drivers and the automobile industry successfully lobbied for rights on city streets (Dispenza 1995; McShane 1994). Working-class Americans did not organize to lobby, and, unlike in the 1880s, American producers ignored their problems. By 1910, bicycles were disappearing from American cities (McShane 1994). Conversely, French magazines reported increasing urban cycling (*L'Industrie des Cycles* Jan 1907).

By the 1920s, American bicycle production shrank to levels seen in the 1880s (Herlihy 2004). Automobiles may have driven cyclists off American streets anyway, but bicycle industry caution made it inevitable. The French industry, responsive to demand, thrived.

Discussion and Conclusion

Tracing early French and American bicycle markets illustrates this conceptualization of markets. Producers marketed to consumers, helped them on conditions of use, developed new designs, and responded to demand fluctuations. Consumers informed producers about product usability, increasingly entered the market after design improved, and entered more when prices dropped. Also, both groups dealt with socioeconomic environments. Producers made bicycles with available techniques, overproduced when few other products did well, and sometimes avoided pursuing consumers. Gender expectations limited potential consumers, elite opinion limited more of them—until it changed—and inter-class relations eventually led these markets in different directions.

Many results here, such as attention to demand and to prices, are not new. Others, such as institutions limiting demand, varying industrial fortunes in the 1890s, and firms ignoring their customers, are more intriguing. Most importantly, the back-and-forth between the industries and consumers never stopped because the markets and environments changed and both groups had to respond.

Yet most scholars of the economy ignore at least some of these issues. This market conceptualization synthesizes concepts about markets drawn from economic studies of phenomena that are integrated in real life but divided academically. Thus, it contributes to interdisciplinary debates on markets. The main concept—markets as cycles of ongoing interactions between an industry and its base—is not theorized enough (Fine and Leopold 1993; Pietrykowski 2009; Zelizer 2005). This article is a first attempt. Producer-consumer interaction exists in time, and the product life-cycle is a stylized market history, but few accounts inquire how institutions affect sales trajectories. More studies can help scholars better understand consumer markets, and thus understand industries.

While producers have a greater stake—survival—in any market than consumers do (Fligstein 2001: 31), survival clearly rests on consumer expenditures. This implies treating marketing as an institution, a practice now neglected (Araujo, Finch, and Kjellberg 2010). Yet marketing clearly is an institution, one that Callon (1998) argues "performs" economists' ideas. Examining marketing practices—market research and promotion—as institutions, subject to historical and geographic differences, would help us understand markets better.

Most scholars now acknowledge institutional influences on industries, but few economists address sources of consumer preferences, while most sociologists ignore sales. Relating purchase to use in this study means endogenizing preferences (Hodgson 1988). Institutions influencing use clearly influence purchase, and could be studied more. Furthermore, individual studies of consumption regimes (Bourdieu 1984; Holt 1998) and comparisons of national varieties of production (Streeck 2011) together imply the existence of national varieties of capitalist consumption, another under-studied topic.

These cases are limited by product, by historical period, and by geographic setting. Studies of other products, other historical periods, and other countries would tell us more about producer-consumer interaction and national environments. The conceptualization applies only to consumer markets, but still makes possible much new research that could teach us more about markets in general.

References

Altschuler, G. C. (1982). *Race, Ethnicity and Class in American Social Thought, 1865–1919.* Arlington Heights: H. Davidson.

American Bicycling Journal. (1877–1879). Boston.

Anderson, P., and M. L. Tushman. (1990). "Technological Discontinuities and Dominant Designs: A Cyclical Model of Technical Change." *Administrative Science Quarterly* 35: 604–633.

Araujo, L., J. Finch, and H. Kjellberg. (2010). *Reconnecting Marketing to Markets.* New York: Oxford University Press.

Aspers, P. (2007). "Theory, Reality, and Performativity in Markets." *American Journal of Economics and Sociology* 66(2): 379–398.

Atack, J. (1993). "Industrial Structure and the Emergence of the Modern Corporation." In *Historical Perspectives on the American Economy: Selected Readings.* Eds. R. Whaples and D. C. Betts. New York: Cambridge University Press.

Auslander, L. (1996). *Taste and Power: Furnishing Modern France.* Berkeley: University of California Press.

Baker, W. E. (1984). "The Social Structure of a National Securities Market." *American Journal of Sociology* 89(4): 775–811.

Bass, F. (1980) "The Relationship Between Diffusion Rates, Experience Curves, and Demand Elasticities for Consumer Durable Technological Innovations." *Journal of Business* 53: S51–S67.

Baudry de Saunier, L. (1891). *Histoire générale de la vélocipédie.* Paris: Paul Ollendorf.

Beltran, A., and P. Griset. (1994). *L'économie française, 1914–1945.* Paris: A. Colin.

Berlanstein, L. (1984). *The Working People of Paris, 1871–1914.* Baltimore: Johns Hopkins University Press.

Berto, F. (2006). "The Electric Streetcar and the End of the First American Bicycle Boom." *Cycle History 17: Proceedings of the 17th International History Conference.* San Francisco: Cycle Publishing/Van der Plas Publications.

Bicycling World. (1879–1918). Boston, MA: Bicycling World Company.

Bijker, W. (1995). *Of Bicycles, Bakelites, and Bulbs: Toward a Theory of Sociotechnical Change.* Cambridge, MA: MIT Press.

Blackford, M. G., and K. A. Kerr. (1986). *Business Enterprise in American History.* Boston: Houghton Mifflin.

Blois, K. J. (1972). "Vertical Quasi-Integration." *Journal of Industrial Economics* 20(3): 253–272.

Blumin, S. M. (1989). *The Emergence of the Middle Class: Social Experience in the American City, 1760–1900.* New York: Cambridge University Press.

Bourdieu, P. (1984). *Distinction: A Social Critique of the Judgment of Taste.* Trans. Richard Nice. Cambridge: Harvard University Press.

Braudel, F., and E. Labrousse. (1976). *Histoire économique et sociale de la France,* V. II-III. Paris: Presses universitaires de France.

Bruchey, S. (1990). *Enterprise: The Dynamic Economy of a Free People.* Cambridge: Harvard University Press.

Bryson, B. (1996). "'Anything But Heavy Metal': Symbolic Exclusion and Musical Dislikes." *American Sociological Review* 61: 884–899.

Burgwardt, C. (1996). "A Landscape of Early Bicycle History." In *Cycle History 7: Proceedings of the 7th International Cycle History Conference.* Ed. R. van der Plas. Anaheim: Rob van der Plas.

Burt, R. S. (1988). "The Stability of American Markets." *American Journal of Sociology* 94: 356–395.

Callon, M. (1998). "Introduction: The Embeddedness of Economic Markets in Economics." In *The Laws of the Markets.* Ed. M. Callon. Malden, MA: Blackwell/Sociological Review.

Cameron, R., and C. E. Freedeman. (1983). "French Economic Growth: A Radical Revision." *Social Science History* 7: 3–30.

Caron, F. (1979). *An Economic History of Modern France.* New York: Columbia University Press.

City of Detroit. (1898–1908). *Annual Report of the City of Detroit.* Detroit: Thos. Smith Printing.

City Engineer. (1896–1911). *Annual Reports of the Various City Officers of the City of Minneapolis, Minnesota.* Minneapolis: City of Minneapolis.

Clément et Cie. (1880, 1897). Catalog.

Cott, N. F., ed. (2000). *No Small Courage: A History of Women in the United States.* New York: Oxford University Press.

Cowan, R. S. (1987). "The Consumption Junction: A Proposal for Research Strategies in the Sociology of Technology." In *The Social Construction of Technological Systems. New Directions in the Sociology and History of Technology.* Eds. W. E. Bijker, T. P. Hughes, and T. J. Pinch. Cambridge: MIT Press.

Cycle Age and Trade Review. (1897–1901). Chicago: Cycle Age Company.

Cycle and Automobile Trade Journal. (1902–1914). Philadelphia: Chilton.

Cycle et Automombile Industriels. (1897–1903). Paris.

De Mooij, M. (2004). *Consumer Behavior and Culture: Consequences for Global Marketing and Advertising.* Thousand Oaks, California: SAGE.

DiMaggio, P. J., and H. Louch. (1998). "Socially Embedded Consumer Transactions: For What Kinds of Purchases Do People Most Often Use Networks?" *American Sociological Review* 63: 619–637.

Dispenza, M. E. (1995). *"From Elite Social Club to Motoring Service Organization: The Automobile Club of Buffalo, 1900–1920."* Ph.D. dissertation, State University of New York, Buffalo.

Dobbin, F. (2005). "Comparative and Historical Approaches to Economic Sociology." In *Handbook of Economic Sociology*. Eds. N. Smelser and R. Swedberg, pp. 26–48, 2nd edition. Princeton and New York: Princeton University Press and Russell Sage Foundation.

Dowell, G., and A. Swaminathan. (2000). "Racing and Back-Pedaling into the Future: New Product Introduction and Organizational Mortality in the US Bicycle Industry, 1880–1918." *Organization Studies* 2: 405–431.

Dunham, N. L. (1956). "The Bicycle Era in American History." Ph.D. dissertation, Harvard University.

Durry, J. (1973). *La véridique histoire des géants de la route*. [s.l.]: Edita, Denöel.

Engerman, S. L., and R. E. Gallman, eds. (1996). *Cambridge Economic History of the United States. Volume II: The Long Nineteenth Century*. New York: Cambridge University Press.

Epperson, B. (1999). "Failed Colossus: Albert A. Pope and the Pope Manufacturing Company, 1876–1900." In *Cycle History 9: Proceedings of the 9th International Cycle History Conference*. Eds. G. Norcliffe and R. van der Plas. Sausalito, CA: Bicycle Books.

———. (2001). "How Many Bikes? An Inquiry into Bicycle Production." In *Cycle History 11: Proceedings of the 11 International Cycle History Conference*. Eds. A. Ritchie and R. van der Plas. Sausalito, CA: Bicycle Books.

Evans, P., and J. E. Rausch. (1999). "Bureaucracy and Growth: A Cross-National Analysis of the Effects of 'Weberian' State Structures on Economic Growth." *American Sociological Review* 64(5): 748–765.

Fine, B., and E. Leopold. (1993). *The World of Consumption*. London and New York: Routledge.

Firmin-Didot, A. (1857–1908). *Annuaire-almanach du commerce, de l'industrie, de la magistrature et de l'administration*. Paris: Firmin-Didot frères.

Fischer, C. (1992). *America Calling: A Social History of the Telephone to 1940*. Berkeley: University of California Press.

Fligstein, N. (1990). *The Transformation of Corporate Control*. Cambridge, MA: Harvard University Press.

———. (2001). *The Architecture of Markets: An Economic Sociology of Twenty-First-Century Capitalist Societies*. Princeton: Princeton University Press.

Flink, J. J. (1975). *America Adopts the Automobile, 1895–1910*. Cambridge, Massachusetts: MIT Press.

Galambos, L., and J. Pratt. (1988). *The Rise of the Corporate Commonwealth: U.S. Business and Public Policy in the Twentieth Century*. New York: Basic Books.

Gottdiener, M. (1985). "Hegemony and Mass Culture: A Semiotic Approach." *American Journal of Sociology* 90: 979–1001.

Granovetter, M. (1973). *Getting a Job: A Study of Contacts and Careers.* Cambridge, MA: Harvard University Press.

Gutman, H. G. (1987). *Power & Culture: Essays on the American Working Class.* Ed. I. Berlin. New York: Pantheon Books.

Hall, P. A., and D. Soskice. (2001). *Varieties of Capitalism: The Institutional Foundations of Comparative Advantage.* Oxford: Oxford University Press.

Hamilton, G. G., B. Senauer, and M. Petrovic. (2011). *The Market Makers: How Retailers are Reshaping the Global Economy.* New York: Oxford University Press.

Harper's Weekly. (1878–1902). New York: [s.n].

Harrison, A. E. (1969). "The Competitiveness of the British Cycle Industry." *Economic History Review,* new series 22(2): 287–303.

Herlihy, D. (2004). *Bicycle: The History.* New Haven and London: Yale University Press.

Hirschman, A. O. (1970). *Exit, Voice, and Loyalty: Responses to Decline in Firms, Organizations, and States.* Cambridge, MA: Harvard University Press.

Hodgson, G. (1988). *Economics and Institutions: A Manifesto for a Modern Institutional Economics.* Philadelphia: University of Pennsylvania Press.

Holt, D. B. (1998). "Does Cultural Capital Structure American Consumption?" *Journal of Consumer Research* 25(1): 1–25.

Hounshell, D. A. (1984). *From the American System to Mass Production, 1800–1932: The Development of Manufacturing Technology in the United States.* Baltimore and London: Johns Hopkins University Press.

Johnson, R. (1986–1987). "What is Cultural Studies, Anyway?" *Social Text* 16: 38–80.

Journal des Machines à Coudre et Vélocipèdes. (1890–1903) Paris: [s.n.].

Kemp, T. (1971). *Economic Forces in French History.* London: Dennis Dobson.

Klein, M., and H. A. Kantor. (1976). *Prisoners of Progress: American Industrial Cities, 1850–1920.* New York: Macmillan.

Kron, K. (1887). *Ten Thousand Miles on a Bicycle.* New York: Karl Kron (Lyman Hotchkiss Bagg).

L'Industrie des Cycles. (1898–1914). Saint-Étienne: Chambre Syndicale.

L'Industrie Vélocipédique. (1882–1914). Paris: [s.n.].

La Vie Parisienne. (1885–1897). Saint Maur: Vie parisienne magazine.

Lamoreaux, N. R. (1985). *The Great Merger Movement in American Business, 1895–1904.* New York: Cambridge University Press.

Lancaster, K. J. (1966). "A New Approach to Consumer Behavior." *Journal of Political Economy* 74(2): 132–157.

Langlois, R. N., and P. L. Robertson. (1995). *Firms, Markets and Economic Change: A Dynamic Theory of Business Institutions.* London and New York: Routledge.

Levy-Léboyer, M. (1976). "Innovation and Business Strategies in Nineteenth- and Twentieth-Century France." In *Enterprise and Entrepreneurs in*

Nineteenth- and Twentieth-Century France. Eds. E. C. Carter II, R. Forster, and J. N. Moody. Baltimore: Johns Hopkins University Press.

Liljenberg, A. (2005). "A Socio-Dynamic Understanding of Markets: The Progressive Joining Forces of Economic Sociology and Austrian Economics." *American Journal of Economics and Sociology* 64(4): 999–1023.

Mahoney, J., and D. Rueschemeyer. (2003). *Comparative Historical Analysis in the Social Sciences*. Cambridge: Cambridge University Press.

Mason, P. P. (1957). "The League of American Wheelmen and the Good-Roads Movement, 1880–1905." Ph.D. dissertation, University of Michigan

Mathias, P., and Postan, M. M. eds. (1978). *Cambridge Economic History of Europe. Volume VII. The Industrial Economies: Capital, Labor, and Enterprise*. London and New York: Cambridge University Press.

Matt, S. (2003). *Keeping Up with the Joneses: Envy in American Consumer Society, 1890–1930*. Philadelphia: University of Pennsylvania Press.

McKay, J. P. (1976). *Tramways and Trolleys: The Rise of Urban Mass Transport in Europe*. Princeton, NJ: Princeton University Press.

McMillan, J. (2000). *France and Women, 1789–1914: Gender, Society and Politics*. New York: Routledge.

McShane, C. (1994). *Down the Asphalt Path: The Automobile and the American City*. New York: Columbia University Press.

Meldrum, M., and M. McDonald. (2007). *Marketing in a Nutshell: Key Concepts for Non-Specialists*. Burlington, MA: Elsevier.

Ministère du commerce, de l'industrie, des postes et des télégraphes. (1885–1915). *Annuaire statistique de la France*. Paris: Statistique générale.

Mintz, S. (1986). *Sweetness and Power: The Place of Sugar in Modern History*. New York: Viking.

Monkkonen, E. (1988). *America Becomes Urban: The Development of U.S. Cities and Towns, 1780–1980*. Berkeley: University of California Press.

New York Times. (1893–1903). New York: H.J. Raymond & Co.

Ogden, P. E., and P. E. White. (1989). *Migrants in Modern France: Population Mobility in the Late Nineteenth and Twentieth Centuries*. Boston: Unwyn Hyman.

Pietrykowski, B. (2009). *The Political Economy of Consumer Behavior: Contesting Consumption*. London: Routledge.

Pope Mfg. Co. (1880–1899). Catalog. Boston: Pope Mfg. Co.

Poyer, A. (2003). *Les premiers temps de la véloce-clubs: Apparition et diffusion du cyclisme associative français entre 1867et 1914*. Paris: L'Harmattan.

Price, R. (1981). *An Economic History of Modern France, 1730–1914*. London: Macmillan.

———. (1987). *A Social History of Nineteenth-Century France*. London: Hutchinson.

Rampolla, M. L. (2010). *A Pocket Guide to Writing in History*. Boston: St. Martins.

Revue du Sport Vélocipédique. (1886–1890). Paris: [s.n.].
Revue Mensuelle du Touring-Club de France. (1891–1910). Paris: Touring-Club de France.
Revue Vélocipédique. (1882–1886). Troyes: [s.n.].
Richardson, G. B. ([1960]1990). *Information and Investment: A Study in the Working of the Competitive Economy.* Oxford: Clarendon Press.
Ritchie, A. (1975). *King of the Road: An Illustrated History of Cycling.* Berkeley: Ten Speed Press.
Rosenbaum, E. (2000). "What is a Market? On the Methodology of a Contested Concept." *Review of Social Economy* 58(4): 455–482.
Sawyer, M. (1999). "Market Structure." In *Encyclopedia of Political Economy.* London: Routledge.
Schwinn, F. (1993). Frank W. Schwinn's Personal Notes on the Bicycle Industry. Unpublished manuscript. From the archives of the Bicycle Museum of America.
Scribner's Monthly. (1895). New York: Scribner & Company.
Segal, A. J. (1995). "The Republic of Goods: Advertising and National Identity in France, 1875–1914." Ph.D. dissertation, University of California, Los Angeles.
Shah, S., and M. Tripsas. (2007). "The Accidental Entrepreneur: The Emergent and Collective Process of User Entrepreneurship." *Strategic Entrepreneurship Journal* 1(1): 123–140.
Simmel, G. ([1904]1971). *On Individuality and Social Forms: Selected Writings.* Chicago: University of Chicago Press.
Smith, R. (1972). *A Social History of the Bicycle: Its Early Life and Times in America.* New York: American Heritage Press.
Sorlin, P. (1969). *La société française. I: 1840–1914.* Paris: B. Arthaud.
Spahr, C. B. (1896). *An Essay on the Present Distribution of Wealth in the United States.* New York: Thomas Y. Crowell & Company.
Sport Vélocipédique. (1880–1886). Paris: [s.n.].
Steele, V. (1998). *Paris Fashion: A Cultural History.* 2nd edition. New York: Oxford University Press.
Stinson, M. A., and C. R. Bhat. (2003). "Commuter Cyclist Route Choice: Analysis Using a Stated Preference Survey." *Transportation Research Record*, 1828. Washington, DC: National Academy Press.
Strasser, S. (1989). *Satisfaction Guaranteed: The Making of the American Mass Market.* New York: Pantheon Books.
Streeck, W. (2011). "E Pluribus Unum? Varieties and Commonalities of Capitalism." In *The Sociology of Economic Life.* Eds. M. Granovetter and R. Swedberg. 3rd edition. Boulder: Westview.
Swedberg, R. (1994). "Markets as Social Structures." In *Handbook of Economic Sociology.* Eds. N. J. Smelser and R. Swedberg. Princeton and New York: Princeton University Press and Russell Sage Foundation.

Szostak, R. (2009). *The Causes of Economic Growth*. Dordrecht: Springer.
The Wheel and Cycling Trade Review. (1889–1898). New York: Wheel and Cycling Trade Review.
Thévin, F., and C. Houry. (1892–1901). *Annuaire général de la vélocipédie et des industries qui s'y rattachent*. Paris: Thévin & Houry.
Thompson, C. S. (1997). "The Third Republic on Wheels: A Social, Cultural, and Political History of Bicycling in France from the Nineteenth Century to World War II." Ph.D. dissertation, New York University.
Tiersten, L. (2001). *Marianne in the Market: Envisioning Consumer Society in Fin-de-Siècle France*. Berkeley: University of California Press.
U.S. Bureau of the Census. (1910). Census. Washington: Government Printing Office.
Vant, A. (1993). *L'industrie du cycle dans la région stephanoise*. Lyon: Éditions Lyonnaises d'Art et d'Histoire.
Veblen, T. ([1899]1953). *Theory of the Leisure Class*. New York: New American Library.
Véloce-Sport. (1891–1895). Paris and Bordeaux: [s.n.].
Wall Street Journal. (1907). New York: Dow, Jones & Company.
Weber, E. (1986). *France, Fin-de-Siècle*. Cambridge, MA: Belknap Press.
White, H. C. (1981). "Where Do Markets Come From?" *American Journal of Sociology* 87: 517–547
Wright, G. (1995). *France in Modern Times*. New York: W.W. Norton.
Zelizer, V. (2005). "Circuits Within Capitalism." In *The Economic Sociology of Capitalism*. Eds. V. Nee and R. Swedberg. Princeton: Princeton University Press.

No End to the Consensus in Macroeconomic Theory? A Methodological Inquiry

By JOHN McCOMBIE and MAUREEN PIKE*

ABSTRACT. After the acrimonious debates between the New Classical and New Keynesian economists in the 1980s and 1990s, a consensus developed, namely, the New Neoclassical Synthesis. However, the 2007 credit crunch exposed the severe limitations of this approach. This article presents a methodological analysis of the New Neoclassical Synthesis and how the paradigmatic heuristic of the representative agent, namely, market clearing subject to sticky prices, excluded the Keynesian notion of involuntary unemployment arising from lack of effective demand. It shows these models may be modified to produce Keynesian results, but are ruled out of consideration by proponents of the New Neoclassical approach by weak incommensurability. It concludes that because of this the New Neoclassical Synthesis, in spite of its failure to explain the sub-prime crisis, is likely to resist successfully the resurgence in Keynesian economics.

Introduction

Consider the following two quotations. The first is from Nordhaus. "American macroeconomists are in disarray. Like a shell-shocked army, barraged by criticism because of poor forecasts . . . confused because of divided intellectual leadership, they are unsure which way to retreat. Out of the ashes of defeat rises a new phalanx of competing theories, a ragtag collection of discarded ideas from the past as well as unproved fancies for the future." Commenting on this, Solow could not have been in more agreement. "Why, then, is macroeconomics is

*John McCombie is Director, Cambridge Centre for Economics and Public Policy, University of Cambridge, UK and Fellow in Economics, Downing College, Cambridge; E-mail address: jslm2@cam.ac.uk. Maureen Pike is Senior Lecturer in the Department of Accounting, Finance, and Economics, Oxford Brookes University, Wheatley, Oxford, UK and Associate Member, Cambridge Centre for Economics and Public Policy, University of Cambridge, UK; E-mail address: mpike@brookes.ac.uk. They are grateful for the helpful comments of two anonymous referees.

No End to the Consensus in Macroeconomic Theory? 239

disarray? 'Disarray' is an understatement. Thoughtful people in other university departments look on with wonder. Professional disagreements exist in their field too . . . but, as outsiders, they are shocked at the way alternative schools of thought in macroeconomics describe each other as wrong from the ground up. They wonder what kind of subject economics is."

When were these words written? In 2008 or 2009 when the failure of mainstream (neoclassical) macroeconomics adequately to account for the credit crunch was being widely debated in the press?[1] The answer is ironically "No." The words were written as long ago as 1983 (Nordhaus 1983: 247; Solow 1983: 279) when there was an acrimonious debate between the New Keynesians and the New Classical economists, which Mankiw (2006: 38) has described as "vitriol among intellectual giants." Yet, paradoxically, over the subsequent years there arose a synthesis of these two schools of thought, to give what is known as the New Neoclassical Synthesis (Goodfriend and King 1997; Goodfriend 2004, 2007) or alternatively the New Macroeconomic Consensus (Meyer 2001; Arestis 2007).[2] The general consensus in mainstream economics was that there were no longer any substantial methodological controversies left in macroeconomics. See, for example, Chari and Kehoe (2006), and Blanchard (2008).

At the theoretical level, the New Neoclassical Synthesis essentially consists of a general dynamic stochastic general equilibrium model, based on what are seen as rigorous microfoundations. The model assumes rational expectations, which had initially proved so controversial in the late 1970s, but are now widely accepted by even the New Keynesians (but not by the Post Keynesians), and the intertemporal optimization of utility by households, with production given by, and shocks reflected in, the real business cycle model. It is a consensus because rigidities from the New Keynesian assumptions of imperfect competition, optimal mark-ups, and price rigidities arising from, for example, menu costs are now included in the New Neoclassical Synthesis model, but the benchmark is still the real business cycle (Goodfriend 2004).

However, the sub-prime crisis of 2007 and the accompanying dramatic fall in output and rise in unemployment exposed the limitations of the New Neoclassical Synthesis as destructively as the Great

Depression had of the pre-Keynesian Classical economics (Allington, McCombie, and Pike 2011, 2012). In 2009, Blanchflower (2009: 7), a former member of the Bank of England's Monetary Policy Committee wrote: "As a monetary policy maker I have found the 'cutting edge' of current macroeconomic research totally inadequate in helping to resolve the problems we currently face" (see also Buiter 2009).

What is interesting is that it was the external event of the sub-prime crisis that caused this radical reassessment of the state of macroeconomics. It was not because of the build-up of anomalies or the econometric specification, testing, and progressive refutations of certain aspects of the model. Major economic crises, such as in the early 1970s or the Great Depression, that cannot be explained by the dominant paradigm are more effective in challenging the mainstream paradigm than statistical testing of the models. The reassessment concerned the very foundations of the discipline and the pressing policy implications (DeLong 2009a, 2009b). The critics, in Solow's (1983) words, saw the New Neoclassical Synthesis as "wrong from the ground up." See, for example, Krugman (2009) and the rejoinder by Cochrane (2009).

The level and type of debate discussed above represents *par excellence* a Kuhnian paradigmatic crisis. Of course, some do not see a crisis at all. As Kuhn (1970: 248) notes, it could be that two scientists (economists) "reach different judgements in concrete cases, one man seeing a cause of crisis where another sees only evidence of limited talent for research." In this article we analyze this methodological crisis in macroeconomics within the Kuhnian framework (Kuhn 1970, 1977, 1999) for the general economist. We emphasise the importance of rhetoric in paradigmatic choice (although drawing different conclusions from McCloskey (1985, 1994)).

Paradigms and Their Incommensurability

Kuhn approached the methodology of the physical sciences from the viewpoint of a historian of science. He found that scientific theories were not immediately abandoned after a single or even several refutations. He showed that it was possible to identify a scientific school of thought or paradigm within which certain assumptions were made untestable by fiat. The paradigm sets the agenda and provides the scientist with the legitimate problems or "puzzles" to be investigated. It also provides the methods or tools with which these puzzles can be solved, while ensuring it will only be the lack of a scientist's ingenuity that prevents this from happening. The paradigm protects the scientist for most of the time from the deeply disturbing problems that can question the whole rationale of his/her discipline and that may lead to a sense of nihilism. What is considered the acceptable method of scientific inquiry is not explicitly laid down but occurs through demonstration and the teaching of exemplars through the textbooks. Thus the paradigm is essentially socially determined. See, for example, the Strong Programme of Barnes, Bloor, and Henry (1996) and also Hands (2004).

But in the natural sciences, with their emphasis on controlled experiments, anomalies accumulate and become more and more difficult to ignore, which eventually leads to a shift to a competing paradigm. However, the reason to change from one paradigm to another is not made for objective reasons. This is because some problems become non-problems and some concepts have no meaning within the new paradigm. In other words, competing paradigms have elements of incommensurability. This concept is essential for the understanding of controversies in macroeconomics.[3,4]

Certain concepts in one paradigm will either have no meaning in the other or there will be meaning change. What are deemed to be the important questions and the standards will also change. Kuhn cites the concepts of the Newton and Einstein mechanics as being incommensurable and having different meanings that are untranslatable in the different paradigms. A favorite example of Kuhn (1970: 115, 128–129, 130–134) of exensional meaning change is that after the Copernican revolution the earth became a planet while the sun and moon ceased to be called that. Because paradigms are not completely commensurable, then there is no objective way of deciding between them.

In the 1980s, Kuhn turned from a discussion of incommensurability in terms of a gestalt switch to one in linguistic terms and also narrowed the term to a more local concept. It is local in that it does not apply to all concepts in competing paradigms. Kuhn draws on the analogy of two languages that an individual may learn, but there may be certain concepts in one language that are not possible to express in the other. Not all the concepts employed in both theories change meaning in the transition to a new paradigm. There is only local incommensurability, otherwise "anomaly would be everywhere, and correspondingly unrecognizable" (Kuhn 1999: 34).

This allows a refutation of the charge of relativism: "It is not the case that a proportion (sic) [proposition] true in one language (or within one paradigm) can be false in another. It is rather that some proposition which may be true (or false) in one language cannot even be formulated in another. It is not truth value but effability that varies with language" (Kuhn 1999: 35). A further misunderstanding of Kuhn is that incommensurability implies incomparability and discontinuity, which is not the case (see Hoyningen-Huene 1993: 218–222).

McCombie (2001) dichotomized incommensurability into strong and weak incommensurability. Strong incommensurability is where theoretical terms in one paradigm have literally no explanatory meaning in another, even though their explanatory domains may be similar. An example of this is the fact that the central tenets of the Marxian paradigm are the concepts of class, viz., labor and capitalists, together with economic power, the labor theory of value, and the rate of exploitation or surplus value. These terms as an explanation of economic phenomena have no role to play in the neoclassical theory of price. Conversely, the approach of methodological individualism with "agents" maximizing utility subject to a budget constraint has no explanatory meaning in the Marxian schema. In the neoclassical aggregate production function, capital and labor enter as factor inputs on the same footing. But in the Marxian paradigm it is labor that ultimately provides value. Consequently, there is strong incommensurability between the neoclassical and the Marxian paradigms.

But in economics especially there are problems where the same concepts (and indeed the same mathematical notation) are used, but their interpretation is still incommensurable. This is weak incommensurability. For example, Fisher's (1992) theoretical work that showed the impossibility of aggregating micro-production functions into an aggregate production function was essentially a critique within the neoclassical paradigm (Felipe and Fisher 2003). He regarded reswitching and capital reversing as nothing more than a logical consequence of the more general aggregation problem. For Harcourt (1976: 29) there is much more to it than this: "What is involved [in the Cambridge capital theory controversies] is the relevant 'vision' of the economic system and the historical processes associated with its development."

Yet the neoclassical participants saw it rather as Fisher does, as an interesting, but not vital technical (Kuhnian) "puzzle." It can be seen here that there is *weak* incommensurability. It is "weak" because the debate centred on the *same* models and concerned matters of logical inference, not empirical issues that could be subject to different interpretations. In this regard, there was agreement over the formal results, but not over their implications. Many of the debates in macroeconomics can best be understood in terms of weak incommensurability.

The boundaries of what are acceptable puzzles are determined by the *paradigmatic pseudo-assumptions* or the *paradigmatic heuristics*. The term pseudo-assumption is used because, in the natural sciences, these assumptions are a hybrid of analytic-synthetic, or quasi-analytic, statements. They are analytic because they are deemed not falsifiable by fiat. They are taken as self-evident and demarcate the paradigm. But they are synthetic in that they may initially have been part of the empirical basis of the paradigm, but "they are by no means the product of arbitrary definitional stipulations. They are rather in part the products of painstaking empirical and theoretical research" (Hoyningen-Huene 1993: 210). Hence, it is in this sense that they are termed pseudo-assumptions rather than just assumptions. An example that Kuhn gives is Newton's second law of motion. Though it was derived after many years of observation, it "behaves for those committed to Newton's theory very much like a purely logical statement that no amount of observation could refute" (Kuhn 1970: 78). It is these paradigmatic pseudo-assumptions that change between paradigms.

Within economics, the pseudo-assumptions are not necessarily, or indeed usually, based on empirical testing, but may be simply theoretical presuppositions. An example, which we shall elaborate below, is that the New Classical assumption of price flexibility and market clearing means that there can be no such thing as "involuntary unemployment." For this reason, we shall use the term "paradigmatic heuristic."

Economics differs from the natural sciences in that, as we have seen, there can be a "reswitching" of economic paradigms. For example, the New Classical economics is seen by some as the formalization and development of the neoclassical economics after the Keynesian interregnum. In turn, the sub-prime crisis has led to a resurgence of interest in, for some, the previously discredited Keynesian economics. There was, for example, a rediscovery of the insights of Minsky (1976). Kuhn, in an attempt to refute the charge that his methodology was "mere relativism," was at pains to argue that if a scientist were to consider two scientific paradigms, there are sufficient criteria that "would enable an uncommitted observer to distinguish the more recent theory time after time" and crucially one of these criteria was the "accuracy of prediction, particularly of quantitative prediction." "Scientific development is, like biological, an unidirectional and irreversible process" (Kuhn 1970: 206.)

Yet within economics, while we can usually tell which of two economic theories is the latter merely by its degree of formalism and mathematical technique, if we were to reconstruct it in verbal terms or to compare them in terms of their conclusions, could we be so certain? Certainly, in no sense is the development of economics "an unidirectional and irreversible process." The reason why this is the case lies in Kuhn's revealing phrase, "the accuracy of prediction." Paradigmatic crisis occurs in the natural sciences by the build up of anomalies, largely the result of repeated controlled experiments.

Within economics, econometrics can never have this role, as was initially shown by the Keynes-Tinbergen debate (Garrone and Marchionatti 2004). Summers (1991) convincingly argues that econometric results rarely if ever affect the "profession's belief" and considers a couple of influential econometric papers that substantiate his point. Mankiw (1990: 1648) argues that had there been confidence in the underlying Keynesian macroeconomic model, the stagflation of the 1970s could have been explained in terms of OPEC supply shocks. "The remainder could always have been attributed to a few large residuals. Heteroskedasticity has never been a reason to throw out an otherwise good model." Hendry and Ericisson's (1985) "Assertion without Empirical Basis," which was a devastating econometric critique of Friedman and Schwartz (1982), had little or no impact on the adherents to monetarism. Kenny and Williams (2001) provide a compelling critique of Barro-type growth regression models. Leamer (2010) provides more general criticisms.

We have also seen that while some see a linear change of mainstream macroeconomics from the "economics of Keynes" through Keynesian economics (the IS-LM and AD-AS models), New Classical and New Keynesian economics to the New Neoclassical Synthesis, the sub-prime crisis has resulted in a reconsideration of macroeconomic theory from a Keynesian/Minskian view (see, for example, Posner 2009; Skidelsky 2009). It should be noted that other paradigms such as the Post Keynesian and Sraffian have also co-existed with the dominant neoclassical paradigm. Kuhn puts such a proliferation down to the immaturity of the social sciences (Kuhn 1970: 179).

In the light of these comments, how is it that paradigmatic revolutions can ever occur in economics? To understand this it is necessary to consider the literature of the sociology of knowledge and the use of rhetoric (McCloskey 1985, 1994). Garnett (2004) provides a good overview. How do economists persuade? McCloskey, most notably, has used the tools of literary criticism and rhetorical analysis to understand the "economic conversation." There is not space here to discuss this and it should be noted that McCloskey's rhetorical use of rhetoric is controversial. Most notable is her insistence that the "market in ideas" will ensure the most worthy ideas will eventually dominate. (This is itself a rhetorical use of a metaphor from neoclassical economics, which provides support for mainstream neoclassical economics, with obvious self-referential problems.) However, she does admit that rhetoric, or the power of persuasion, "may block science for years" by allowing a paradigm to persist. For a more detailed discussion, see McCombie (1998: 49–56) and the references cited therein. But the main message is clear: there are no objective, or logical, foundations for paradigmatic choice, as this article will confirm.

We next turn to a methodological assessment of the debate concerning the New Neoclassical Synthesis paradigm and consider first its heuristic. But our discussion ranges more broadly than this, contrasting the New Neoclassical Synthesis and Keynesian approach.

The New Neoclassical Synthesis Paradigm

Microfoundations and the Representative Agent

One of the paradigmatic heuristics of the New Neoclassical Synthesis is the need to explain the workings of the macroeconomy in terms of agents maximizing an objective function subject to appropriate constraints. In other words, macroeconomics needs to rest on sound microfoundations and theory must be exclusively modeled using mathematics. Much of the debate concerning these assumptions has been directed at the New Classical economics, but they apply equally to the New Keynesian models (on this see Wren-Lewis 2007). We therefore emphasize the New Classical economics, which, as we noted above, is seen as the benchmark model. Given the complexity of constructing mathematical models with heterogeneous individuals and disparate production technologies, recourse is made to the representative agent model, where the economy is simply taken to be a blown-up version of the representative agents as households and producers. Moreover, although not often discussed by the New Neoclassical Synthesis economists, there is a mistaken belief that the analysis is firmly and successfully grounded in Walrasian general equilibrium theory and hence is supported, if at one remove, by rigorous microfoundations.

Hoover (2009) identifies three types of reductionist arguments, with the first two closely related. The first is the view that there is no useful distinction between microeconomics and macroeconomics and he cites Lucas (1987: 107–108) as a proponent of this view. As all economic outcomes are ultimately the result of human actions, any scientific explanation must be couched in terms of the agents' optimizing behavior. This is the neoclassical "primitive notion" in terms of which all explanation must eventually be reduced. The second is the view that macroeconomics is essentially just a subfield of microeconomics, distinguished only by the material it covers. The third admits different methods between macroeconomics and microeconomics and "sees macroeconomics only as a pragmatic compromise with the complexity of applying microeconomics to economy-wide problems. This view asserts that macroeconomics reduces to microeconomics in principle but, because the reduction is difficult, we are not there yet" (Hoover 2009: 388). We may term the first two types *strong* reductionism and the last one *weak* reductionism.

The approach taken by Keynes and the Post Keynesians may seem initially to be a case of weak reductionism, but there are important differences. Keynes gave an intuitive explanation of macroeconomic phenomenon in terms of individuals' behavior, but not within an explicit maximizing model. For example, Keynes explained the consumption function in terms of individual preferences (the "fundamental psychological laws") and the liquidity preference. Trevithick (1992: 111–113), for example, uses the representative firm in his discussion of the procyclicality of wages, as does Kaldor (1961) (see Harcourt 2006: 117). Nevertheless, the fallacy of composition, emphasized by both Keynes and Post Keynesians, cannot be reduced to microeconomic principles, as it is an emergent property of the economic system.

Strong reductionism uses the explicit functional forms of the individual agent's utility function and a firm's production function within the context of mathematical models. A specific form of reductionism is the use of the representative agent, which is used in order to make the mathematical solutions of the model tractable. While early New Classical models were not based on the representative agent model (Hartley 1997), the latter was later used to provide the "deep structural" parameters (from the representative utility and production functions), which were assumed by Lucas to be constant and hence immune from the Lucas critique.

Kirman (1992) has presented further serious problems that the representative agent faces. There is simply no correspondence between individual and collective behavior, even when the former acts in a rational optimizing way. Even the weak axiom of revealed preference does not carry over with aggregation. Collectively, x may be preferred to y in one situation and the converse in another. It is also possible for a representative agent to prefer situation a to b

while all the agents that are "represented" prefer *b* to *a* (see Kirman 1992: 124–125 for an intuitive explanation). In an early critique, Mishan (1961: 1) came to the conclusion that the "[practicing economist] would be no worse off if he remained ignorant of all theories of consumer behaviour, accepting the obvious indispensible 'Law of Demand' on trust."

The production side of the model also faces equally serious problems. It has long been established that identical micro-production functions obeying all the standard assumptions of neoclassical production theory cannot be aggregated to give a well-behaved aggregate production function, *even as an approximation* (Fisher 1992; Felipe and Fisher 2003). These are essentially intra-paradigmatic criticisms as they are logical challenges to the theoretical assumptions within the New Neoclassical Synthesis paradigm.

Kirman's (1992: 119) conclusions are extremely damaging for the New Neoclassical Synthesis paradigm. "The way to develop appropriate microfoundations for macroeconomics is not to be found by starting with the study of individuals in isolation, but rests in an essential way on studying the aggregate activity resulting from the direct interaction between different individuals. Even if this is too ambitious a project in the short run, it is clear that the 'representative' agent deserves a decent burial, as an approach to economic analysis that is not only primitive, but fundamentally erroneous."

But these criticisms have been simply ignored. The defense of the New Neoclassical Synthesis paradigm is primarily an instrumental one. Primacy is given to the articulation of aggregate models derived from the representative agent approach that closely mimic the observed path of the economy (Lucas 1977). What matters is that there should be a fully articulated model based on the paradigmatic heuristic that has been shown to be capable of replicating the path of the economy using either, preferably, calibration or else econometric techniques. It is not that the new classical model can "satisfactorily account for all the main features of the observed business cycle. Rather we have simply argued that no sound reasons have yet been advanced which even suggest that these models are, as a class, *incapable* of providing a satisfactory business cycle" (Lucas and Sargent 1979: 14, emphasis in the original).[5]

Market Clearing and the Irrelevance of Involuntary Unemployment

The New Classical economics has two further paradigmatic heuristics, namely, that agents or households maximize utility and what Lucas calls the "equilibrium discipline" that "markets always clear." De Vroey (2007: 331) argues that the change brought about by Lucas was "not only of substance, it was also methodological." He also states that "it [the claim that markets clear and agents act in their own self-interest] is considered so obvious and universally accepted that no justification for it seems required" (De Vroey 2004: 400).

> Cleared markets is simply a principle, not verifiable by direct observation, which may or may not be useful in constructing successful hypotheses about the behavior of these series [employment and wage rates]. (Lucas and Sargent 1979: 211)

It is a methodological imperative that has been made irrefutable, because Lucas and Sargent continue:

> Alternative principles, such as the postulate of the existence of a third-party auctioneer inducing wage rigidity and uncleared markets are similarly "unrealistic" in the not especially important sense of not offering a good description of observed labor market institutions.

Consequently, while it is conceded that in principle it may be possible to test these assumptions (otherwise how could they be deemed unrealistic), the paradigmatic heuristic is "whether [for example] actual contracts can be adequately accounted for within an equilibrium model, that is, a model in which agents are proceeding in their own best interests" (Lucas and Sargent 1979). At the heart of the equilibrium assumption is that if there were any unexploited opportunities in markets they would eventually be exploited. The only "scientific" explanation can be, it is argued, in terms of individual agent's optimization (as modeled by the representative agent) and that markets clear. Consequently, there can be no coordination failures leading to lack of effective demand and therefore there can be no involuntary unemployment. Indeed, the very term is an empty theoretical concept that was introduced by Keynes, and, as such, there is no need for modern economists (that is, New Classical theorists) to explain it. It also means that "meaningless phrases" such as full capacity and slack are absent. The problem is "to explain why people allocate time to a particular *activity*—like unemployment—we need to know why they prefer it to *all* other available activities" (Lucas 1987: 54, emphasis in the original).

This methodological view of Lucas, especially with respect to Keynes's notion of involuntary unemployment, has been analyzed in detail by De Vroey (2004). It is sufficient for our purposes to note how the paradigmatic heuristics, including the use of the representative agent, lead inexorably to this conclusion. If markets are assumed to clear, then by definition, all unemployment must be voluntary (if frictional unemployment is included in the latter term). The Keynesian view that *all* firms may simultaneously lay off workers because of lack of effective demand has no meaning in the New Classical paradigm. Neither does the proposition that unemployment may exceed vacancies in all industries. Moreover, it may not even be profitable for a worker to sell apples on a street corner, as Lucas (1978) suggests, in view of the competition and low prices from the large supermarkets. (Weitzman (1982) somewhat controversially has argued that the presence of increasing returns is a necessary condition for involuntary unemployment for this reason.) Consequently, Blinder's (1987) recourse to empirical evidence in his methodological discussion of "Keynes, Lucas and Scientific Progress" is unlikely to influence anyone but the already committed.

Inter-Paradigmatic Criticisms

In this section, we consider two criticisms that have arisen from the Post Keynesian paradigm and that illustrate the role of weak incommensurability.

Risk, Uncertainty, and the Investment Demand Schedule

The first criticism concerns how the future is modeled, in other words it involves the fundamental distinction between both rational expectations and risk *vis-à-vis* uncertainty. The importance of the last was the central point of Keynes's (1936) *General Theory* and has been repeatedly emphasised by Post Keynesians, such as Davidson

(1982–1983, 2007). The most succinct statements of Keynes's views on the instability of the capitalist economy are to be found in Chapter 12 of the *General Theory*, "The State of Long-Term Expectation," and in his rejoinder to his critics in the 1937 *Quarterly Journal of Economics*. In this he outlined the way fluctuations in investment and hence aggregate demand could lock the economy into a period of sustained unemployment. "Given the psychology of the public, the level of output and employment as a whole depends on the amount of investment. I put it in this way ... because it is usual in a complex system to regard as the *causa causans* that factor which is more prone to sudden and wide fluctuations" (Keynes 1937: 122). The key is the volatility of "conventional expectations," expectations that in the presence of uncertainty, rather than Knightian risk, are formed by conventions.

The parting of the ways came with Hicks's formalization of the *General Theory* as a simple equilibrium IS-LM model. This, and the comparative static exercises that followed from it, exclude the role of volatile expectations or "animal spirits." Hicks himself later partially realized this when his whole methodological approach to economics changed (Hicks 1980). He increasingly emphasized the importance of temporal (not logical) time and the role of history (Pasinetti and Mariutti 2008). An inter-paradigm critique of the New Neoclassical Synthesis is, as Davidson repeatedly pointed out, that the world is *non-ergodic* not *ergodic*. With rational expectations, the effect of Knightian uncertainty is assumed away. The fact that the world is not deterministic is modeled by simply the introduction of a stochastic element characterized by well-defined probability distributions.

A good example of the way the Hicks IS-LM model abstracts from uncertainty is through the treatment of the investment schedule and the IS curve in comparative static analyses. A form of IS curve appears in the New Macroeconomic Consensus but is derived from an explicit optimization process within the representative agent model (Meyer 2001). Nevertheless, it is convenient for expositional purposes to use the Hicks model.

A fall in the interest rate in the IS-LM and AD-AS models increases the volume of investment through the investment schedule. This assumes away any adverse changes in expectations. Thus the investment schedule is assumed not only to be downward sloping with respect to the interest rate, but is stable and not affected by changes in expectations concerning the future net revenue stream. However, suppose that in the presence of falling demand, the interest rate is cut by the central bank. If it is not clear that demand will necessarily rise because of coordination failures, then with this uncertainty, the expectations about the size of the net revenues from a new investment will fall. In these circumstances, as Keynes and Davidson have argued, the firm will stay liquid and not invest. This has the effect of shifting the investment schedule to the left. If expectations worsen to the extent that total investment and demand might actually fall, notwithstanding the decline in the interest rate, this leads to a self-fulfilling prophecy. This means that it is not possible to determine within the comparative static framework of the IS-LM whether or not output will unambiguously increase or decrease, although one can, of course, show the various possible outcomes within this framework.[6] With the representative agent model, of course, this problem does not arise as the act of investment must *pari passu* raise demand as there cannot, by definition, be any coordination failure.

We may illustrate this argument by considering the investment decision facing a typical firm that is deciding whether or not to purchase a piece of capital equipment.[7] It is assumed that the payback period is five years. Consequently, the decision of the firm is whether or not at time $t=0$ to irrevocably commit funds (any expenditure is subsequently sunk costs) to this investment, which comes on-stream a year later. The expected net present value of the machine $E(V)$ is given by:

$$E(V) = \sum_{t=1}^{5} \frac{E(R_t)}{(1 + E(i_t))^t} \qquad (1)$$

where R is the net revenues of the goods produced by the machine and i is the cost of borrowing (which is a function of the bank rate). All values are in real terms. E(.), which denotes the anticipated value of the variable, may not be well defined mathematically, as a non-ergodic world is assumed.

To see the importance of expectations, let us assume that at time $t=0$, the real rate of interest is 5 percent per annum and at this value,

$V = V^*$ and $R = R^*$ where the superscript * denotes the Marshallian critical value at which it pays to invest in the machine, that is,

$$V^* = \sum_{t=1}^{5} \frac{R_0^*}{(1+i_0)^t} \qquad (2)$$

For simplicity, we assume that R_t does not vary over the five years, although its value is uncertain at time $t = 0$. Suppose the economy moves into recession and it is announced that the real interest rate will be cut substantially by 5 percentage points to zero from $t = 1$, and this is credible. It may be easily shown that if the expected revenues fall by more than 13.5 percent, compared with R_0, then notwithstanding the cut in interest rates, it will not be profitable to invest.[8]

The illustrative 13.5 percent may seem large, but in fact the expected fall in total revenue of the firm will be much smaller than this because, by definition, the production from this new machine is the *marginal* output. For example, suppose that the new investment equals a net addition to the firm's capacity of 10 percent. Then it would only require a downturn of 1.2 percent in total revenues to cause the 13.5 percent decline of the proposed new machine's revenues and hence for the investment not to be undertaken. The picture is more complicated than this because we have abstracted from vintage effects and scrapping, but the argument follows through.

A key variable in the firm's decision is the expected revenue, which will be a function of what it expects other firms do and *vice versa*. Hence, the reason for the crucial role of Keynesian conventional expectations in the investment decision.

Dixit (1992) has incorporated a measure of risk into the net present value equation that shows how, with an increase in risk, it becomes optimal for the firm to delay investing. The measure of risk is simply taken as the volatility of the revenue stream and is assumed to follow a geometric Brownian motion. Nevertheless, the model shows how in principle uncertainty may lead to an inward shift of the aggregate investment schedule, especially if the degree of uncertainty is a function of other firms' investment decisions.

One of the reasons why these criticisms have had little effect within the New Neoclassical Synthesis paradigm is that they lead to ambiguous results. It raises the problem of how to construct models when the relationships are not stable. Nevertheless, recent work by Frydman and Goldberg (2008, 2010) has shown a way forward in terms of modeling expectations more realistically, which necessitates abandoning the rational expectations hypothesis.

The Neoclassical Labor Market and the Fallacy of Composition

The second problem with the Hicks IS-LM model was that while it showed the importance of demand and provided a pedagogical explanation of the Keynesian revolution, it contained the seeds of its own destruction. This was the absence of an explicit supply side; it was assumed that the supply of labor was infinitely elastic at the given price level. This ushered in the first or "Samuelson" neoclassical synthesis, namely, the AD-AS model where the price level was endogenized. As the model is short run and the capital stock is fixed, the demand for labor is given by the neoclassical marginal product of labor based on the representative firm's profit maximization and the supply of labor is determined by households' optimization, trading off leisure for work depending upon the real wage.

In the early models, this led to the "old" neoclassical synthesis conclusion that Keynesian "involuntary" unemployment was the result of the real wage being too high. This follows from the paradigmatic heuristic that the labor market is the same as any other competitive market with excess supply the result of the price being above the market-clearing level.[9] The following draws partly on McCombie (1985–1986).

Figure 1 displays the standard textbook neoclassical labor market diagram where the demand for labor is given by the marginal product of labor curve. It should be emphasized that we are examining the case where the neoclassical analysis breaks down, even though we still make the assumptions of the existence of a well-behaved production function and the marginal product theory of factor pricing. Like Keynes, we are trying to show the problems of the (neo)classical economists by granting them all their standard concepts.

In anticipation of our later discussion, let us assume a classical savings function where all profits are invested and total wages go to consumption. This is usually omitted in the standard discussion as the

Figure 1

The Neoclassical Labor Market

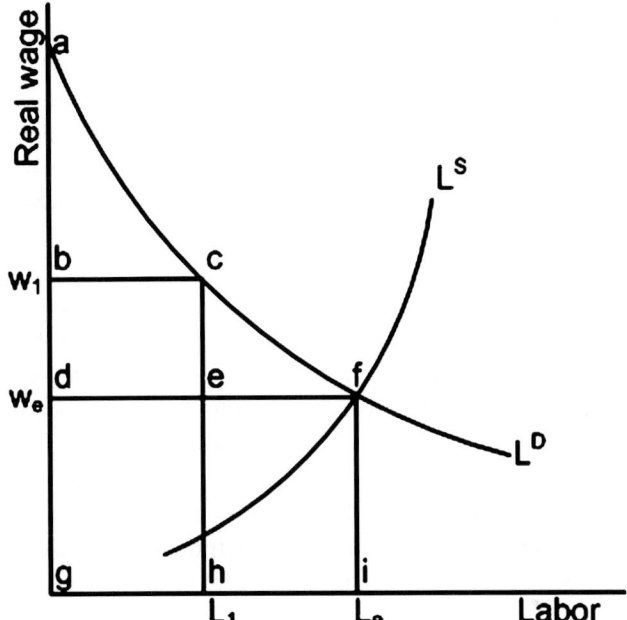

driving force behind the model is seen as the flexibility of the real wage. (Assuming workers do not save is not essential for the argument, but helps the exposition.)

Consequently, if the real wage is w_1, then total investment (profits) is given by the area *abc* and total wages (consumption) by the area *bchg*. The amount of labor employed is L_1 and is below the market-clearing level of L_e. The proximate cause of "involuntary" unemployment in this scenario is the fact that the real wage is above its market-clearing value, w_e. It can be seen that if the real wage falls to w_e for whatever reason, the labor market *must* clear and employment must increase to L_e. Output and profits *must* increase to *afig* and *afd*, respectively, by the construct of the model. (This is a "paradigmatic prediction," a result that is in principle empirically testable, but that is assumed to hold by dint of the paradigmatic heuristic.) In effect,

Say's law holds and the determination of the volume of investment by, say, animal spirits as discussed in the last section is ruled out, *ab initio*.

However, a stylized fact is the real wage moves procyclically not contracyclically as Keynes originally thought. Dunlop (1938) and Tarshis (1939) first drew attention to this (Keynes 1939).[10] This is incompatible with the analysis discussed above. As there are some econometric results where this is not the case, one paradigmatic strategy is to shelve the finding as an anomaly to await further estimates. The other is to develop a model that can allow for this procyclicality, while still maintaining the crucial paradigmatic heuristic of the representative firm and optimization. The New Classical model does this by relaxing the assumption that the technology is constant and allows for productivity shocks. Within the context of the one-sector model depicted in Figure 2, an increase in the level of technology from A_1 to A_2 (a positive shock) shifts the labor demand curve upwards. The labor supply is assumed to shift upwards to the left as a consequence of a fall in the interest rate (from i_1 to i_2) and the intertemporal optimization by households. There is a simultaneous adjustment process. Firms produce extra output and increase the wage rate. It can be seen that the equilibrium level of employment must, as a consequence of the paradigm, move from L_{e1} to L_{e2} and the real wage moves procyclically. Optimizing households, given the increase in the wage rate, increase their employment (that is, move up their supply curve) and thereby their demand for goods and services, which matches the increased output supply. The equilibrium occurs where households are on their labor supply curve. In terms of Figure 2, this is at point *b*. Employment can never be constrained by aggregate demand to be off its supply function because there is no independent determinant of demand through, for example, a separate investment function where animal spirits can play a crucial role. The position is slightly more complex when prices are sticky, but essentially the argument is the same.

The above is a simplification of the New Neoclassical Synthesis model, where firms have a mark-up pricing policy and, in imperfectly competitive markets, they are willing to supply as much as is demanded as the wage is below the marginal product of labor

Figure 2

The New Classical Labor Market

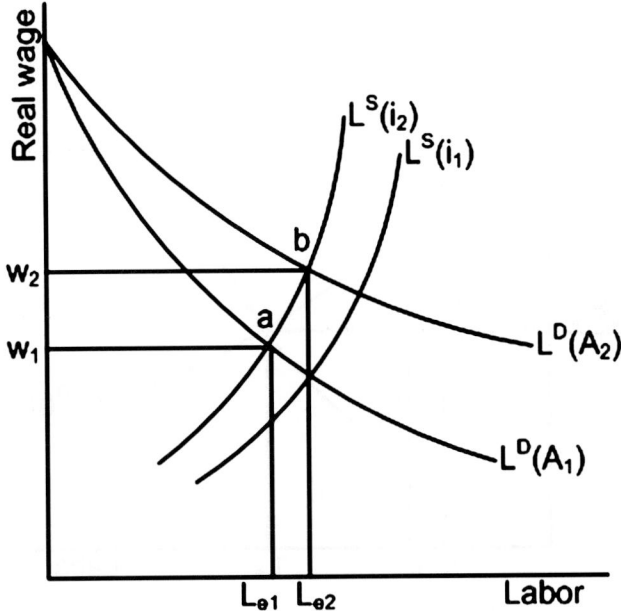

(Goodfriend 2004). There is thus a "Keynesian" transmission mechanism because if demand increases, firms will raise the wage to attract the extra labor necessary to supply the output. Thus, through the production function, the demand for output determines the supply, which in turn determines the level of employment. But at the same time, "the classical perspective takes the view that the actual employment ... must equal labor willingly supplied by households ... *regardless of the strength of aggregate demand*" (Goodfriend 2004: 30, emphasis added). Employment is determined exactly as in the core real business cycle. The answer to this conundrum, at the risk of over-simplification, is that aggregate demand here is not Keynes's concept of aggregate demand.

But the "Old" and the New Neoclassical Synthesis suffer from the fallacy of composition and once this is taken into account,

Figure 3

The Post Keynesian Labor Market

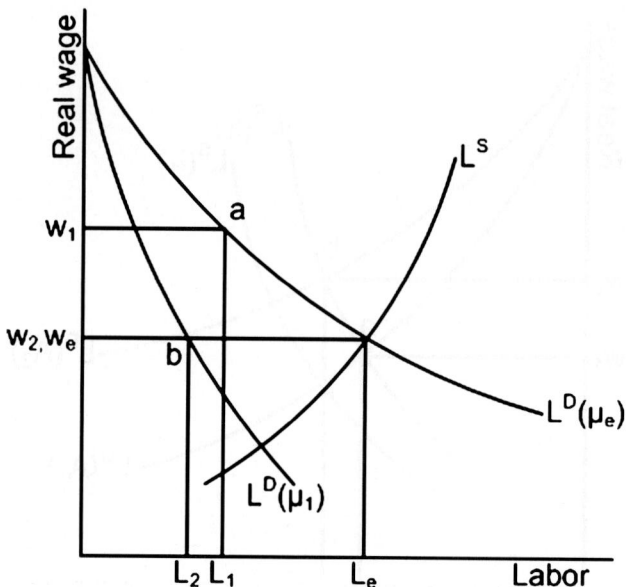

involuntary unemployment, in Keynes's sense of the term, can occur. The short-run production function is given by $Y = f(\mu \bar{K}, L)$, where Y is output, $\bar{K}$ is the fixed capital stock, μ is the rate of capacity utilization, and L is employment. There is a family of marginal product of labor curves, conditional on the rate of capacity utilization. For example, Figure 3 shows two such functions, one where there is full capacity utilization μ_e and one where, with a reduction in the use of the capital stock, capacity utilization has declined to μ_1. Although capital is a sunk cost, it is assumed that, given the costs of rehiring labor and the damage to worker morale, it is optimal for a profit-maximizing firm not to allow labor to bear the whole brunt of the fall in production and for labor hoarding to occur.[11] A fall in worker morale, for example, means that less labor services are forthcoming for any given level of employment, which, in the absence of any effective control mechanisms by the firm, in terms of Figure 1 has the aggregate effect of shifting the marginal productivity curve to the left and reducing total profits.[12]

As the real wage falls, with some simple dynamics, so does aggregate demand. Consequently, inventories will accumulate and firms will begin to cut back on production. In the light of this, they are reluctant to commit themselves to their present level of investment, even though the real interest rate may have fallen, as discussed in the previous section. Capacity utilization falls, the labor demand curve shifts to the left, and labor is laid off. The path of the economy is from *a* to *b* in Figure 3. For expositional purposes, it is assumed that the real wage falls to $w_2 = w_e$. (Note that we are still adopting the neoclassical assumption that the wage rate is equal to the marginal product of labor.) At this point, the level of aggregate demand, determined by the level of investment, has fallen enough to extinguish the excess inventories. After a period of time, capital scrapping will occur and so the L^D (μ_1) curve becomes the full capacity utilization labor demand curve. At this point the equilibrium levels of employment and the wage rate are now lower than previously, even though firms are profit maximizing and the labor supply function is given by the optimization of households. The neoclassical model (without excess capacity and a shift in the marginal product of labor curve) cannot handle this case, as the above analysis is logically incompatible with employment increasing as w_1 falls to w_e in Figure 1.

This critique is a case of weak incommensurability because the same neoclassical concepts are used. Namely, firms and households optimize and the demand for labor is given by the neoclassical aggregate production function. The only difference is that the model now allows for excess capacity and a dynamic adjustment process such that a falling real wage drives down demand and hence employment. We thus get involuntary unemployment, notwithstanding the existence of real wage flexibility.

The New Neoclassical Synthesis has to explain the observed fluctuations in capacity utilization in terms of an optimizing framework. It does so by assuming that changes in capacity utilization implausibly reflect the optimal amount of time that is used for maintenance (Greenwood, Hercowitz, and Huffman 1988; Barro 2008: ch. 9). No direct test of this hypothesis is provided by Greenwood, Hercowitz, and Huffman (1988), who merely adopted the standard calibration exercise and find that the variance of the macroeconomic variables are close to those observed in the real data. It should be noted that the detailed discussion of the empirics of capacity utilization by Corrado and Mattey (1997: 166) make no reference to variations in it being due to changes in maintenance, but attributes it explicitly to variations in aggregate demand.

New Keynesian Menu Costs, Unemployment, and the Fallacy of Composition

As Caplin and Spulber (1987) show, the fallacy of composition equally applies to the New Keynesian model of pricing policy under menu and other adjustment costs. These adjustment costs imply that firms do not adjust prices until a trigger point is reached where the increased profits from raising the price exceeds their implementation costs. The New Keynesians, thus, see unemployment occurring because of the lack of instantaneous price flexibility, which is due to an optimal pricing policy by firms. It also leaves a role for monetary policy. (This stands in contrast to the Post Keynesians who do not see price rigidity as the *cause* of involuntary unemployment.) Thus, the price stickiness of the representative firm (although the firms are assumed to have staggered price setting) provides the microfoundations for price stickiness at the macroeconomic level. However, Caplin and Spulber show that money shocks do not have aggregate real effects when price changes are endogenously determined in response to the size of monetary shocks, rather than occurring at preset times with fixed-length contracts, as in many such models. On aggregating across firms, price stickiness disappears even when the timing of price adjustments is staggered. Hence, monetary shocks are neutral and the New Keynesian explanation of cyclical fluctuations in employment is considerably weakened.

Caballero (1992) constructs a simple probabilistic model that also shows the effects of the fallacy of composition. He considers the asymmetric case where employment creation by a firm during an upswing is less than employment destruction in a downswing, but occurs with greater frequency. This is due to asymmetric adjustment costs. The outcome is that if all firms have identical adjustment costs and face the same (that is, perfectly correlated) demand shocks, then this will carry through to the macroeconomic level and will cause cyclical fluctuations in employment. In other words, this can be analyzed using a representative agent model. But if the firms' shocks are not perfectly correlated with each other then in the aggregate, these employment asymmetries are washed out and aggregate causes are required to explain the employment fluctuations. While Caballero argues that this does not mean that the microeconomic forces are irrelevant to the explanations of aggregate phenomenon, he does concede that *"direct application of microeconomic explanations to aggregate data can be seriously misleading, since they typically do not consider the natural probability forces that tend to undo such explanations"* (1992: 1291, emphasis in the original). This reinforces the problems of using the representative firm as the basis of the explanation given the problems posed by the fallacy of composition.

Both the Caplin and Spulber (1987) and Caballero (1992) arguments are intra-paradigmatic critiques and ironically strengthen the New Classical emphasis at the expense of the New Keynesian in the New Neoclassical Synthesis. Given these results, the alternative explanation for cyclical fluctuations in employment is that they are due to fluctuations in aggregate demand in Keynes's sense of the term and emphasized by the Post Keynesians. But, as we have seen above, this explanation, which involves the existence of involuntary unemployment, is ruled out by the neoclassical paradigmatic heuristic.

Conclusions

In this article a Kuhnian approach has been followed in an attempt to understand the continuing controversies in macroeconomics. First, the *intra*-paradigm criticisms of the New Neoclassical Synthesis that go beyond the puzzle solving of normal science were discussed. They challenge the logical foundations of the paradigm and therefore should not be shelved as anomalies, although with respect to the New Neoclassical Synthesis they are. These critiques include the problems concerning the stability of equilibrium (the Sonnenschein-Mantel-Debreu theorem—see Kirman 1989) and the insuperable problems of aggregating both household utility functions and micro-production functions. The last two invalidate the use of the representative agent.

Secondly, we discussed the *inter*-paradigm criticisms that involve weak incommensurability, where many of the variables and assumptions are the same, but the paradigmatic heuristics differ. Most notably, we considered the effect of uncertainty on the investment schedule and the introduction of an assumption, the possibility of excess capacity, that vitiates the result that "markets always clear" and that employment fluctuations (even with price stickiness) are always optimal, that is, the assumption that labor is always on its supply curve.

Given that the paradigm heuristic is determined by the textbooks, worked examples, and demonstration, the neoclassical approach with its emphasis on the representative agent and methodological individualism has a powerful inertia effect. We have shown how a Keynesian explanation of unemployment can be couched in neoclassical terms, but because of weak incommensurability is not persuasive for neoclassical economists. In spite of the sub-prime crisis, the New Neoclassical Synthesis is seen by many to be relatively unscathed (but with the imperative to build in assumptions that allow for debt default and bankruptcy) and the erroneous Treasury view of the 1920s has returned to U.K. macroeconomic policy. The latter is that cutting government expenditure and reducing the budget deficit in the depths of a recession will somehow revitalize the private sector and increase its investment. It is as if the Keynesian revolution had never occurred.

Notes

1. Krugman's title of his *New York Times* (September 6, 2009) article on the 2008 crisis says it all: "How Did Economists Get it So Wrong?"

2. The former term is normally applied to the theoretical models and the latter to the applied work resulting from these models on monetary policy, including inflation targeting.

3. See, for example, Hoyningen-Huene (1993: 207, fn. 58), Hoyningen-Huene and Sankey (2001), and Soler, Sankey, and Hoyningen-Huene (2008).

4. The work of Lakatos, which is essentially an interpretation of Kuhn within a Popperian framework, has proved an attractive alternative to the paradigm. However, the great weakness of Lakatos is his belief that any

putative incommensurable theories can be made comparable by the use of a suitable "dictionary" (Lakatos 1970: 79, fn 1).

5. However, in an unguarded moment Lucas (2004: 23) noted: "The problem that the new theories, the theories embedded in general equilibrium dynamics of the sort that we know how to use pretty well now—there's a residue of things they don't let us think about. They don't let us think about the U.S. experience in the 1930s or about financial crises and their real consequences in Asia and Latin America, They don't let us think, I don't think (*sic*), very well about Japan in the 1990s." As Laidler (2010: 42) comments, "some residue!"

6. See Bibow (1998) for a discussion of the interrelationship between confidence, investment, and the liquidity preference.

7. See Baddeley (2003) for a discussion of the various theories of investment and the empirical evidence.

8. To see this assume that $R_0 = R^*$ is 100. With an interest rate of 0.05, the net present value of the machine is 433, which we assume is the price of the machine. If i falls to zero, *ceteris paribus*, the net present value rises to 500. Under these circumstances, if there is then a fall in total net revenues by 13.5 percent over the five years due to a fall in demand, the net present value declines to 433 again, the critical value. Any further fall beyond 13.5 percent will make the investment unprofitable even though the interest rate is zero.

9. This is notwithstanding the argument of some Post Keynesians (see especially Davidson 1983) that there is a direction of casualty absent in the neoclassical paradigm. Aggregate demand determines output, which in turn determines the level of employment (via the production function) and then, in turn, the real wage via the marginal product of labor. More fundamental problems are that the aggregate marginal product of labor curve theoretically does not exist (Fisher 1992). Nor can econometric testing provide any support for the proposition that it can be treated as an approximation, as the results are merely a statistical artefact (Felipe and McCombie 2009).

10. See Bils (1985) and Solon, Barsky, and Parker (1994).

11. An alternative explanation is to assume a putty-clay production function and that there are *ex post* fixed coefficients of production, but this is not the normal neoclassical approach.

12. This is related to the efficiency-wage hypothesis.

References

Allington, N. F. B., J. S. L. McCombie, and M. Pike. (2011). "The Failure of the New Macroeconomic Consensus: From Non-Ergodicity to the Efficient Markets Hypothesis and Back Again." *International Journal of Public Policy* 7(1/2/3): 4–21.

———. (2012). "Lessons Not Learnt: From the Collapse of Long-Term Capital Management to the Subprime Crisis." *Journal of Post Keynesian Economics* 34(4): 555–582.

Arestis, P. (ed.) (2007). *Is There a New Consensus in Macroeconomics?* Basingstoke: Palgrave Macmillan.

Baddeley, M. C. (2003). *Investment. Theories and Analysis*. Basingstoke: Palgrave Macmillan.

Barnes, B., D. Bloor, and J. Henry. (1996). *Scientific Knowledge: A Sociological Analysis*. Chicago: University of Chicago Press.

Barro, R. J. (2008). *Macroeconomics. A Modern Approach*. Mason: Thompson South-Western.

Bibow, J. (1998). "On Keynesian Theories of Liquidity Preference." *Manchester School* 66(2): 238–273.

Bils, M. J. (1985). "Real Wages Over the Cycle: Evidence from Panel Data." *Journal of Political Economy* 93(4): 666–689.

Blanchard, O. J. (2008). "The State of Macro." National Bureau of Economic Research, Working Paper No. 14259.

Blanchflower, D. (2009). "The Future of Monetary Policy." Lecture given at Cardiff University, March 24, 2009.

Blinder, A. S. (1987). "Keynes, Lucas, and Scientific Progress." *American Economic Review, Papers and Proceedings* 77(2): 130–136.

Buiter, W. (2009). "The Unfortunate Uselessness of Most 'State of the Art' Academic Monetary Economics." Available at http://blogs.ft.com/maverecon/2009/03/the-unfortunate-uselessness-of-most-state-of-the-art-academic-monetary-economics/ (accessed December 21, 2011).

Caballero, R. J. (1992). "A Fallacy of Composition." *American Economic Review* 82(5): 1279–1292.

Caplin, A. S., and D. F. Spulber. (1987). "Menu Costs and the Neutrality of Money." *Quarterly Journal of Economics* 102(4): 703–726.

Chari, V. V., and P. J. Kehoe. (2006). "Modern Macroeconomics in Practice: How Theory is Shaping Policy." *Journal of Economic Perspectives* 20(4): 3–28.

Cochrane, J. (2009). "How Did Paul Krugman Get it So Wrong?" Available at http://modeledbehavior.com/2009/09/11/john-cochrane-responds-to-paul-krugman-full-text/ (accessed December 21, 2011).

Corrado, C., and J. Mattey. (1997). "Capacity Utilization." *Journal of Economic Perspectives* 11(1): 151–167.

Davidson, P. (1982–1983). "Rational Expectations: A Fallacious Foundation for Studying Crucial Decision Making Processes." *Journal of Post Keynesian Economics* 5(2): 182–197.

———. (1983). "The Marginal Product Curve is Not the Demand Curve for Labor and Lucas's Labor Supply Function is Not the Supply Curve for Labor in the Real World." *Journal of Post Keynesian Economics* 6(1): 105–117.

———. (2007). *John Maynard Keynes*. Basingstoke: Palgrave Macmillan.
De Vroey, M. (2004). "Lucas on Involuntary Unemployment." *Cambridge Journal of Economics* 28(3): 397–411.
De Vroey, M. (2007). "Did the Market-Clearing Postulate Pre-Exist New Classical Economics? The Case of Marshallian Theory." *Manchester School* 75(3): 328–348.
DeLong, B. (2009a). Shichinin no Economusutai–NOT!! September 20. Available at http://delong.typepad.com/sdj/2009/09/a-magnificent-seven.html (accessed December 21, 2011).
———. (2009b). "The State of Modern Cutting Edge Macro: Narayana Kocherlakota Leaves Me Puzzled." Available at http://delong.typepad.com/sdj/2009/09/the-state-of-modern-cutting-edge-macro-narayana-kocherlakota-leaves-me-puzzled.html (accessed December 21, 2011).
Dixit, A. (1992). "Investment and Hysteresis." *Journal of Economic Perspectives* 6(1): 107–132.
Dunlop, J. T. (1938). "The Movement of Real and Money Wages." *Economic Journal* 48(191): 413–434.
Felipe, J., and F. M. Fisher. (2003). "Aggregation in Production Functions: What Applied Economists Should Know." *Metroeconomica* 54(2&3): 208–262.
Felipe, J., and J. S. L. McCombie. (2009). "Are Estimates of Labour Demand Functions Mere Statistical Artefacts?" *International Review of Applied Economics* 23(2): 147–168.
Fisher, F. M. (1992). *Aggregation. Aggregate Production Functions and Related Topics*. Ed. J. Monz. London: Harvester Wheatsheaf.
Friedman, M., and A. J. Schwartz. (1982). *Monetary Trends in the United States and the United Kingdom: Their Relation to Income, Prices, and Interest Rates, 1867–1975*. Chicago: University of Chicago Press.
Frydman, R., and M. D. Goldberg. (2008). "Macroeconomic Theory for a World of Imperfect Knowledge." Centre on Capitalism and Society at Columbia University, Working Paper, No. 24, May.
———. (2010). "Efficient Markets: Fictions and Reality." Paper given to the Institute for New Economic Thinking, Cambridge, UK, April.
Garnett, R. R. (2004). "Rhetoric and Postmodernism in Economics." In *The Elgar Companion to Economics and Philosophy*. Eds. J. B Davis, A. Marciano, and J. Runde, pp. 231–259. Cheltenham: Edward Elgar.
Garrone, G., and R. Marchionatti. (2004). "Keynes on Econometric Method. A Reassessment of His Debate with Tinbergen and Other Econometricians, 1938–1943." Department of Economics, University of Turin, working paper, 01/2004.
Goodfriend, M. (2004). "Monetary Policy in the New Neoclassical Synthesis: A Primer." *Economic Quarterly*, Federal Reserve Bank of Richmond 90(3): 21–45.

———. (2007). "How the World Achieved Consensus on Monetary Policy." *Journal of Economic Perspectives* 21(4): 47–68.

Goodfriend, M., and R. King. (1997). "The New Neoclassical Synthesis and the Role of Monetary Policy." *NBER Macroeconomics Annual* 1997 12 (September): 231–296.

Greenwood, J., Z. Hercowitz, and G. W. Huffman. (1988). "Investment, Capacity Utilization, and the Real Business Cycle." *American Economic Review* 78(3): 402–417.

Hands, D. W. (2004). "Constructivism: The Social Construction of Scientific Knowledge." In *The Elgar Companion to Economics and Philosophy*. Eds. J. B. Davis, A. Marciano, and J. Runde, pp. 197–212. Cheltenham: Edward Elgar:

Harcourt, G. C. (1976). "The Cambridge Controversies: Old Ways and New Horizons—Or Dead End?" *Oxford Economic Papers* 28(1): 25–65.

———. (2006). *The Structure of Post-Keynesian Economics. The Core Contributions of the Pioneers.* Cambridge: Cambridge University Press.

Hartley, J. E. (1997). *The Representative Agent in Macroeconomics*, Routledge Frontiers of Political Economy. London: Routledge.

Hendry, D. F., and N. R. Ericisson. (1985). "Assertion Without Empirical Basis: An Econometric Appraisal of *Monetary Trends in . . . the United Kingdom*, Federal Reserve Board, International Finance Discussion Papers, No. 270. Available at http://www.federalreserve.gov/pubs/ifdp/1985/270/default.htm (accessed December 21, 2011)

Hicks, J. R. (1980). "IS-LM: An Explanation." *Journal of Post Keynesian Economics* 3(2): 139–154.

Hoover, K. D. (2009). "Microfoundations and the Ontology of Macroeconomics." In *The Oxford Handbook of Philosophy of Economics*. Eds. H. Kincaid and D. Ross, pp. 386–409. Oxford: Oxford University Press.

Hoyningen-Huene, P. (1993). *Reconstructing Scientific Revolutions. Thomas S. Kuhn's Philosophy of Science.* Chicago: Chicago University Press.

Hoyningen-Huene, P., and H. Sankey. (2001). *Incommensurability and Related Matters.* Dordrecht: Klumer Academic.

Kaldor, N. (1961). "Capital Accumulation and Economic Growth." In *The Theory of Capital.* Eds. F. A. Lutz and D. C. Hague, pp. 177–222. London: Macmillan.

Kenny, C., and D. Williams. (2001). "What Do We Know About Economic Growth? Or, Why Don't We Know Very Much?" *World Development* 29(1): 1–22.

Keynes, J. M. (1936). *The General Theory of Employment, Interest, and Money.* London: Macmillan.

———, (1937). "The General Theory of Employment." *Quarterly Journal of Economics* 51(2): 209–223.

——. (1939). "Relative Movements of Real Wages and Output." *Economic Journal* 49(139): 34–51.
Kirman, A. (1989). "The Intrinsic Limits of Modern Economic Theory: The Emperor Has No Clothes." *Economic Journal* 99(395): 126–139.
——. (1992). "Whom or What Does the Representative Individual Represent?" *Journal of Economic Perspectives* 6(2): 117–136.
Krugman, P. (2009). "How Did Economists Get it So Wrong?" *New York Times*, September 2. Available at http://www.nytimes.com/2009/09/06/magazine/06Economic-t.html?pagewanted=all (accessed December 21, 2011).
Kuhn, T. S. (1970). *The Structure of Scientific Revolutions*. Chicago: University of Chicago Press (2nd Edition).
——. (1977). *The Essential Tension: Selected Studies in Scientific Tradition and Change*. Chicago: University of Chicago.
——. (1999). "Remarks on Incommensurability and Translation." In *Incommensurability and Translation. Kuhnian Perspectives on Scientific Communication and Theory Change*. Eds. R. R. Favretti, G. Sandri, and R. Scazzeri, pp. 33–37. Cheltenham: Edward Elgar,
Laidler, D. (2010). "Lucas, Keynes, and the Crisis." *Journal of the History of Economic Thought* 32(1): 39–62.
Lakatos, I. (1970). "Falsification and the Methodology of Scientific Research Programmes." In *Criticism and the Growth of Knowledge*. Eds. I. Lakatos and A. Musgrave, pp. 91–195. Cambridge: Cambridge University Press.
Leamer, E. E. (2010). "Tantalus on the Road to Asymptopia." *Journal of Economic Perspectives* 24(2): 31–46.
Lucas, R. E. (1977). "Understanding Business Cycles." *Carnegie-Rochester Conference Series on Public Policy* 5(1): 7–29.
——. (1978). "Unemployment Policy." *American Economic Review, Papers and Proceedings* 68(2): 353–357.
——. (1987). *Models of Business Cycles*. Oxford: Basil Blackwell.
——. (2004). "My Keynesian Education." *History of Political Economy*, Annual Supplement, 36: 12–24. Available at http://www.nytimes.com/2009/09/06/magazine/06Economic-t.html?pagewanted=all
Lucas, R. E., and T. J. Sargent. (1979). "After Keynesian Macroeconomics." *Quarterly Review*, Federal Reserve Bank of Minneapolis, 3(2)(Spring). Available at http://www.minneapolisfed.org/research/qr/qr321.pdf (accessed December 21, 2011)
Mankiw, N. G. (1990). "A Quick Refresher Course in Macroeconomics." *Journal of Economic Literature* 28(4): 1645–1660.
——. (2006). "The Economist as Scientist and Engineer." *Journal of Economic Perspectives* 20(4): 29–46.

McCloskey, D. [1985] (1998). *The Rhetoric of Economics*. Maddison: University of Wisconsin Press (2nd Edition).

——. (1994). *Knowledge and Persuasion in Economics*. Cambridge: Cambridge University Press.

McCombie, J. S. L. (1985–1986). "Why Cutting Real Wages Will Not Necessarily Reduce Unemployment—Keynes and the 'Postulates of the Classical Economics'." *Journal of Post Keynesian Economics* 8(2): 233–248.

——. (1998). "Rhetoric, Paradigms and the Relevance of the Aggregate Production Functions." In *Method, Theory and Policy in Keynes: Essays in Honour of Paul Davidson*. Ed. P. Arestis, pp. 44–68. Cheltenham: Edward Elgar.

——. (2001). "Reflections on Economic Paradigms and Controversies in Economics." *Zagreb International Review of Economics and Business* 4(1): 1–25.

Meyer, L. H. (2001). "Does Money Matter?" *Federal Reserve Bank of St. Louis Review* May: 1–16.

Minsky, H. P. [1976] (2008). *John Maynard Keynes*. Columbia: Columbia University Press (2nd Edition).

Mishan, E. J. (1961). "Theories of Consumer's Behaviour: A Cynical View." *Economica* 28(109): 1–11.

Nordhaus, W. D. (1983). "Macroconfusion: The Dilemmas of Economic Policy." In *Macroeconomics, Prices and Quantities: Essays in Memory of Arthur M. Okun*. Ed. J. Tobin, pp. 247–284. Washington, DC: Brookings Institution.

Pasinetti, L. L., and G. P. Mariutti. (2008). "Hick's "Conversion"—from J.R. to John." In *Markets, Money and Capital. Hicksian Economics for the Twenty First Century*. Eds. R. Scazzieri, A. Sen, and S. Zamagni, pp. 52–71. Cambridge: Cambridge University Press.

Posner, R. A. (2009). "How I Became a Keynesian. Second Thoughts in a Recession." *New Republic* September 23: 34–39.

Skidelsky, R. (2009). *Keynes. The Return of the Master*. London: Allen Lane.

Soler, L., H. Sankey, and P. Hoyningen-Huene. (2008). *Rethinking Scientific Change and Theory Comparison*. Dordrecht: Springer.

Solon, G., R. Barsky, and J. A. Parker. (1994). "Measuring the Cyclicality of Real Wages: How Important is Composition Bias?" *Quarterly Journal of Economics* 109(1): 1–25.

Solow, R. M. (1983). "'Comment' on Nordhaus." In *Macroeconomics, Prices and Quantities: Essays in Memory of Arthur M. Okun*. Ed. J. Tobin, pp. 279–284. Washington, DC: Brookings Institution.

Summers, L. (1991). "The Scientific Illusion in Empirical Macroeconomics." *Scandinavian Journal of Economics* 93(2): 129–148.

Tarshis, L. (1939). "Changes in Real and Money Wages." *Economic Journal* 49(193): 150–154.

Trevithick, J. A. (1992). *Involuntary Unemployment: Macroeconomics from a Keynesian Perspective.* Hemel Hempstead: Harvester Wheatsheaf Books.

Weitzman, M. L. (1982). "Increasing Returns and the Foundations of Unemployment Theory." *Economic Journal* 92(368): 787–804.

Wren-Lewis, S. (2007). "Are There Dangers in the Microfoundations Consensus?" In *Is There a New Consensus in Macroeconomics?* Ed. P. Arestis, pp. 43–60. Basingstoke: Palgrave Macmillan.

Index

for

STUDIES IN ECONOMIC REFORM AND SOCIAL JUSTICE: MARKETS, COMPETITION, AND THE ECONOMY AS A SOCIAL SYSTEM

A
Absentee Ownership (Veblen), 169
academic disciplines, 7, 27n4, 48
acting person, 120n5
Administration for Children and Families, 92
advertising, 169, 171, 172, 182–183
agency, Luhmann on, 25, 30n37
agent behavior, 108–109, 120nn4–6. *See also* methodological individualism
Aglietta, M., 19, 29n26
Agresti, A., 95
Ahn, T. K., 51
Akerlof, G. A., 35, 135, 141
Allaire, G., 103, 107, 113, 136
Allington, N. F. B., 240
Allison, P. D., 95
Almond, B., 72
Altschuler, G. C., 225
Altvater, E., 136
Amable, B., 128
American Journal of Economics and Sociology, 1–2
Anderson, P., 215, 221, 223
Andrews, P. W. S., 170
anthropology, 43–44
Araujo, L., 211–212, 230
Arestis, P., 239
Arndt, J., 171
Arthur, W. B., 23, 29n25
Aspers, P., 144, 151, 174, 212
Atack, J., 216
Auslander, L., 211, 213, 216
Australia, 144–151, 154n7, 159–163
Austrian School, 63. *See also* Methodenstreit

autopoietic systems, 11, 16–17, 28n12, 29n19
Ayres, C. E., 106

B
Baker, D., 130
Baker, W. E., 46, 210
Bales, R. F., 72
banking system, 12, 15
Baran, P., 189, 190, 193, 200
Barba, A., 71
Barnes, B., 241
Barnes, John, 44
Barr, M. S., 71
Barro, R. J., 259
Bass, F., 214
Baudry de Saunier, L., 217, 218, 219, 220
Baumol, W., 167, 170
Becker, G. S., 36, 72
Beckert, J., 177
Beckert, Jens, 7, 16, 25, 29n23
Belsley, D. A., 96
Beltran, A., 222
Benjamin, Walter, 29n19
Berger, Peter, 37
Berlanstein, L., 225
Berto, F., 225
Bhat, C. R., 228
Bichler, S., 50
bicycle market cycle case study, 216–230
  early markets (1867–1875), 216–217
  market revival (1875–1885), 217–219

design ferment (1885–1892), 220–221
popularity (1893–1898), 221–224
diverging markets (1899–1905), 224–226
different markets (1903–1914), 227–229
Bijker, W., 212, 217, 220
Blackford, M. G., 216, 218
Blanchard, O. J., 239
Blanchflower, D., 240
Blank, R. M., 71
Blaug, M., 34, 134, 135
Blinder, A. S., 199, 250
Blois, K. J., 227
Bloor, D., 241
Blumin, S. M., 216, 219
Blundell, R., 84
Bögenhold, D., 46, 49
Bogenhold, D., 175
Boorman, S. A., 44–45
Bott, Elizabeth, 44
Bourdieu, P., 50–51, 196, 211, 213, 230
Bowles, S., 74, 76, 91, 108, 110, 113, 118, 177
Boyer, R., 91, 134, 136, 137–138, 140, 141, 142, 151, 152
brand loyalty, 169–170, 174
Braudel, F., 216, 218, 223
Breiger, R. L., 44–45
Bruchey, S., 219, 222, 223
Brunner, Elisabeth, 170
Bryson, B., 211, 213
Bucks, B. K., 94
Buiter, W., 240
Bunge, M., 49
Burgwardt, C., 218
Burns, A., 168
Burt, R. S., 46, 47, 50, 51, 211

C
Caballero, R. J., 260–261
Caldwell, B., 60
Caldwell, B. J., 106
Callon, M., 103, 136, 210, 230
Cameron, R., 222
capitalism, 119n2. *See also* capitalist system instability

capitalist system instability, 188–203
and business enterprise market governance, 198–200
and debt dependency, 190–193, 203nn2,3
financial, 189–190
heterodox economics on, 188–189, 203n1
and New Neoclassical Synthesis, 250–251
and optimal outcomes as illusion, 196–197, 203n6
social foundations of, 193–195
and state regulation, 194, 200–202, 203n4
Caplin, A. S., 260, 261
Carlson, S. M., 74
Caron, F., 218, 223
Carrier, J. G., 130, 132, 138
Carrington, P. J., 47
Carroll, M. C., 41
Carter, S. B., 92
Chalupnicek, P., 52
Chamberlin, E., 169, 170
Chamlee-Wright, E., 52
Chang, H-J., 132, 133, 136
Chari, V. V., 239
Chester, L., 144, 146
Chick, V., 23, 24, 25
Clark, J. M., 167
Cloward, R. A., 77
Coase, R. H., 133, 135
Cochrane, J., 240
Colander, D. C., 34
Coleman, J., 50, 51
Collins, J. L., 72
Collins, R., 43, 49, 72
Collins, S. D., 77
Commons, J. R., 110, 154n5, 165
communication, 8–9, 14, 23, 28n17, 30nn33,34
comparative historical sociology, 215
competition, 164–184
and advertising, 169, 171, 172, 182–183
horizontal (consumer vs. consumer), 173–176
horizontal (seller vs. seller), 165–167

and ideology, 164–165, 177
institutional/post-Keynesian
  economics on, 114, 121nn13–15
Luhmann on, 19–20
mode simultaneity, 181–182
neoclassical economics on, 115,
  121n14, 166
and regulation, 180–181
and social embeddedness/
  interactivity, 177–179
vertical, 167–173
conception of control, 171–172
consumers. See market cycles;
  markets
consumption regimes, 213, 216
contractual agreements, 110, 120n9
Coontz, S., 73
Coriat, B., 103, 110, 128, 129, 136,
  137
Cornehls, J. V., 200
corporate market control, 197–200,
  203n7, 204nn8,9
Corrado, C., 260
Cott, N. F., 219
Cowan, R. S., 212
Creed, G. W., 73
critical realism, 107, 120n7
Crofton, S., 173
Cromwell, J. B., 94
Crotty, J. R., 194
Crouch, C., 128, 134
culture. See social embeddedness
  concept
Cyert, R. M., 109

D
Dallery, T., 191, 198, 200
Danziger, S., 72, 84
Darby, M., 170
Dauter, L., 175
Davidson, P., 112, 250–251
Dawid, H., 22
debt dependency, 190–193,
  203nn2,3
Dehmer, M., 47
DeLong, B., 240
de Mooij, M., 211
Dequech, D., 108, 110, 112,
  115
De Vroey, M., 249, 250

Dickinson, J., 73
difference, 9
differentiation, 9, 15, 18, 28n6
DiMaggio, P. J., 211
D'Ippoliti, C., 62, 63, 66
Dispenza, M. E., 229
Dixit, A., 253
Dixit, A. K., 197
Dobbin, F., 215
domesticated markets, 171
dominant design, 215, 223
Dorfman, J., 38
Dorsch, M., 183
Dosi, G., 115
double circular flow, 11–12
double contingency, 15
Dow, S., 23, 24, 25
Dowd, D. F., 194
Dowell, G., 223
Downward, P., 106, 199
Dugger, W. M., 117, 118
Dunham, N. L., 217, 219, 220
Dunlop, J. T., 256
Dunn, S. P., 115, 116
Durkheim, Emile, 41
Durlauf, S. N., 23, 29n24
Durry, J., 222, 227

E
Earl, P., 170, 181
Earl, P. E., 113
Easley, D., 47, 52
ecological economics, 22, 30n30
the economic, Luhmann on, 21
economic sociology, 20, 27n4, 103,
  136–137, 211
economic theory, 27n4
economy as social system, 1–2.
  See also Luhmann on economy
  as social system
Edwards, R., 74
Egidi, M., 115
Eichner, A. S., 121n15, 194, 199
Ellison, C. G., 36
Elsner, W., 133
Elster, J., 38, 108
empirical market analysis, 127–153
  application of, 144–145, 154n6
  electricity market, 145–146,
    154n7, 159–163

Index

employment services market, 148, 159–163
framework for, 137–144, 152
low-income housing market, 147–148, 159–163
need for, 129–130, 152–153
water market, 146–147, 159–163
Engels, F., 73, 190, 193
Engerman, S. L., 223
environment
Luhmann on, 10, 18, 22, 28nn7,15, 29n24, 30n30
and market cycles, 213
Epperson, B., 219, 220, 222, 223, 226, 227
Ericisson, N. R., 245
Evans, P., 211
exchange relations, 107, 109–110, 111, 120nn8,9, 139–141

F
Fabiani, S., 199
Fagiolo, G., 22
fallacy of composition, 247, 257–258, 260–261, 263nn11,12
family economic deterioration, 70–96
data notes, 92–96
historical institutional analysis, 72–73, 75–82, 96n1
research neglect of, 71, 72
time-series models, 83–89, 94–96, 96n4, 97nn5,6
Faust, K., 47
Felipe, J., 243, 248
Fernández-Huerga, E., 108
Field, John, 52
Finch, J., 211–212, 230
Findlay, M. C., 110
Fine, B., 66, 210, 212, 230
Finlay, B., 95
Firat, A. F., 182
firm behavior, 109, 120n6
Firmin-Didot, A., 216, 218
Fischer, C., 212
Fisher, F. M., 242–243, 243, 248
Fleetwood, S., 106, 107
Fligstein, N., 45, 103, 110, 118, 136, 137, 172, 175, 190, 195, 196, 197, 200, 211, 213, 222, 223, 230

Flink, J. J., 224, 228
Foundations of Social Theory (Coleman), 51
Fourie, F. C. v. N., 107, 108, 109, 110, 111, 114, 116, 117
Frank, R., 175
Freedeman, C. E., 222
Freeman, J., 136
free-market rhetoric, 119n2, 127–128, 132–133, 134
and capitalist system instability, 201
and institutional content of markets, 119n3
policy implications of, 128, 144–145
See also markets; neoclassical economics
French bicycle market. *See* bicycle market cycle case study
Friedman, M., 112, 245
Frydman, R., 254
Fukuyama, F., 51–52

G
Galambos, L., 222
Galbraith, J. K., 132, 165, 171, 174–175, 184
Gallman, R. E., 223
game theory, 20
Ganßman, H., 15
Garcia-Parpet, M-F., 130
Garnett, R. R., 245
Garrone, G., 244
Gart, A., 84
General Theory (Keynes), 251
Georgescu-Roegen, N., 108
German Historical School, 53n2, 63. *See also* Methodenstreit
Ghosh, D., 25
Gillespie, M. D., 74
Gintis, H., 108, 110, 113
Girard, R., 19
Giroux, H., 127, 129
Glyn, A., 198
Goldberg, G. S., 77
Goldberg, M. D., 254
Goodfriend, M., 239, 257
Goodman, P. S., 71, 84
Gordon, D. M., 74, 76, 91

Gottdiener, M., 212
Gough, I., 74
Gould, J. P., 144
government. *See* state intervention
Granovetter, M., 136, 178, 210
Granovetter, M. S., 41–42, 46, 136
Great Recession, 70, 71
The Great Transformation (Polanyi), 41
Greenspan, Alan, 131
Greenwood, J., 259–260
Griset, P., 222
Grossman, S., 135
Gruchy, A. G., 196
Grundriß der allgemeinen Volkswirtschaftslehre (Schmoller), 61
Guillén, M. F., 34–35
Günther, Gotthard, 28n11, 30n37
Gutman, H. G., 225

H

Haase Svendsen, G. L., 52
Hahnel, R., 118, 127
Hall, P., 128
Hall, P. A., 211
Haller, M., 49
Hamilton, G. G., 210, 213, 227
Hands, D. W., 241
Hannan, M., 136
Hanson, J., 169, 182
Harcourt, G. C., 242, 247
Härdle, W., 135
Hargreaves Heap, S. P., 194
Harrison, A. E., 221
Harrison, L. E., 36
Hartley, J. E., 247
Harvey, D., 79, 132
Harvey, M., 137, 140, 142
Hassett, K. A., 91
Häußling, R., 47
Haveman, R. H., 84
Hayek, Friedrich, 13
Hays, S., 72
Haythornthwaite, C., 48
Hendry, D. F., 245
Henry, J., 241
Henry, J. F., 194, 195, 200
Hercowitz, Z., 259–260
Herlihy, D., 216, 217, 228, 229

heterodox economics, 188–189, 203n1, 203n2. *See also* institutional/post-Keynesian economics; post-Keynesian economics
Hicks, J. R., 251, 254
Hirsch, F., 174
Hirschman, A. O., 214
historical institutional analysis, 72–73, 75–82, 96n1
Hodgson, G. M., 38, 40, 105, 106, 107, 108, 109, 110, 111, 112, 113, 117, 136, 170, 210, 213, 230
Holt, D. B., 211, 230
homo oeconomicus, 37, 38, 40
homo sociologicus, 42. *See also* social embeddedness concept
Hoover, K. D., 34, 246–247
Hounshell, D. A., 218, 220, 221, 223
Houry, C., 221, 222, 226
Howe, M., 199
Howell, B., 80
Hoyningen-Huene, P., 242, 243
Huffman, G. W., 259–260
Huntington, S. P., 36
Hutter, Michael, 7, 15

I

ideology, 29–30n27, 164–165, 177
incommensurability, 241–243, 262–263n4
inductive vs. deductive reasoning, 60–67, 67n3. *See also* social embeddedness concept
industrial organization studies, 180
institutional content of markets, 106, 107–119
  agent behavior, 108–109, 120nn4–6
  critical realism on, 107, 120n7
  and free-market rhetoric, 119n3
  horizontal relations, 114–117, 121nn13–15
  and market creation, 117–118
  and market cycles, 211, 213, 230
  vertical relations, 109–114, 120nn8–10, 121nn11,12
institutional/post-Keynesian economics, 103, 119n1. *See also* institutional content of markets

International Network for Social Network Analysis, 47
interpenetration, 18
IRS-SOI, 93

J
Jackson, W. A., 105, 107, 109, 110, 111, 113, 114, 116, 118
Jessop, B., 74
Johnson, R., 212
Jones, E. L., 36, 38

K
Kahneman, D., 35
Kaldor, N., 247
Kalecki, M., 190, 191, 193, 194
Kantor, H. A., 216, 218, 221
Karni, E., 170
Keen, S., 133
Kehoe, P. J., 239
Kemp, T., 222
Kenny, C., 245
Kerber, W., 118, 119
Kerr, K. A., 216, 218
Keynes, J. M.
  on capitalist system instability, 194, 250–251
  on macro-vs. micro-analysis, 247
  on monetary production economy, 203n2
  on real wage, 256
  on unemployment, 249
Kilbourne, W., 177, 183
King, R., 239
Kirman, A., 22, 135, 247–248, 261
Kirman, A. P., 22, 130
Kjellberg, H., 211–212, 230
Klein, D. M., 72
Klein, M., 216, 218, 221
Klein, P., 118
Kleinberg, J., 47, 52
Kotz, D. M., 71, 74, 78, 80, 88, 91
Kranton, R. E., 35
Kron, K., 217, 219
Krugman, P., 240
Kuhn, T. S., 240–242, 243, 244, 245, 261
Kysar, D., 169, 182

L
Labrousse, E., 216, 218, 223
Labys, W. C., 94
Laidler, D., 263n5
Laird, P. W., 47
Lakatos, I., 262–263n4
Lamoreaux, N. R., 226
Lancaster, K. J., 210
Landes, David, 37
Lane, D., 23, 29n24
Langlois, R. N., 117, 212, 215, 223
Larner, W., 197
Lauterbach, A., 38
Lavoie, M., 106, 108, 199
Lawson, T., 30n35, 106, 107
Lazonick, W., 191, 192
Leamer, E. E., 245
Lee, Frederic S., 38, 106, 133, 196, 197, 198, 199
Leonardi, R., 51
Leopold, E., 210, 212, 230
Levine, D. P., 201
Lévi-Strauss, C., 43
Levy-Léboyer, M., 222
Lie, J., 106
Liljenberg, A., 105, 118, 210, 212, 214
Lindblom, C. E., 132
Loasby, B. J., 108, 112, 113, 117, 118
Louch, H., 211
Louzek, M., 60–61, 62, 65, 66, 67n3
Lowry, S. T., 118
Lucas, R. E., 246, 247, 248, 249, 250, 263n5
Luhmann, Niklas, 27n1. *See also* Luhmann on economy as social system
Luhmann on economy as social system, 6–27
  and academic disciplines, 7, 27n4
  agency, 25, 30n37
  autopoietic systems, 11, 16–17, 28n12, 29n19
  communication, 8–9, 14, 23, 28n17, 30nn33,34
  competition, 19–20
  differentiation, 9, 15, 18, 28n6
  and ecological economics, 22, 30n30
  the economic, 21

environment, 10, 18, 22, 27n5, 28nn7,15, 29n24, 30n30
and equilibrium method, 10, 28n8
and ideology, 29–30n27
markets, 17–20, 29nn20,21,24,25
and methodological individualism, 9–10, 21–23, 30n32
money as symbolic in, 14–16, 29n18
open/closed systems, 10–11, 12, 23–25, 28n10, 30n35
payments, 11–12, 28n16
polycontextual systems, 18, 28n11
price, 12–14, 22, 28n16
and Quesnay, 11, 28n13
rational expectations theory, 18–19, 29n23
reproduction, 11, 16–17, 28n14

M

MacKenzie, D., 130, 136
macro-vs. micro-analysis, 1
and Luhmann on economy as social system, 22
and New Neoclassical Synthesis, 246–248
and social network analysis, 34, 49–50
Maguire, J., 176
Mahoney, J., 215
Mankiw, N. G., 239, 244
Mantzavinos, C., 133
March, J. G., 109
Marchionatti, R., 244
Marcovich, A., 37
Mariutti, G. P., 251
market clearing, 249–250, 254–260, 263nn9,11,12
market control, 196–203, 203n6
business enterprise governance, 197–200, 203n7, 204nn8–11
neoclassical economics on, 203n5
optimal outcomes as illusion, 196–197, 203n6
market cycles, 209–215
conceptual model of, 212–215
theoretical neglect of, 210–212, 230
See also bicycle market cycle case study

market failure
and capitalist system instability, 201
and competition, 166, 181
empirical analysis of, 150n11
and information rules, 141
neoliberalism on, 132, 133
policy implications of, 128
and state intervention, 135, 154n3
markets, 102–119
as basis of public policy, 128, 144–145, 151–152, 154n2
canonization of, 127–128
central theoretical role of, 102–103
economic sociology on, 136–137
and exchange relations, 107, 109–110, 111, 120nn8,9, 139–141
as identified with capitalism, 119n2
interactivity in, 177–179
interrelationships among, 151
Luhmann on, 17–20, 29nn20,21,24,25
rules in, 140–142
social network analysis on, 45–46, 53n5
types of, 137–139
See also competition; empirical market analysis; free-market rhetoric; institutional content of markets; market control; market cycles; neoclassical economics
Marschall, J., 46, 49
Martinez, M. A., 136
Marx, Karl
on capitalist system instability, 189, 190, 193, 194
on communication, 28n17
on family, 73
on monetary production economy, 203n2
and social embeddedness, 39
Mason, P. P., 219
Mason, R., 174
Mathias, P., 216, 225
Matt, S., 224, 225
Mattey, J., 260
Maturana, H. R., 28n12

Mauss, M., 43
Mayer, V., 72
McCloskey, D., 240, 245
McCloskey, Deirdre, 30n34
McCombie, J. S. L., 240, 242, 245, 254
McDonagh, P., 183
McDonald, M., 212, 213, 214, 215
McDonough, T., 77
McGuire, P., 136
McKay, J. P., 228
McLean, B., 71
McMillan, J., 219
McShane, C., 225, 228, 229
Meldrum, M., 212, 213, 214, 215
Melmies, J., 199
Ménard, C., 105, 107, 110, 117
Menger, Karl, 39–40. *See also* Methodenstreit
Methodenstreit, 39–40, 60–67
methodological individualism, 65, 67, 68n4
  Luhmann's rejection of, 9–10, 21–23, 30n32
Meurs, M., 117, 118
Meyer, L. H., 239, 251
Meyer, P. B., 190, 197, 200, 201
Michalowski, R. J., 74
Mikl-Horke, G., 39
Mill, John Stuart, 62, 64–65, 66
Miller, E. S., 196
Millo, Y., 103, 136
Mills, C. W., 73, 175
Milonakis, D., 66
Minsky, H., 169–170, 189–190, 193, 194, 202, 244
Mintz, S., 212
Mirowski, Ph., 23
Mishan, E. J., 248
Mitchell, Clyde, 44
Mittelstaedt, J., 177
Mittelstaedt, R., 177
Moati, P., 119
monetary production economy, 203n2. *See also* debt dependency
money
  institutional/post-Keynesian economics on, 112–113, 121n12
  as symbolic, 14–16, 29n18

Monkkonen, E., 225, 226, 228
Moody, K., 132
Moore, A., 91
Morgan, M., 39
Morgen, S., 79
Morris, A., 146
Mott, T., 200
Mukerjee, R., 165
Münch, R., 16
Muniesa, F., 103, 136

N
Nanetti, R. Y., 51
Nelson, P., 170
Nelson, S., 135, 151
neoclassical economics
  in Australian economy, 144–145
  on competition, 115, 121n14, 166
  identification of capitalism with markets, 119n2
  and institutional content of markets, 119n3
  and market canonization, 127–128
  on market control, 203n5
  on market types, 138
  overviews, 104–107, 131–135
  on state intervention, 132, 133, 134, 135, 154n3, 203n4
  and vertical market relations, 121n12
  vs. social embeddedness concept, 36, 37–38, 39–40
  See also free-market rhetoric; neoclassical economics on markets; neoliberalism
neoliberalism, 131, 132–133, 134, 144–145. *See also* neoclassical economics
Neubeck, K. J., 76
New Classical economics, 247, 249, 250, 256. *See also* New Neoclassical Synthesis
New Keynesian economics, 239. *See also* New Neoclassical Synthesis
New Macroeconomic Consensus. *See* New Neoclassical Synthesis
Newman, K. S., 72
Newman, M., 47
New Neoclassical Synthesis, 246–262

development of, 238–239
fallacy of composition in, 247, 257–258, 260–261, 263nn11,12
market clearing, 249–250, 254–260, 263n9
microfoundations, 246–248, 263n%
sub-prime crisis challenge to, 239–240
terms for, 239, 262n2
uncertainty in, 250–254, 263n8
Nielsen, A. C., 173
Nitzan, J., 50
Nocera, J., 71
Nordhaus, W. D., 238, 239
North, D. C., 135

O
observation, 18–19, 20, 25, 30n36
O'Connor, J., 74
Ogden, P. E., 224
O'Hara, P. A., 74, 200
oligopoly, 168–169, 171, 172
open/closed systems
 critical realism on, 107
 Luhmann on, 10–11, 12, 23–25, 28n10, 30n35
 neoclassical economics on, 106
Orhangazi, Ö., 198
Orléans, A., 19, 29n26
Ostrom, E., 51
O'Sullivan, M., 191, 192

P
Panzar, J., 167, 170
paradigm theory, 240–246, 262–263n4
Parsons, Talcott, 14, 16, 18, 23, 29n18, 30n32, 72
Parsons, W., 175
Pasinetti, L. L., 251
Pattillo-McCoy, M., 72
payments, 11–12, 28n16
Pearson, H., 37, 60
Peck, J., 136
Penaloya, L., 182
Petrovic, M., 210, 213, 227
Pietrykowski, 210, 211, 212, 213, 230
Pike, M., 240

Pistaferri, L., 84
Piven, F. F., 77, 95
Pivetti, M., 71
Polanyi, Karl, 1, 9, 41, 136, 196, 197
Pollay, R., 183
polycontextual systems, 18, 28n11
positivism, 106, 107
Posner, R. A., 245
Postan, M. M., 216, 225
post-Keynesian economics, 239, 247, 263n9. *See also* institutional content of markets; institutional/post-Keynesian economics
Poyer, A., 217, 219, 220, 224, 225, 227
Prasch, R. E., 114, 116, 136, 137, 139, 140, 141, 142
Pratt, J., 222
Prechel, H., 190, 196, 199, 201
Prechel, 196, 199, 201
Pressman, S., 71, 84, 194
Preston, I., 84
Price, R., 216, 218, 219, 226
price
 and competition, 168, 180
 and institutional content of markets, 111–112, 113, 116, 121nn11,15
 Luhmann on, 12–14, 22, 28n16
 and market control, 198–199, 204n11
 neoclassical economics on, 105, 115
procedural rationality, 108, 120n4
product differentiation, 168–169, 170
Putnam, R. D., 51

Q
Quesnay, François, 11, 28n13

R
Rabin, M., 38
Radcliffe-Brown, A., 44
Rampolla, M. l., 215
Randles, S., 137, 140, 142
rational expectations theory, 18–19, 29n23
Rausch, J. E., 211
Redmond, W., 172

regulation. *See* state intervention
regulation theory, 203n1
Reich, M., 74
Reinhart, C. M., 71
reserved capacity, 198, 204n10
Richardson, G. B., 223
Ritchie, A., 217
Robertson, P. L., 212, 215, 223
Rochon, L-P., 112
Rodgers, D. T., 34
Rogers, E. M., 47
Rogoff, K. S., 71
Rosenbaum, E. F., 102, 107, 109, 111, 114, 210, 213
Ross, D., 22
Ross, David, 166, 167, 183
Rota, M. F., 47
Rueschemeyer, D., 215
Russell, B., 73

S
Sabatini, F., 52
Samuels, W. J., 106, 107, 118, 194
Samuelson, P., 30n37
Sargent, T. J., 248, 249
Sawyer, M., 210, 214
Sawyer, M. C., 105, 111, 113, 114, 115, 116
Scherer, F. M., 166, 167, 183
Scherer, K. R., 38
Schmölders, G., 37
Schmoller, Gustav, 39–40, 60–67
Schor, J., 176
Schülein, J. A., 49
Schumpeter, J. A., 35, 37, 48
Schwartz, A. J., 245
Schwinn, F., 227
Scitovsky, T., 170
Scott, J., 35, 44, 45, 47
Scott, R., 71, 84
Searle, J., 118
Seefeldt, K. S., 72
Segal, A. J., 218
Sen, A., 130
Senauer, B., 210, 213, 227
Shackle, G. L. S., 45
Shah, S., 212
Sherman, H. J., 200
Shi, D., 175
Shiller, R. J., 35

Shinn, T., 37
Shipman, A., 182
Sidel, R., 72
Simmel, G., 211, 213
Simmel, Georg, 42
Simon, H., 135
Simon, H. A., 108, 109
Siu, L., 136
Skidelsky, R., 131–132, 245
Slater, D., 177
Smelser, N. J., 38
Smith, Adam, 13, 166
Smith, R., 215
social aggregates, 65–66, 67
social capital, 50–52
social class
 and capitalist system instability, 189, 194
 and market cycles, 216, 218–219, 221, 222, 224–225, 227–228
 SSA theory on, 73–74
 and status competition, 175
social embeddedness concept, 1, 34–35
 and competition, 177–179
 concept development, 40–42
 and innovative nature of social network analysis, 36–38
 Methodenstreit, 39–40
 vs. neoclassical economics, 36, 37–38, 39–40
social-institutional analysis, 72
social network analysis, 34–52
 influence of, 47–48
 innovative nature of, 36–38
 and macro-vs. micro-analysis, 34, 49–50
 on markets, 45–46, 53n5
 origins of, 42–45
 quantitative vs. qualitative methods in, 47
 and social capital, 50–52
 as theory vs. method, 48–50
 as useful for studying social embeddedness, 34–35, 36–38
social status. *See* status competition
social structure of accumulation (SSA) theory, 73–74, 75–82, 96n1, 203n1
social theory, 27n4

sociology, 35, 40–41, 65, 66, 210–211. *See also* economic sociology
Soederberg, S., 190, 191, 192, 198, 200, 201
Solow, R. M., 238–239, 240
Solskice, D., 211
Sombart, Werner, 40
Sorkin, A. R., 71
Sorlin, P., 216, 224
Soskice, D., 128
Spahr, C. B., 219
Spiegel, J. W., 84
Spillman, L., 165
Spulber, D. F., 260, 261
Sraff, 28n14
SSA (social structure of accumulation) theory, 73–74, 75–82, 96n1, 203n1
Stanfield, J. R., 41
Starr, M., 182
state intervention
  and capitalist system instability, 194, 200–202, 203n4
  and competition, 166, 174, 180–181
  economic sociology on, 137
  and institutional content of markets, 110–111, 112–113, 120n10
  neoclassical economics on, 132, 133, 134, 135, 154n3, 203n4
status competition, 174–176, 183
Steele, V., 218, 221
Stegbauer, C., 47
Steindl, J., 193
Stern, N., 132
Stets, J. E., 38
Stiglitz, J. E., 135, 154n3
Stigum, B., 25
Stinson, M. A., 228
Strasser, S., 218
Streeck, W., 211, 213, 230
sub-prime crisis (2007), 239–240
Summers, L., 244
Svendsen, Gert Tinggaard, 52
Swaminathan, A., 223
Swedberg, R., 38, 45, 103, 107, 167–168, 173, 196, 210

Sweezy, P. M., 189, 190, 193, 194, 200
Swenson, D., 72
Szostak, R., 213

T

Talmud, I., 50
Tarshis, L., 256
Teece, D., 115
Teplin, A. M., 93
Terraza, M., 94
Theodore, N., 136
theory falsification, 67n3
The Theory of the Leisure Class (Veblen), 174
Thévin, F., 221, 222, 226
Thompson, C. S., 225
Thompson, D., 174
Tiersten, L., 218, 224
Tilman, R., 178
time-series models, 83–89, 94–96, 96n4, 97nn5,6
Tonkiss, F., 177
Tordjman, H., 103, 110, 113, 137, 140–141, 142, 143
Trevithick, J. A., 247
Trigg, A., 176
Tripsas, M., 212
Tsakalotos, E., 108, 113, 118, 136
Turner, J., 38, 49
Turner, L. J., 72
Tushman, M. L., 215, 221, 223
Tyagi, A. W., 72

U

unemployment. *See* market clearing
Urien, B., 183
U.S. bicycle market. *See* bicycle market cycle case study
U.S. Census Bureau, 71

V

Vant, A., 221
Varela, F. J., 28n12
Veblen, T.
  on capitalist system instability, 189, 190, 193, 194, 196
  on competition, 168, 169
  on consumption regimes, 211, 213

on debt dependency, 191
on market control, 196, 199, 200
on monetary production economy, 203n2
and social embeddedness, 53n3
on status competition, 174, 175, 183
Venkatesh, A., 182
Vernego, M., 112
Vignes, A., 130
Viskovatoff, Alex, 7, 10, 13, 22, 29n24

W
Wakeley, T., 170
Waller, W., 194
Warren, E., 72
Wasserman, S., 47
Waterson, M., 172, 182
Weber, E., 225
Weber, Max
  on competition, 165
  and Luhmann, 27n1
  on market control, 196
  and social embeddedness, 40, 53n3
  on status competition, 175, 176
Weinstein, O., 103, 110, 128, 129, 136, 137

Weisskopf, T. E., 74, 76, 91
Weitzman, M. L., 250
Wellman, B., 44, 45, 48, 49
White, Harrison C., 17, 44–45, 46
White, H. C., 136, 210–211
White, J. M., 72
White, P. E., 224
Wicksell, Knut, 34
Williams, D., 245
Williams, E. E., 110
Williamson, O., 135
Willig, R., 167, 170
Wilson, W. J., 72
Wirtschaft der Gesellschaft (Luhmann), 6, 11, 27n1
Wolfson, M. H., 74, 78
workable competition, 167
Wray, L. R., 112, 198
Wren-Lewis, S., 246
Wright, G., 219, 221

Y
Yakubovich, Valery, 136

Z
Zaretsky, E., 73
Zelizer, V. A., 136, 137, 211, 230
Zimmerman, J.-B., 22
Zukin, S., 176

WILEY